BLACK&DECKER®

THE COMPLETE GUIDE TO

CONTEMPORARY
SHEDS

Complete Plans for 12 Sheds, including:

- Garden Outbuilding
- Storage Lean-to
- Playhouse
- Woodland Cottage
- Hobby Studio
- Lawn Tractor Barn

by Philip Schmidt

Creative Publishing
international

MINNEAPOLIS, MINNESOTA
www.creativepub.com

Creative Publishing international

Copyright © 2008
Creative Publishing international, Inc.
400 First Avenue North
Suite 300
Minneapolis, Minnesota 55401
1-800-328-3895
www.creativepub.com
All rights reserved

Printed at R.R. Donnelley

10 9 8 7 6 5 4 3 2 1

Library of Congress Cataloging-in-Publication Data

Schmidt, Philip.
  The complete guide to contemporary sheds : complete plans for 12 sheds,
including playhouse, garden outbuilding, storage lean-to, lawn tractor barn,
hobby studio, woodland cottage / by Philip Schmidt.
      p. cm. -- (Complete guide)
  At head of title: Branded by Black & Decker
  Summary: "Provides practical information for planning and building sheds
of all types"--Provided by publisher.
  Includes index.
  ISBN-13: 978-1-58923-335-5 (soft cover)
  ISBN-10: 1-58923-335-2 (soft cover)
  1. Sheds--Design and construction--Amateurs' manuals. 2. Toolsheds--
Design and construction--Amateurs' manuals. 3. Outbuildings--Design and
construction--Amateurs' manuals. I. Black & Decker Corporation (Towson,
Md.) II. Title. III. Title: Branded by Black & Decker. IV. Series.

TH4962.S53 2008
690.89--dc22

2007039143

President/CEO: Ken Fund
Vice President for Sales & Marketing: Peter Ackroyd

Home Improvement Group

Publisher: Bryan Trandem
Managing Editor: Tracy Stanley
Senior Editor: Mark Johanson
Editor: Jennifer Gehlhar

Creative Director: Michele Lanci-Altomare
Senior Design Manager: Brad Springer
Design Managers: Jon Simpson, Mary Rohl

Lead Photographer: Steve Galvin
Photo Coordinator: Joanne Wawra
Shop Manager: Bryan McLain
Shop Assistant: Cesar Fernandez Rodriguez

Production Managers: Linda Halls, Laura Hokkanen

Author: Philip Schmidt
Page Layout Artist: Danielle Smith
Photographers: Peter Caley, Andrea Rugg, Joel Schnell
Shop Help: Dan Anderson, Tami Helmer, John Webb,
   Glenn Austin, Scott Boyd, Lyle Ferguson, David Hartley,
   Russ Reininger, Syd Thomas, Kevin Weber
Technical Review: Arien Cartrette

The Complete Guide to Contemporary Sheds
Created by: The Editors of Creative Publishing international, Inc., in cooperation with Black & Decker.
Black & Decker® is a trademark of The Black & Decker Corporation and is used under license.

NOTICE TO READERS

For safety, use caution, care, and good judgment when following the procedures described in this book. The Publisher and Black & Decker cannot assume responsibility for any damage to property or injury to persons as a result of misuse of the information provided.

   The techniques shown in this book are general techniques for various applications. In some instances, additional techniques not shown in this book may be required. Always follow manufacturers' instructions included with products, since deviating from the directions may void warranties. The projects in this book vary widely as to skill levels required: some may not be appropriate for all do-it-yourselfers, and some may require professional help.

   Consult your local Building Department for information on building permits, codes and other laws as they apply to your project.

Contents

The Complete Guide to Contemporary Sheds

Introduction 4

Essential Outbuildings 6

Building Basics 20

Choosing a Site for Your Shed 22

Working with Construction Drawings 24

Anatomy of a Shed 26

Lumber & Hardware 27

Building Foundations 28

Framing the Structure 40

Roofing 52

Siding & Trim 62

Doors & Windows 70

Ramps, Steps & Decks 74

Shed Projects 84

Clerestory Studio 86

Sunlight Garden Shed 100

Lean-to Tool Bin 114

Convenience Shed 124

Gambrel Garage 138

Simple Storage Shed 154

Gothic Playhouse 166

Timber-frame Shed 180

Service Shed 192

Metal & Wood Kit Sheds 202

Shed with Firewood Bin 220

Additional Shed Plans 230

Resources & Credits 236

Index 238

Clerestory Studio 86

Sunlight Garden Shed 100

Lean-to Tool Bin 114

Convenience Shed 124

Gambrel Garage 138

Simple Storage Shed 154

Gothic Playhouse 166

Timber-frame Shed 180

Service Shed 192

Metal & Wood Kit Sheds 202

Introduction

The contemporary backyard shed is much more than a place to park the lawnmower. Sheds are still great for storage, of course, but many homeowners are finding added value in their sheds' less tangible qualities— privacy, personal expression, a connection to the outdoors. Perhaps most of all, people like the separation from the main house. A shed is the perfect place to forget your duties or your day job and spend a few hours absorbed in a hobby. For many, it's an open invitation to come out and play in the dirt.

Keeping in mind that every shed can have a range of uses, the custom buildings in this book are designed to be versatile, practical, and adaptable. They're also designed for good looks. In terms of property value, a shed can be either an asset or a liability. Everyone can picture the familiar dilapidated tin shed with doors hanging by one wheel and propped shut with concrete blocks. This is a world apart from a handsome building with solid proportions and fitting architectural details. A well-built shed can evoke the character of a miniature house or a small, private cabin or playhouse. A shed can be an appealing outdoor retreat and a solid complement to your home's landscape.

You can acquire a DIY shed in one of two ways: build it from scratch or buy a kit shed made for easy assembly. This book covers both options. Each of the 10 custom shed projects includes a complete set of construction drawings, a detailed materials list, and step-by-step instructions and photos for building the shed from the ground up. For those who prefer the easy-assembly route, there's a full discussion of choosing a kit shed, plus two projects showing the basic steps for assembling popular kit buildings.

If you don't have a lot of experience with carpentry, don't worry—the Building Basics section of the book walks you through the entire construction process. It will also help you choose the right foundation for your shed and give you the knowledge to make custom substitutions to the projects as shown. Many shed kits involve a fair amount of freehand work, as well, so you're covered even if your kit comes without roofing or a floor.

One of the best aspects of building a shed is that it doesn't disrupt daily life in your home. This makes the project infinitely more pleasurable than, say, a complete kitchen remodel. So take your time, enjoy the process, and look forward to years of getting away from it all. You'll find that getting even a few yards away is something special.

Essential Outbuildings

Ask a dozen people what they would do with a basic shed in their backyard and you're bound to hear as many different answers. Some would certainly use the outbuilding for storage—yard and garden supplies, play equipment, bicycles, and other spillover items from the garage. Others would claim the shed for more specific pursuits: raising exotic flowers, turning pottery, watching sports on a big-screen TV. Some may even imagine the shed as a fully equipped home office or, going in the opposite direction, a simple, quiet retreat for reading and meditation.

Regardless of the answers you get, one note would ring true: Each person could picture himself in that same building, doing his own thing and filling the space with personal stuff. That's what sheds are all about. Like a house, a good shed offers more than shelter and square footage; it's also an opportunity for self-expression. Perhaps best of all, a shed offers the additional advantage of privacy. You don't have to clean it up for guests or worry about tracking mud on the carpet. And if you set it up just right, you won't even hear the doorbell ringing in the house ("Sorry, I must have been out in my workshop. . . .").

The following pages feature backyard sheds of all descriptions and for any number of personal uses. See if you can picture yourself in some of them. Then try to identify features that make those sheds special to you. Chances are, you can apply those same ideas when building your own backyard getaway.

Whether it's perched at the water's edge or tucked away in the trees, a well-appointed outbuilding can feel a lot like a vacation home.

Believe it or not, this graciously ornamented shed is easily built from a panelized kit. Special details like the dormer appear to be the work of a highly skilled carpenter but can actually be assembled by the average do-it-yourselfer.

Door placement impacts a shed's appearance and its interior layout. This centralized door flanked with windows transforms an ordinary shed into a quaint cottage.

No need to get fancy. This humble shed has plenty of charm and blends perfectly with its surroundings.

Designed to suit the setting, this shed's rustic materials and antique windows add an air of timelessness and easy country living.

Garden folly, playhouse, or work of art? Any of those would be an accurate description. And you can bet the owners had fun building this one.

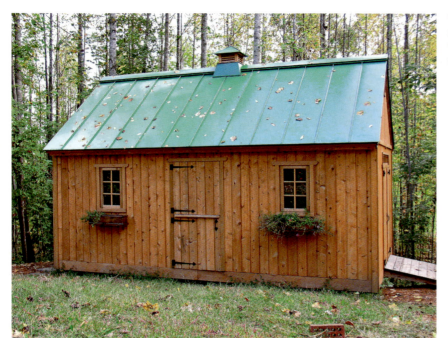

While kit sheds are based on efficient, modern building concepts, you can still find them in traditional styles with nice, custom details, such as this metal roof.

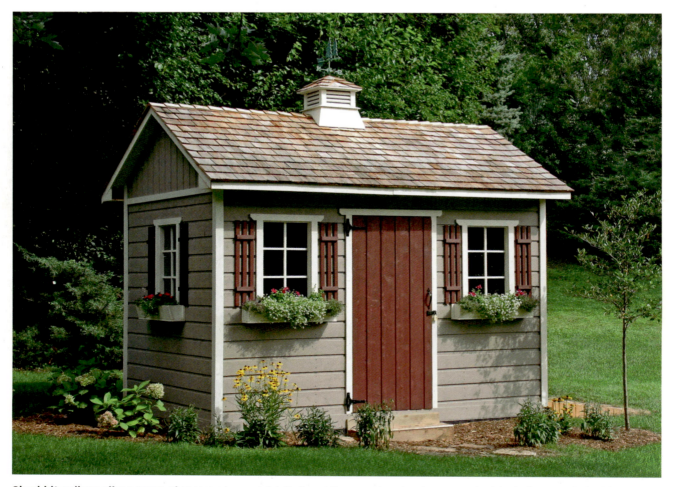

Shed kit sellers offer a range of accessories and details for adding a custom touch to your shed, including practical add-ons like window flower boxes and decorative trim.

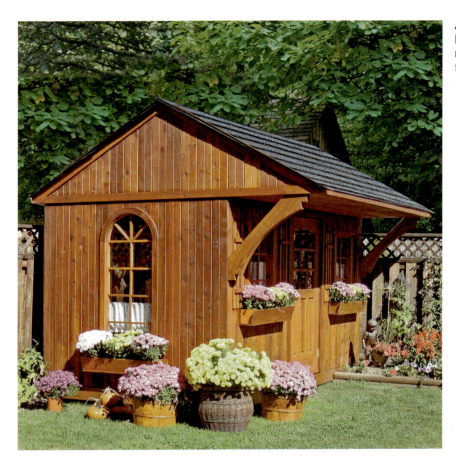

A deep roof overhang adds character but also shelters windows from hot midday sun—an important consideration for working sheds.

Not everyone wants a large, freestanding building in the backyard. Plenty of kit sheds are designed for discreet placement against a house wall or a tall fence.

Integrating a shed into a patio plan can help define the space, block unwanted views, and provide shade and handy storage for patio items.

A traditional saltbox shed may look complicated but is nothing more than a simple gabled building with a shed-style addition.

This handsome shed demonstrates how a little trim and some custom details, such as window boxes, shutters, a dutch door, and a chimney, can turn a basic gable structure into something extraordinary.

In this abundant garden setting, two gambrel-roofed buildings evoke the farming traditions of the American landscape.

Knotty pine paneling and roof sheathing were given a diluted whitewash to create a rustic yet elegant backdrop for this inviting country shed interior.

Cedar shingles and open eaves create a seaside-cottage feeling in this shed, even in the middle of a wooded lot.

The tranquil and graceful character of Asian garden structures has inspired countless Western designers.

On the outside, this artist's retreat displays the proud utility of classic New England architecture (left), while the lovingly decorated interior (this page) bears the personal mark of its owners. With the finished ceiling, fireplace, and double-hung windows, this furnished shed functions as a guest house.

Because sheds are relatively small, materials upgrades, such as cedar shingles instead of asphalt roofing or plywood siding, can still be affordable.

Used as a sunroom in cooler weather, this shed greatly enhances the function and beauty of this outdoor gathering place.

Greenhouses have inspired many versatile shed designs. Windows on the roof bring in plentiful light for growing.

Building Basics

Almost everything you've ever wanted to know about building a shed is in this section. Each element of the construction project is covered in detail—from selecting a site to building the foundation to framing the floor, walls, and roof. You'll also learn about buying lumber and hardware. After your shed is built, return to this section for help with adding a ramp, deck, or steps.

Because the various elements are presented à la carte, you can pick and choose the designs and materials you like best. For the foundation, it makes sense to choose a type based on the shed's location. Several drawings in this book call for a wooden skid foundation (which is the easiest to build), but a concrete block foundation may be a better choice for a sloping site.

Be sure to have your project plans approved by the local building department before starting construction. This is especially important if you're making substitutions to the plans featured in the Shed Projects section.

In This Chapter:

- Choosing a Site for Your Shed
- Working with Construction Drawings
- Anatomy of a Shed
- Lumber & Hardware
- Building Foundations
- Framing the Structure
- Roofing
- Siding & Trim
- Doors & Windows
- Ramps, Steps & Decks

Choosing a Site for Your Shed

The first step in choosing a site for your building doesn't take place in your backyard but at the local building and zoning departments. By visiting the departments, or making calls, you should determine a few things about your project before making any definite plans. Most importantly, find out whether your proposed building will be allowed by zoning regulations and what specific restrictions apply to your situation. Zoning laws govern such matters as the size and height of the building and the percentage of your property it occupies, the building's location, and its position relative to the house, neighboring properties, the street, etc.

From the building side of things, ask if you need a permit to build your structure. If so, you'll have to submit plan drawings (photocopied plans from this book should suffice), as well as specifications for the foundation and materials and estimated cost. Once your project is approved, you may need to buy a permit to display on the building site, and you may be required to show your work at scheduled inspections.

Because outbuildings are detached and freestanding, codes typically govern them loosely. Many impose restrictions or require permits only on structures larger than 100, or even 120, square feet. Others draw the line with the type of foundation used. In some areas, buildings with concrete slab or pier foundations are classified as "permanent" and thus are subject to a specific set of restrictions (and taxation, in some cases), while buildings that are set on skids and can—in theory at least—be moved are considered temporary or accessory and may be exempt from the general building codes.

Once you get the green light from the local authorities, you can tromp around your yard with a tape measure and stake your claim for the new building. Of course, you'll have plenty of personal and practical reasons for placing the building in a particular area, but here are a few general considerations to keep in mind:

Soil & drainage: To ensure that your foundation will last (whatever type it is), plant your building on solid soil, in an area that won't collect water.

Access: For trucks, wheelbarrows, kids, etc. Do you want access in all seasons?

Utility lines: Contact local ordinances to find out where the water, gas, septic, and electrical lines run through your property. Often, local ordinances and utility companies require that lines are marked before digging. This is an essential step not only because of legalities, but also because you don't want your building sitting over lines that may need repair.

Setback requirements: Most zoning laws dictate that all buildings, fences, etc., in a yard must be set back a specific distance from the property line. This setback may range from 6" to 3 feet or more.

Neighbors: To prevent civil unrest, or even a few weeks of ignored greetings, talk to your neighbors about your project.

View from the house: Do you want to admire your handiwork from the dinner table, or would you prefer that your outbuilding blend in with the outdoors? A playhouse in plain view makes it easy to check on the kids.

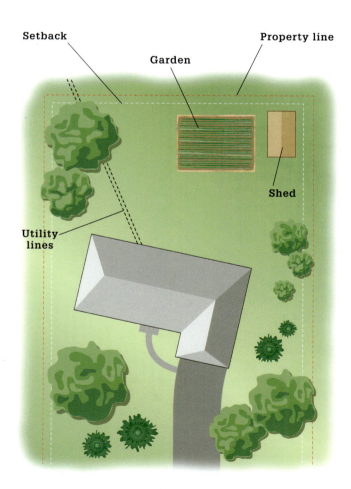

Setback   Garden   Property line   Shed   Utility lines

Siting for Sunlight

Like houses, sheds can benefit enormously from natural light. Bringing sunlight into your backyard office, workshop, or garden house makes the interior space brighter and warmer, and it's the best thing for combating a boxy feel. To make the most of natural light, the general rule is to orient the building so its long side (or the side with the most windows) faces south. However, be sure to consider the sun's position at all times of the year, as well as the shadows your shed might cast on surrounding areas, such as a garden or outdoor sitting area.

SEASONAL CHANGES

Each day the sun crosses the sky at a slightly different angle, moving from its high point in summer to its low point in winter. Shadows change accordingly. In the summer, shadows follow the east-west axis and are very short at midday. Winter shadows point to the northeast and northwest and are relatively long at midday.

Generally, the south side of a building is exposed to sunlight throughout the year, while the north side may be shaded in fall, winter, and spring. Geographical location is also a factor: as you move north from the equator, the changes in the sun's path become more extreme.

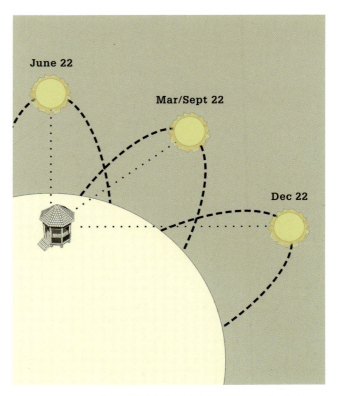

The sun moves from its high point in summer to its low point in winter. Shadows change accordingly.

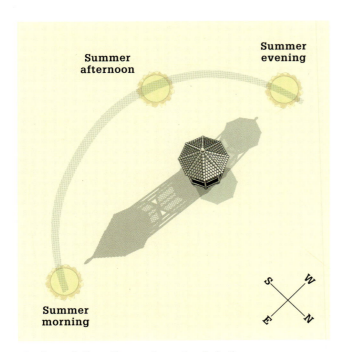

Shadows follow the east-west axis in the summer.

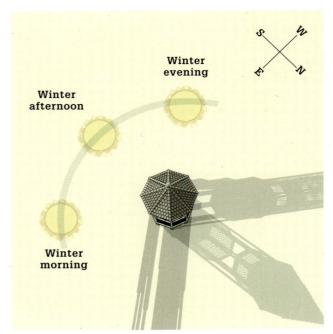

Winter shadows point to the northeast and northwest and are relatively long at midday.

Working with Construction Drawings

The projects in this book include complete construction drawings in the style of architectural blueprints. If you're not familiar with reading plans, don't worry; they're easy to use once you know how to look at the different views. Flipping back and forth between the plan drawings and the project's step-by-step photos will help you visualize the actual structure.

Note: The drawings in this book are accurately proportioned, but they are not sized to a specific scale. Also, dimensions specified in the drawings are given in feet and inches (for example, 6'-8"), the standard format for architectural plans. For your convenience, the written instructions may give dimensions in inches so you don't have to make the conversion.

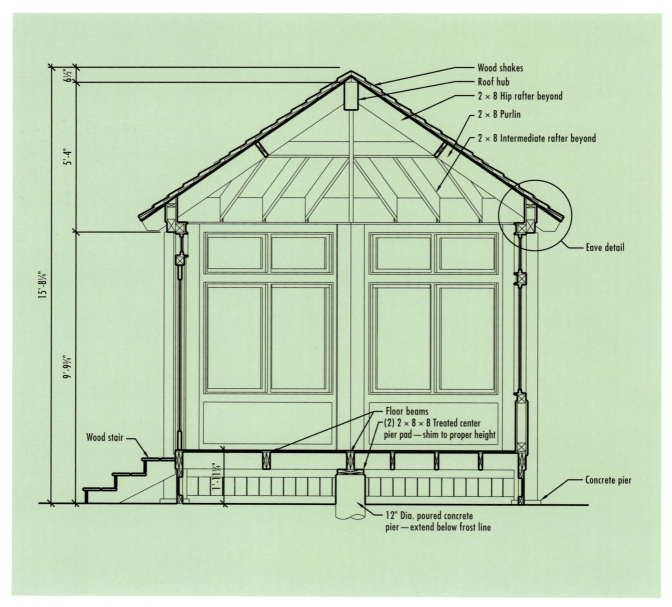

The building section is the most comprehensive drawing, giving you a side view of the structure sliced in half down the middle. It shows both the framing and finish elements.

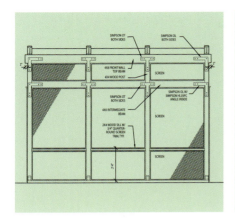
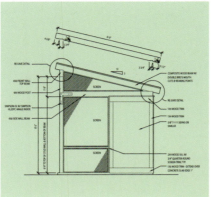
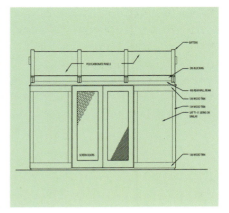

Elevations give you a direct, exterior view of the building from all sides. Drawings may include elevations for both the framing and the exterior finishes.

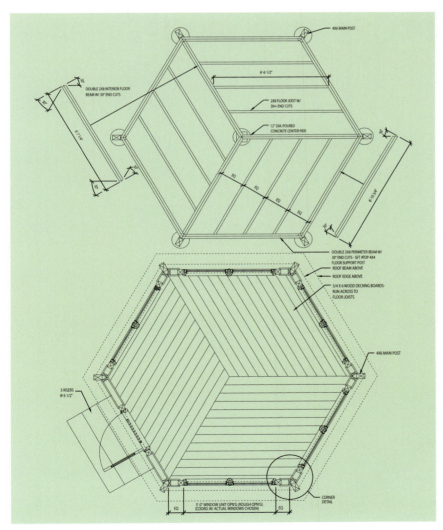

Plan views are overhead views looking straight down from above the structure. Floor plans show the layout of the walls or upright supports, with the top half of the structure sliced off. There are also foundation plans, roof framing plans, and other plan views.

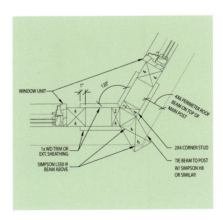

Detail drawings and templates show a close-up of a specific area or part of the structure. They typically show a side or overhead view.

Anatomy of a Shed

Shown as a cutaway, this shed illustrates many of the standard building components and how they fit together. It can also help you understand the major construction stages—each project in this book includes a specific construction sequence, but most follow the standard stages in some form:

1. Foundation—including preparing the site and adding a drainage bed;
2. Framing—the floor is first, followed by the walls, then the roof;
3. Roofing—adding sheathing, building paper, and roofing material;
4. Exterior finishes—including siding, trim, and doors and windows.

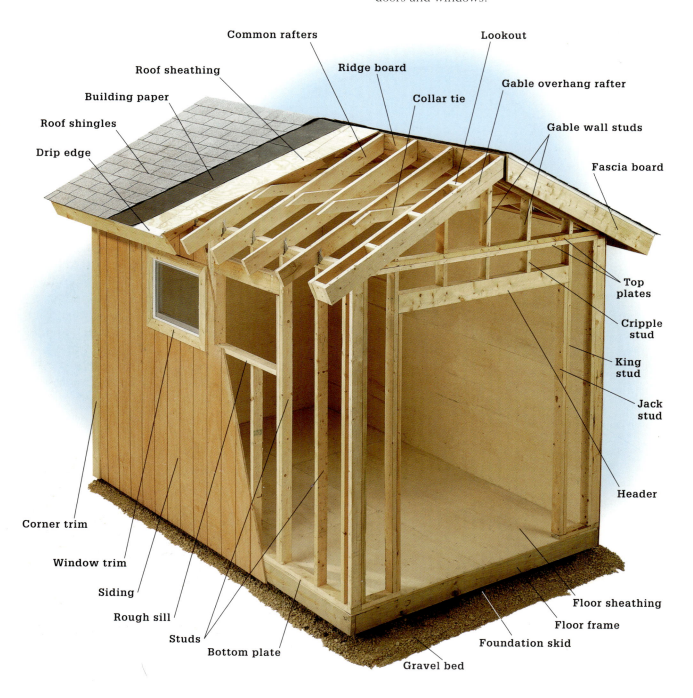

Common rafters

Roof sheathing

Building paper

Roof shingles

Drip edge

Ridge board

Lookout

Collar tie

Gable overhang rafter

Gable wall studs

Fascia board

Top plates

Cripple stud

King stud

Jack stud

Header

Corner trim

Window trim

Siding

Rough sill

Studs

Bottom plate

Gravel bed

Foundation skid

Floor frame

Floor sheathing

Lumber & Hardware

Lumber types most commonly used in outbuildings are pine—or related softwoods—or cedar, which is naturally rot-resistant and is less expensive than most other rot-resistant woods. For pine to be rot-resistant, it must be pressure-treated, typically with a chemical mixture called CCA (Chromated Copper Arsenate).

Pressure-treated lumber is cheaper than cedar, but it's not as attractive, so you may want to use it only in areas where appearance is unimportant. Plywood designated as exterior-grade is made with layers of cedar or treated wood and a special glue that makes it weather-resistant. For the long run, though, it's a good idea to cover any exposed plywood edges to prevent water intrusion.

Framing lumber—typically pine or pressure-treated pine—comes in a few different grades: Select Structural (SEL STR), Construction (CONST) or Standard (STAND), and Utility (UTIL). For most applications, Construction Grade No. 2 offers the best balance between quality and price. Utility grade is a lower-cost lumber suitable for blocking and similar uses but should not be used for structural members, such as studs and rafters. You can also buy "STUD" lumber: construction-grade 2 × 4s cut at the standard stud length of 92⅝". *Note: Treated lumber should be left exposed for approximately 6 months before applying finishes. Finishes will not adhere well to treated lumber that is still very green or wet. Lumber manufacturers likely have recommended times for their product.*

Board lumber, or finish lumber, is graded by quality and appearance, with the main criteria being the number and size of knots present. "Clear" pine, for example, has no knots.

All lumber has a nominal dimension (what it's called) and an actual dimension (what it actually measures). A chart on page 237 shows the differences for some common lumber sizes. Lumber that is greater than 4" thick (nominally) generally is referred to as timber. Depending on its surface texture and type, a timber may actually measure to its nominal dimensions, so check this out before buying. Cedar lumber also varies in size, depending on its surface texture. S4S (Surfaced-Four-Sides) lumber is milled smooth on all sides and follows the standard dimensioning, while boards with one or more rough surfaces can be over ⅛" thicker.

When selecting hardware for your project, remember one thing: All nails, screws, bolts, hinges, and anchors that will be exposed to weather or rest on concrete or that come in contact with treated lumber must be corrosion-resistant. The best all-around choice for nails and screws is hot-dipped galvanized steel, recognizable by its rough, dull-silver coating. Hot-dipped fasteners generally hold up better than the smoother, electroplated types, and they're the recommended choice for pressure-treated lumber. Aluminum and stainless steel are other materials suitable for outdoor exposure; however, aluminum fasteners corrode some types of treated lumber. While expensive, stainless steel is the best guarantee against staining from fasteners on cedar and redwood.

Another type of hardware you'll find throughout this book is the metal anchor, or framing connector, used to reinforce wood framing connections. All of the anchors called for in the plans are Simpson Strong-Tie® brand (see Resources), which are available at most lumberyards and home centers. If you can't find what you need on the shelves, look through one of the manufacturer's catalogs or visit the manufacturer's website. You can also order custom-made hangers. Keep in mind that metal anchors are effective only if they are installed correctly—always follow the manufacturer's installation instructions, and use exactly the type and number of fastener recommended.

Finally, applying a finish to your project will help protect the wood from rot, fading and discoloration, and insects. Pine or similar untreated lumber must have a protective finish if it's exposed to the elements, but even cedar is susceptible to rot over time and will turn gray if left bare. If you paint the wood, apply a primer first—this helps the paint stick and makes it last longer. If you want to preserve the natural wood grain, use a stain or clear finish.

A combination of sheet stock, appearance-grade lumber, and structural lumber is used in most sheds.

Building Foundations

Your shed's foundation provides a level, stable structure to build upon and protects the building from moisture and erosion. In this section you'll learn how to build five of the most common types of shed foundations. All but the concrete pier foundation are "on-grade" designs, meaning they are built on top of the ground and can be subject to rising and lowering a few inches during seasonal freezing and thawing of the underlying soil. This usually isn't a problem since a shed is a small, freestanding structure that's not attached to other buildings. However, it can adversely affect some interior finishes (wallboard, for example).

When choosing a foundation type for your shed, consider the specific site and the performance qualities of all systems in various climates; then check with the local building department to learn what's allowed in your area. Some foundations, such as concrete slabs, may classify sheds as permanent structures, which can affect property taxes, among other consequences. Residents in many areas may need to install special tie-downs or ground anchors according to local laws. If your building department requires a "frost-proof" foundation (so the building won't move with the freezing ground), you should be able to pass inspection by building your shed on concrete piers (see page 32). *Note: Information for forming, reinforcing, and bracing deeper foundation walls is not included here. A safe rule of thumb is that the depth required to get below the frost line in cold climates is 4 feet, though colder places like Canada and Alaska can have frost depths up to 8 feet.*

Wooden Skid Foundation

A skid foundation couldn't be simpler: two or more treated wood beams or landscape timbers (typically 4 × 4, 4 × 6, or 6 × 6) set on a bed of gravel. The gravel provides a flat, stable surface that drains well to help keep the timbers dry. Once the skids are set, the floor frame is built on top of them and is nailed to the skids to keep everything in place.

Building a skid foundation is merely a matter of preparing the gravel base, then cutting, setting, and leveling the timbers. The timbers you use must be rated for ground contact. It is customary, but purely optional, to make angled cuts on the ends of the skids—these add a minor decorative touch and make it easier to skid the shed to a new location, if necessary.

Because a skid foundation sits on the ground, it is subject to slight shifting due to frost in cold-weather climates. Often a shed that has risen out of level will correct itself with the spring thaw, but if it doesn't, you can lift the shed with jacks on the low side and add gravel beneath the skids to level it.

Tools & Materials ▸

Shovel	Circular saw
Rake	Square
4-ft. level	Treated wood timbers
Straight, 8-ft. 4 × 4	Compactible gravel
Hand tamper	Wood sealer-preservative

How to Build a Wooden Skid Foundation

STEP 1: PREPARE THE GRAVEL BASE

A. Remove 4" of soil in an area about 12" wider and longer than the dimensions of the building.
B. Fill the excavated area with a 4" layer of compactible gravel. Rake the gravel smooth, then check it for level using a 4-ft. level and a straight, 8-ft.-long 2 × 4. Rake the gravel until it is fairly level.
C. Tamp the gravel thoroughly using a hand tamper or a rented plate compactor. As you work, check the surface with the board and level, and add or remove gravel until the surface is level.

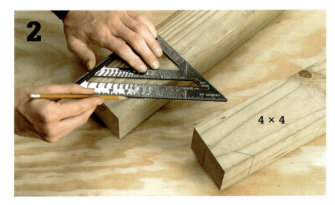

Excavate the building site and add a 4" layer of compactible gravel. Level, then tamp the gravel with a hand tamper or rented plate compactor (inset).

STEP 2: CUT & SET THE SKIDS

A. Cut the skids to length, using a circular saw or reciprocating saw. (Skids typically run parallel to the length of the building and are cut to the same dimension as the floor frame.)

B. To angle-cut the ends, measure down 1½" to 2" from the top edge of each skid. Use a square to mark a 45° cutting line down to the bottom edge, then make the cuts.

C. Coat the cut ends of the skids with a wood sealer-preservative and let them dry.

D. Set the skids on the gravel so they are parallel and their ends are even. Make sure the outer skids are spaced according to the width of the building.

STEP 3: LEVEL THE SKIDS

A. Level one of the outside skids, adding or removing gravel from underneath. Set the level parallel and level the skid along its length, then set the level perpendicular and level the skid along its width.

B. Place the straight 2 × 4 and level across the first and second skids, then adjust the second skid until it's level with the first. Make sure the second skid is level along its width.

C. Level the remaining skids in the same fashion, then set the board and level across all of the skids to make sure they they are level with one another.

If desired, mark and clip the bottom corners of the skid ends. Use a square to mark a 45° angle cut.

Using a board and a level, make sure each skid is level along its width and length, and is level with the other skids.

Concrete Block Foundation

Concrete block foundations are easy and inexpensive to build. In terms of simplicity, a block foundation is second only to the wooden skid. But the real beauty of this design is its ability to accommodate a sloping site: All you have to do is add blocks as needed to make the foundation level.

Blocks suitable for foundations are commonly available at home centers and masonry suppliers. Standard blocks measure 8 × 16" and come in 2" and 4" thicknesses. Be sure to use only solid concrete blocks, not regular building block—the kind with large voids for filling with concrete. Also avoid the various types of decorative block, which may have holes or odd shapes and probably won't be strong enough for this application.

On a level site, you can use a single 4"-thick block for each support point. On a slope, a combination of 4" and 2" blocks should get you close enough to shim

(with lumber or asphalt shingles) the foundation up to level. Setting the blocks on small beds of gravel helps prevent erosion or excess water from undermining the foundation. Avoid excavating and refilling beneath the blocks other than to create a base for compactible gravel, as that may lead to settling. *Note: All reinforcing steel (bars, mesh, or anchor bolts) should have a minimum of 1½" concrete cover. Without this cover, steel will likely rust and cause spalling of concrete.*

Tools & Materials ▸

Mason's lines & stakes	Solid concrete blocks
Excavation tools	Asphalt shingles or
Hand tamper	1 × 8 pressure-
2-ft. level	treated lumber,
4-ft. level	as needed
Long, straight 2 × 4	Construction
Caulking gun	adhesive
Compactible gravel	

Tip ▸

A 2 × 8 mud sill adds strength to a standard 2 × 6 floor frame. First, you fasten the side rim joists to the sill, then you set the assembly on top of the foundation blocks and install the remaining floor joists.

A foundation created with solid concrete blocks on a prepared base is simple to build and makes an easy solution to dealing with low slopes.

How to Build a Concrete Block Foundation

STEP 1: PREPARE THE SITE

A. Using four mason's lines tied to stakes, plot the foundation layout. The foundation exterior should equal the outer dimensions of the floor frame. Use the 3-4-5 method to ensure perfectly square layout lines.

B. Mark the block locations onto the strings, and then onto the ground: Locate the corner blocks at the string intersections, and locate the intermediate blocks at equal intervals between the corner blocks. For an 8×10-ft. or 8×12-ft. shed, one row of four blocks (or block stacks) running down each side of the shed is sufficient.

C. Remove the mason's lines, but leave the stakes in place. At each block location dig a 16×20" hole that is 4" deep. Tamp the soil.

D. Add a layer of compactible gravel in each hole and tamp well, adding gravel if necessary to bring the top of the gravel up to grade. Tamp all added gravel.

STEP 2: SET THE BLOCKS

A. For the first block, retie the mason's lines. At the highest point on the gravel bed, square up a 4"-thick block to the layout lines.

B. Level the block in both directions, adding or removing gravel as needed.

C. Tape a 4-ft. level to the center of a long, straight 2×4.

D. Set up each of the remaining blocks or block stacks, using the level and 2×4 spanning from the first block to gauge the proper height. Start each stack with a 4"-thick block, and make sure the block itself is level before adding more blocks. Use 2" blocks as needed to add height, or shim stacks with trimmed pieces of asphalt shingles or 1×8 pressure-treated lumber.

E. Use the level and 2×4 to make sure all of the blocks and stacks are level with one another.

STEP 3: GLUE THE BLOCK STACKS

A. Glue stacked blocks together with construction adhesive. Also glue any shim material to the tops of the blocks.

B. After gluing, check to make sure all blocks and stacks are level with one another, and that they are on the layout lines, then remove the strings and stakes.

Create a bed of compacted gravel centered at each block location in your layout.

Set a block at the highest point on the site, check it with a level, and adjust as needed. (Inset) Use a level and board spanning across the blocks to establish the height of each stack so all the tops are level.

Bind stacked blocks together with exterior-rated construction adhesive to prevent shifting.

Concrete Pier Foundation

Foundation piers are poured concrete cylinders that you form using cardboard tubes. The tubes come in several diameters and are commonly available from building materials suppliers. For a standard 8 × 10-ft. shed, a suitable foundation consists of one row of three 8"-diameter piers running down the long sides of the shed.

You can anchor the shed's floor frame to the piers using a variety of methods. The simplest method (shown here) is to bolt a wood block to the top of each pier, then fasten the floor frame to the blocks. Other anchoring options involve metal post bases and various framing connectors either set into the wet concrete or fastened to the piers after the concrete has cured. Be sure to consult your local building department for the recommended or required anchoring specifications.

Piers that extend below the frost line—the ground depth to which the earth freezes each winter—will keep your shed from shifting during annual freeze-thaw cycles. This is a standard requirement for major structures, like houses, but not typically for freestanding sheds (check with your building department). Another advantage of the pier foundation is that you can extend the piers well above the ground to accommodate a sloping site. *Note: All concrete should have compacted gravel underneath and against back walls as backfill. All reinforcing steel should have a minimum of 1½" concrete cover.*

How to Build a Concrete Pier Foundation

Tools & Materials ▸

Circular saw	Shovel	2½" screws	Concrete mix
Drill	Posthole digger	Stakes	J-bolts with washers
Mason's line	Reciprocating saw	Nails	and nuts
Sledgehammer	or handsaw	Masking tape	2 × 10 pressure-treated
Line level	Utility knife	Cardboard	lumber (rated for
Framing square	Ratchet wrench	concrete forms	ground contact)
Plumb bob	2 × 4 lumber	Paper	

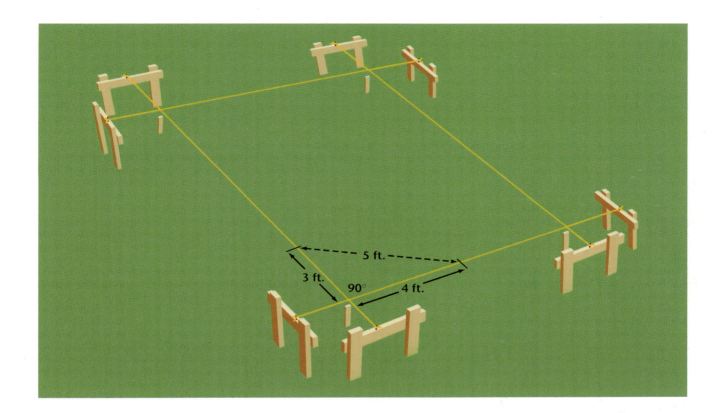

STEP 1: CONSTRUCT THE BATTER BOARDS

A. Cut two 24"- long 2 × 4 legs for each batter board (for most projects you'll need eight batter boards total). Cut one end square and cut the other end to a sharp point, using a circular saw. Cut one 2 × 4 crosspiece for each batter board at about 18".

B. Assemble each batter board using 2½" screws. Fasten the crosspiece about 2" from the square ends of the legs. Make sure the legs are parallel and the crosspiece is perpendicular to the legs.

STEP 2: SET THE BATTER BOARDS & ESTABLISH PERPENDICULAR MASON'S LINES

A. Measure and mark the locations of the four corner piers with stakes, following your project plan.

B. Set two batter boards to form a corner about 18" behind each stake. Drive the batter boards into the ground until they are secure, keeping the crosspieces roughly level with one another.

(continued)

Cut the batter board pieces from 2 × 4 lumber and assemble them with screws.

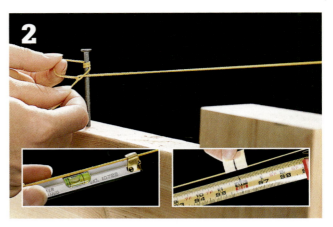

Tie the mason's lines securely to the nails, and level the lines with a line level (inset, left). Use tape to mark points on the lines (inset, right).

C. Stretch a mason's line between two batter boards at opposing corners (not diagonally) and tie the ends to nails driven into the top edge of the crosspieces; align the nails and line with the stakes. Attach a line level to the line, and pull the line very taut, making sure it's level before tying it.

D. Run a second level line perpendicular to the first: Tie off the end that's closest to the first string, then stretch the line to the opposing batter board while a helper holds a framing square at the intersection of the lines. When the lines are perpendicular, drive a nail and tie off the far end.

E. Confirm that the lines are exactly perpendicular, using the 3-4-5 method: Starting at the intersection, measure 3 ft. along one string and make a mark onto a piece of masking tape. Mark the other string 4 ft. from the intersection. Measure diagonally between the two marks; the distance should equal 5 ft. Reposition second string, if necessary, until the diagonal measurement is 5 ft.

STEP 3: MARK THE FOOTING LOCATIONS

A. Following your plan, measure from the existing lines and use the 3-4-5 method to add two more perpendicular lines to form a layout with four 90° corners. Use the line level to make sure the mason's lines are level. The intersections of the lines should mark the centers of the corner piers, not necessarily the outside edge of floor framing.

B. Check the squareness of your line layout by measuring diagonally from corner to corner: when the measurements are equal, the frame is square. Make any necessary adjustments.

C. Plumb down with a plumb bob and place a stake directly under each line intersection. Mark the locations of intermediate piers onto the layout strings, then plumb down and drive stakes at those locations.

D. Untie each line at one end only, then coil the line and place it out of the way. Leaving one end tied will make it easier to restring the lines later.

STEP 4: SET THE FORMS

A. Dig holes for the forms, centering them around the stakes. The holes should be a few inches larger in diameter than the cardboard forms. The hole depth must meet the local building code requirements—add 4" to the depth to allow for a layer of gravel. For deep holes, use a posthole digger or a rented power auger. Add 4" of gravel to the bottom of each hole.

B. Cut each cardboard form so it will extend at least 3" above the ground. The tops of all piers/forms should be level with each other. Also, the top ends of the forms must be straight, so place the factory-cut end up, whenever possible. Otherwise, mark a straight cutting line using a large piece of paper with at least one straight edge: Wrap the paper completely around the form so that it overlaps itself a few inches. Position the straight edge of the paper on the cutting mark, and align the overlapping edges of the paper with each other. Mark around the tube along the edge of the paper. Cut the tube with a reciprocating saw or handsaw.

C. Set the tubes in the holes and fill in around them with dirt. Set a level across the top of each tube to make sure the top is level as you secure the tube with dirt. Pack the dirt firmly, using a shovel handle or a stick.

Use a plumb bob to mark the pier locations. Drive a stake into the ground directly below the plumb bob pointer.

Wrap paper around the form to mark a straight cutting line (inset). Set the forms in the holes on top of a 4" gravel layer.

Fill the forms with concrete, then set the J-bolts. Check with a plumb bob to make sure the bolts are centered.

Anchor a block to each pier with a washer and nut. If desired, countersink the hardware (inset).

STEP 5: POUR THE CONCRETE

A. Restring the mason's lines and confirm that the forms are positioned accurately.

B. Mix the concrete following the manufacturer's directions; prepare only as much as you can easily work with before the concrete sets. Fill each form with concrete, using a long stick to tamp it down and eliminate air pockets in the concrete. Overfill the form slightly.

C. Level the concrete by pulling a 2 × 4 on edge across the top of the form, using a side-to-side sawing motion. Fill low spots with concrete so that the top is perfectly flat.

D. Set a J-bolt into the wet concrete in the center of the form. Lower the bolt slowly, wiggling it slightly to eliminate air pockets. Use a plumb bob to make sure the bolt is aligned exactly with the mark on

the mason's line. *Note: You can set the bolt at 1½" above the concrete so it will be flush with the top of the block, or extend it about 2½" so the washer and nut will sit on top of the block; doing the latter means you won't have to countersink the washer and nut. Make sure the bolt is plumb, then smooth the concrete around the bolt and let the concrete cure.*

STEP 6: INSTALL THE WOOD BLOCKS

A. Cut 8 × 8" square blocks from 2 × 10 pressure-treated lumber that's rated for ground contact.

B. Drill a hole for the J-bolt through the exact center of each block; if you're countersinking the hardware, first drill a counterbore for the washer and nut.

C. Position each block on a pier, then add a galvanized washer and nut. Use the layout strings to align the blocks, then tighten the nuts to secure the blocks.

Concrete Slab Foundation

The slab foundation commonly used for sheds is called a slab-on-grade foundation. This combines a 3½"- to 4"-thick floor slab with an 8"- to 12"-thick perimeter footing that provides extra support for the walls of the building. The whole foundation can be poured at one time using a simple wood form.

Because they sit above ground, slab-on-grade foundations are susceptible to frost heave and in cold-weather climates are suitable only for detached buildings. Specific design requirements also vary by locality, so check with the local building department regarding the depth of the slab, the metal reinforcement required, the type and amount of gravel required for the subbase, and whether plastic or another type of moisture barrier is needed under the slab.

The slab shown in this project has a 3½"-thick interior with an 8"-wide × 8"-deep footing along the perimeter. The top of the slab sits 4" above ground level, or grade. There is a 4"-thick layer of compacted gravel underneath the slab and the concrete is reinforced internally with a layer of 6 × 6" $^{10}/_{10}$ welded wire mesh (WWM). (In some areas, you may be required to add rebar in the foundation perimeter—check the local code.) After the concrete is poured and finished, 8"-long galvanized J-bolts are set into the slab along the edges. These are used later to anchor the wall framing to the slab. *Note: All concrete should have compacted gravel underneath and against the back wall as backfill. All reinforcing steel should have a minimum of 1½" concrete cover.*

Tools & Materials ▸

Circular saw
Drill
Mason's line
Sledgehammer
Line level
Framing square
Shovel
Wheelbarrow
Rented plate compactor
Bolt cutters
Bull float
Hand-held
   concrete float

Concrete edger
Compactible gravel
2 × 3 & 2 × 4 lumber
1¼" & 2½"
   deck screws
¾" A-C plywood
8d nails
5 × 10-ft. welded wire
   mesh (WWM)
1½" brick pavers
J-bolts
2"-thick rigid
   foam insulation

8"-thick perimeter · 4" compacted gravel · Welded wire mesh · Plywood form · Trench sloped 45° · 3½"-thick slab · #4 bars

How to Build a Concrete Slab Foundation

STEP 1: EXCAVATE THE SITE

A. Set up batter boards and run level mason's lines to represent the outer dimensions of the slab. Use the 3-4-5 method to make sure your lines are perpendicular, and check your final layout for squareness by measuring the diagonals.

B. Excavate the area 4" wider and longer than the string layout—this provides some room to work. For the footing portion along the perimeter, dig a trench that is 8" wide × 8" deep.

C. Remove 3½" of soil over the interior portion of the slab, then slope the inner sides of the trench at 45°. Set up temporary cross strings to check the depth as you work.

D. Add a 4" layer of compactible gravel over the entire excavation and rake it level. Compact the gravel thoroughly, using a rented plate compactor. *Note: All areas are to be level (flat).*

Measure down from the layout lines and temporary cross strings to check the depth of the excavation.

Assemble the form pieces with 2½" deck screws, then check the inner dimensions of the form. For long runs, join pieces with plywood mending plates.

Drive stakes every 12" to support the form, using the mason's lines to make sure the form remains straight.

Lay out sheets of wire mesh, tie the rows together, then prop up the mesh with brick pavers or metal bolsters.

STEP 2: BUILD THE FORM

A. Cut sheets of ¾" A-C plywood into six strips of equal width—about 7⅞", allowing for the thickness of the saw blade. To make sure the cuts are straight, use a table saw or a circular saw and straightedge.

B. Cut the plywood strips to length to create the sides of the form. Cut two sides 1½" long so they can overlap the remaining two sides. For sides that are longer than 8 ft., join two strips with a mending plate made of scrap plywood; fasten the plate to the back sides of the strips with 1¼" screws.

C. Assemble the form by fastening the corners together with screws. The form's inner dimensions must equal the outer dimensions of the slab.

STEP 3: SET THE FORM

A. Cut 18"-long stakes from 2 × 3 lumber—you'll need one stake for every linear foot of form, plus one extra stake for each corner. Taper one end of each stake to a point.

B. Place the form in the trench and align it with the mason's lines. Drive a stake near the end of each side of the form, setting the stake edge against the form and driving down to 3" above grade.

C. Measuring down from the mason's lines, position the form 4" above grade. Tack the form to the stakes with partially driven 8d nails (driven through the form into the stakes). Measure the diagonals to make sure the form is square and check that the top of the form is level. Drive the nails completely.

D. Add a stake every 12" and drive them down below the top edge of the form. Secure the form with two 8d nails driven into each stake. As you work, check with a string line to make sure the form sides are straight and the tops are level, and measure the diagonals to check for square.

(continued)

Screed the concrete after filling the form, using two people to screed, while a third fills low spots with a shovel.

Float the slab with a bull float, then set the J-bolts at the marked locations (inset).

STEP 4: ADD THE METAL REINFORCEMENT

A. Lay out rows of 6 × 6" ¹⁰⁄₁₀ welded wire mesh so their ends are 1½" to 2" from the insides of the forms. Cut the mesh with bolt cutters or heavy pliers, and stand on the unrolled mesh as you cut, to prevent it from springing back. Overlap the sheets of mesh by 6" and tie them together with tie wire.

B. Prop up the mesh with pieces of 1½"-thick brick pavers or metal bolsters. The WWM should be just below the center of the slab (about 2" down in a 3½" slab).

C. Mark the layout of the J-bolts onto the top edges of the form, following your plan. (J-bolts typically are placed 4" to 6" from each corner and every 3 ft. in between, but may vary.)

STEP 5: POUR THE SLAB

A. Estimate and order concrete (see page 39). Starting at one end, fill in the form with concrete, using a shovel to distribute it. Use the shovel blade or a 2 × 4 to stab into the concrete to eliminate air pockets and settle it around the wire mesh and along the forms. Fill with concrete to the top of the form.

B. As the form fills, have two helpers screed the concrete, using a straight 2 × 4 or 2 × 6 that spans the form: Drag the screed board along the top of the form, working it back and forth in a sawing motion. Throw shovelfuls of concrete ahead of the screed board to fill low spots. The goal of screeding is to make the surface of the concrete perfectly flat and level, if not smooth.

C. Gently rap the outsides of the form with a hammer to settle the concrete along the inside faces of the form. This helps smooth the sides of the slab, but too much will cause aggregate to settle and concrete will "scale" or "spall."

STEP 6: FINISH THE CONCRETE & SET THE J-BOLTS

A. Immediately after screeding the concrete, make one pass with a bull float to smooth the surface. Add small amounts of concrete to fill low spots created by the floating, then smooth those areas with the float. Floating forces the aggregate down and draws the water and sand to the surface.

B. Set the galvanized J-bolts into the concrete 1¾" from the outside edges of the slab (bottom should turn in toward the slab). Work the bolts into the concrete by wiggling them slightly to eliminate air pockets. The bolts should be plumb and protrude 2½" from the slab surface. After setting each bolt, smooth the concrete around the bolt, using a magnesium or wood concrete float.

C. Watch the concrete carefully as it cures. The bull-floating will cause water (called bleed water) to rise, casting a sheen on the surface. Wait for the bleed water to disappear and the surface to become dull. Pressure-test the concrete for firmness by stepping on it with one foot: if your foot sinks ¼" or less, the concrete is ready to be finished. *Note: Air-entrained concrete may have very little bleed water, so it's best to rely on the pressure test.*

D. Float the concrete with a hand-held magnesium or wood float, working the float back and forth until the surface is smooth. If you can't reach the entire slab from the sides, lay pieces of 2"-thick rigid foam insulation over the concrete and kneel on the insulation. Work backwards to cover up any impressions.

E. Use a concrete edging tool to round over the slab edge, running the edger between the slab and the form. If you want a very smooth finish, work the concrete with a trowel.

F. Let the concrete cure for 24 hours, then strip the forms. Wait an additional 24 hours before building on the slab.

Estimating & Ordering Concrete ▸

A slab for a shed requires a lot of concrete: an 8 × 10-ft. slab designed like the one in this project calls for about 1.3 cubic yards of concrete; a 12 × 12-ft. slab, about 2.3 cubic yards. Considering the amount involved, you'll probably want to order ready-mix concrete delivered by truck to the site (most companies have a minimum order charge). Tell the mixing company that you're using the concrete for an exterior slab.

An alternative for smaller slabs is to rent a concrete trailer from a rental center or landscaping company; they fill the trailer with one yard of mixed concrete and you tow it home with your own vehicle.

If you're having your concrete delivered, be sure to have a few helpers on-hand when the truck arrives; neither the concrete nor the driver will wait for you to get organized. Also, concrete trucks must be unloaded completely, so designate a dumping spot for any excess. Once the form is filled, load a couple of wheelbarrows with concrete (in case you need it) then have the driver dump the rest. Be sure to spread out and hose down the excess concrete so you aren't left with an immovable boulder in your yard.

If you've never worked with concrete, finishing a large slab can be a challenging introduction; you might want some experienced help with the pour.

ESTIMATING CONCRETE

Calculate the amount of concrete needed for a slab of this design using this formula:

Width × Length × Depth, in ft. (of main slab)
Multiply by 1.5 (for footing edge and spillage)
Divide by 27 (to convert to cubic yards)

Example—for a 12 × 12-ft. slab:
12 × 12 × .29 (3½") = 41.76
41.76 × 1.5 = 62.64
62.64 ÷ 27 = 2.32 cubic yards

Timing is key to an attractive concrete finish. When concrete is poured, the heavy materials gradually sink, leaving a thin layer of water—known as bleed water—on the surface. To achieve an attractive finish, it's important to let bleed water dry before proceeding with other steps. Follow these rules to avoid problems:

- Settle and screed the concrete and add control joints immediately after pouring and before bleed water appears. Otherwise, crazing, spalling, and other flaws are likely.
- Let bleed water dry before floating or edging. Concrete should be hard enough that foot pressure leaves no more than a ¼"-deep impression.
- Do not overfloat the concrete; it may cause bleed water to reappear. Stop floating if a sheen appears, and resume when it is gone.

Note: Bleed water does not appear with air-entrained concrete, which is used in regions where temperatures often fall below freezing.

Tips for Pouring Concrete ▸

- Do not overload your wheelbarrow. Experiment with sand or dry mix to find a comfortable, controllable volume. This also helps you get a feel for how many wheelbarrow loads it will take to complete your project.
- Once concrete is poured and floated it must cure. It should not dry. If it is a hot day it is a good idea to spray mist from a hose after it has "set" to keep it moist. Make sure you have a flat, stable surface between the concrete source and the forms.
- Start pouring concrete at the farthest point from the concrete source, and work your way back.

Framing the Structure

Framing is one of the most satisfying phases of a building project. Using basic tools and materials, you'll assemble the skeleton of the structure, piece by piece, and in the process learn the fundamentals of carpentry. The style of framing shown here is standard 2 × 4 framing, also called stick framing. For an alternative style, see the Timber-frame Garden Shed on page 180.

The tools you'll use for most framing are the circular saw (and power miter saw, if you have one), framing square, level, chalk line, and, of course, a framing hammer. Nails used for most framing are called common nails. These have a larger diameter than box nails, making them stronger, but also more likely to split thinner stock. Box nails are better for siding, trim, and other nonstructural materials.

The three most commonly used nailing techniques are shown in the illustrations below. Some framing connections, such as where rafters meet wall plates, require metal connectors for increased strength.

Nailing Techniques ▸

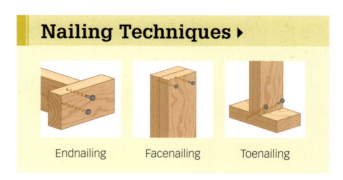

Endnailing   Facenailing   Toenailing

Floor Framing

Floor frames for sheds are simple versions of house floor frames. They have outside, or rim, joists that are set on edge and nailed to the ends of the common joists. On top of floor frames, a layer of tongue-and-groove plywood provides the floor surface and adds strength to the frame. To prevent rot, always use pressure-treated lumber and galvanized nails and hardware for floor frames.

Tools & Materials ▸

Circular saw
Square
Pressure-treated
  2× lumber

8d and 16d galvanized
  common nails
¾" tongue-and-groove
  exterior-grade plywood

How to Build a Shed Floor Frame

STEP 1: CUT THE JOISTS & MARK THE LAYOUT

A. Cut the two rim joists and the common joists to length, making sure both ends are square. Note that rim joists run the full length of the floor, while common joists are 3" shorter than the floor width.

B. Check the rim joists for crowning—arching along the narrow edges. Pick up one end of the board and hold it flat. With one eye closed, sight down the narrow edges. If the board arches, even slightly, mark the edge on the top (convex) side of the arch. This is the crowned edge and should always be installed facing up. If the board is crowned in both directions, mark the edge with the most significant crowning.

Tack together the rim joists, then mark the joist layout. Use a square to transfer the marks to the second rim joist.

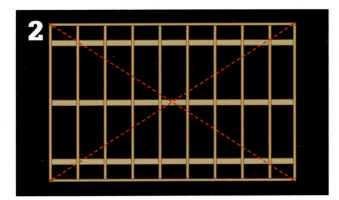

Measure diagonally from corner to corner. If the measurements are equal, the frame is square.

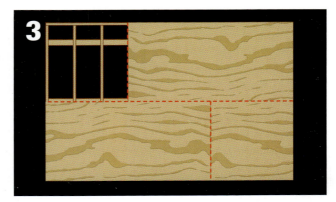

Install the plywood perpendicular to the joists. Start each row with a full sheet and stagger the end-joints between rows.

C. Lay one rim joist flat on top of the other so the edges and ends are flush and the crowned edges are on the same side. Tack the joists together with a few 8d nails. Turn the joists on edge and mark the common joist layout on the top edges: Mark 1½" and 15¼" from the end of one joist. Then, measuring from the 15¼" mark, make a mark every 16"—at 32", 48", 64" and so on, to the end of the board (if the plan calls for 24" spacing, make a mark at 1½" and 23¼", then every 24" from there). Don't worry if the last space before the opposite end joist isn't as wide as the others. Make a mark 1½" in from the remaining end. After each mark, draw a small X designating which side of the line the joist goes—this is a handy framers' trick to prevent confusion. This layout ensures that the edges of a 4-ft. or 8-ft. board or sheet will fall, or break, on the center of a joist.

D. Using a square, draw lines through each of the layout marks, carrying them over to the other rim joist. Draw Xs on the other joist, as well. Separate the joists and remove the nails.

STEP 2: ASSEMBLE & SQUARE THE FRAME

A. Check the two end joists for crowning, then nail them between the rim joists so their outside faces are flush with the rim joist ends and the top edges are flush. Drive two 16d galvanized common nails through the rim joists and into the ends of the end joists, positioning the nails about ¾" from the top and bottom edges.

B. Install the remaining joists, making sure the crowned edges are facing up. Joists should be square to edge of rim joists.

C. Check the frame for squareness by measuring diagonally from corner to corner: when the measurements are equal, the frame is square. To adjust the frame, apply inward pressure to the corners with the longer measurement.

D. If you're building the floor over skids, secure each joist to the outside skids with a metal anchor and toenail the joists to the internal skid(s) with 16d galvanized nails.

STEP 3: INSTALL THE PLYWOOD FLOOR

A. Lay a full sheet of ¾" tongue-and-groove exterior-grade plywood over the frame so the groove side is flush with a rim joist and one end is flush with an end joist. Fasten the plywood to the joists with 8d galvanized nails driven every 6" along the edges and every 8" in the field of the sheet. Do not nail along the tongue edge until the next row of plywood is in place.

B. Cut the second piece to fit next to the first, allowing for a ⅛" gap between the sheets. Install the second sheet with its outside edges flush with the frame.

C. Start the next row with a full sheet (ripped to width, if necessary). Install the sheet starting from the corner opposite the first sheet, so the joints between rows are offset. Make sure the tongue-and-groove joint is tight; if necessary, use a wood block and a sledgehammer to close the joint. Try to align factory edges to meet adjacent sheets.

D. Cut and install the remaining piece of plywood.

Wall Framing

Standard framed walls have vertical 2 × 4 studs nailed between horizontal top and bottom plates. The top plates are doubled to provide additional support for the roof frame and to strengthen the wall connections. Door and window frames are made up of king studs; a header, which supports cripple studs above the opening; and jack studs, which support the header. A window frame also has a rough sill and cripple studs below the opening. The opening defined by the frame is called the rough opening. Wall frames gain rigidity from plywood sheathing, siding, or diagonal 1× lumber braces. If you plan to store automobiles in your shed, use #3 or #4 bars 12" on-center (in lieu of WWM).

Building walls involves three major phases: laying out and framing the walls; raising the walls; and tying the walls together and adding the double top plates. *Note: If your building has a concrete slab floor, use pressure-treated lumber for the bottom plates and anchor the plates to the J-bolts set in the slab (see page 38).*

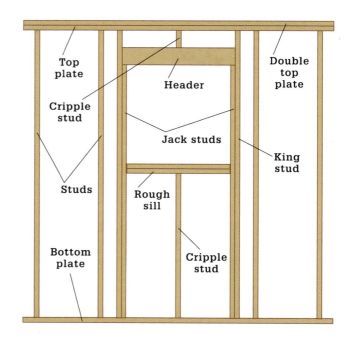

Tools & Materials ▶

Broom	Square	2× lumber	½" plywood
Circular saw or power miter saw	4-ft. level	8d, 10d, and 16d common nails	Construction adhesive
	Handsaw		

How to Frame Walls

STEP 1: MARK THE BOTTOM-PLATE LAYOUT LINES

A. Sweep off the floor and make sure it's dry. Cut a short (about 4 to 6") piece of plate material to use as a spacer. Position the spacer at one corner of the floor, with its outside edge flush with the outside of the floor frame. Mark a pencil line along the inside edge of the spacer.

B. Use the spacer to mark the wall ends at each corner of the floor (eight marks total). Snap chalk lines through the marks. These lines represent the inside edges of the bottom plates.

STEP 2: LAY OUT THE PLATES

A. Measure along the plate layout lines to find the lengths of the plates. *Note: Follow your project*

Use a block cut from plate material to lay out the bottom plates. Mark at the ends of each wall, then snap a chalk line.

2

End stud

Extra corner stud

Through wall

Butt wall

Mark the stud layout onto the wall plates, designating the stud locations with Xs. Through walls have an extra corner stud 2¾" from each end.

3

2 × 6

½" Plywood

2 × 6

Construct the headers from 2× lumber and a ½" plywood spacer.

plans to determine which walls run to the edges of the building (called through walls) and which butt into the other walls (called butt walls).

B. Select straight lumber for the plates. Cut a top and bottom plate for the first wall, making sure their dimensions are the same. Use a circular saw or a power miter saw, but make sure both ends are square. Lay the bottom plate flat on the floor and set the top plate on top of it. Make sure their edges and ends are flush, then tack the plates together with a few 8d nails.

C. Turn the plates on edge and mark the stud layout onto the front edges. If the wall is a through wall, make a mark at 1½" and 2¾" to mark the end stud and extra corner stud. Then, mark at 15¼" (for 16" on-center spacing) or 23¼" (for 24" on-center spacing)—measuring from this mark, make a mark every 16" (or 24") to the end of the plates. Make marks 1½" and 2¾" in from the opposite end. Following your plan, draw an X next to each mark, designating to which side of the line the stud goes. Mark the king and jack studs with a K and J respectively, and mark the cripple studs with a C. If the wall is a butt wall, mark the plate at 1½", then move the tape so the 3½" tape mark is aligned with the end of the plate. Keeping the tape at that position, mark at 15¼" (for 16" spacing) or 23¼" (for 24" spacing) then mark every 16" (or 24") from there. The 3½" that are "buried" account for the width of the through wall.

D. Using a square, draw lines through each of the layout marks, carrying them over to the other plate. Draw Xs on the other plate, as well.

STEP 3: CUT THE STUDS & BUILD THE HEADERS

A. Cut the studs to length, following the framing plan; make sure both ends are square. (Before cutting, give each stud a quick inspection to check for excessive bowing or crowning; reserve any bad studs for scrap or blocking.)

B. Select straight lumber for the door-frame studs. Cut the jack studs to equal the height of the rough opening minus 1½" (this accounts for the thickness of the bottom plate); cut the jack studs for the window frame to equal the height of the top of the rough opening minus 1½". Cut the king studs the same length as the common studs.

C. To build the headers, cut two pieces of 2× lumber (using the size prescribed by the plans) to equal the width of the rough opening plus 3". Check the boards for crowning, and mark the top edges. Cut a piece of ½" plywood to the same dimensions as the lumber pieces.

D. Apply two wavy beads of construction adhesive to each side of the plywood and sandwich the lumber pieces around the plywood, keeping all edges flush. Nail the header together with pairs of 16d common nails spaced about 12" apart. Drive the nails at a slight angle so they won't protrude from the other side. Nail from both sides of the header.

(continued)

Frame the walls with 16d nails endnailed through the plates into the studs. Toenail cripples to headers with 8d nails.

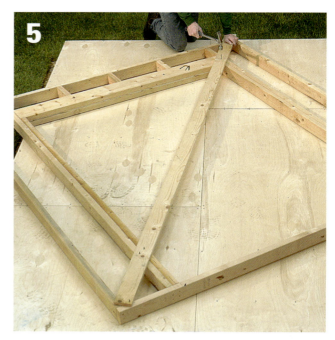

Install a diagonal brace to keep the wall square. Make sure the brace ends won't interfere with the construction.

STEP 4: ASSEMBLE THE WALL

A. Separate the marked plates and remove the nails. Position the plates on edge, about 8 ft. apart, with the marked edges facing up.

B. Set the studs on edge between the plates, following the layout marks. Crown all common and king studs to the same side. Before setting the door- or window-frame studs, facenail the jack studs to the inside faces of the king studs with 10d common nails staggered and spaced every 12"; make sure the bottom ends and side edges are flush.

C. Nail all of the studs to the bottom plate, then to the top plate. Position each stud on its layout mark so its front edge is flush with the plate edge (stud ends square to length of plates), and nail through the plate and into the stud end with two 16d common nails (use galvanized nails on the bottom plate if your floor is concrete). Drive the nails about ¾" in from the plate edges.

D. Set the header in place above the jack studs and nail through the king studs and into the header ends with 16d nails—use four nails on each end for a 2 × 6 header, and six for a 2 × 8 header. For a window frame, measure up from the bottom of the bottom plate and mark the top of the sill on the inside faces of the jack studs—this defines the bottom of the rough opening. Cut two sill pieces to fit between the jack studs and nail them together with 10d nails. Toenail the sill to the jack studs with 16d nails.

E. Cut the cripple studs to fit between the header and the top plate (and the sill and bottom plate, for window frames). Toenail the cripple studs to the plates and headers (and sill) with two 8d nails on one side and one more through the center on the other side.

STEP 5: SQUARE THE WALL FRAME

A. Check the wall frame for squareness by measuring diagonally from corner to corner: When the measurements are equal, the frame is square. To adjust the frame, apply inward pressure to the corners with the longer measurement.

B. When the frame is perfectly square, install a temporary 1 × 4 or 2 × 4 brace diagonally across the studs and plates. Nail the brace to the frame with 8d nails. Use two nails on the plates and on every other stud. To stabilize the structure, leave the wall braces in place until the walls are sheathed or sided.

C. At each end of the wall, attach a board to brace the wall upright after it is raised; nail it to the end stud with one 16d nail. *Note: Install only one end brace for the second and third walls; no end brace is needed for the final wall.*

STEP 6: RAISE THE WALL

A. With a helper, lift the top end of the wall and set the bottom plate on the layout lines you snapped in Step A. Swing out the free ends of the end braces and tack them to the floor frame to keep the wall upright. If you have a slab floor, nail the braces to stakes in the ground.

B. Fine-tune the wall position so the bottom plate is flush with the chalk line, then nail the plate to the floor with 16d nails. Drive a nail every 16" and stagger them so that half go into the rim joist and half go into the common joists. Do not nail the plate inside the door opening.

C. Pull the nails at the bottom ends of the end braces, and adjust the wall until it is perfectly plumb, using a 4-ft. level; set the level against a few different studs to get an accurate reading. Reattach the end braces with 16d nails.

STEP 7: COMPLETE THE WALL FRAMES & INSTALL THE DOUBLE TOP PLATES

A. Build and raise the remaining walls, following the same procedure used for the first wall. After each wall is plumbed and braced in position, nail together the end studs of the adjacent walls with 16d nails, driven every 12". Make sure the wall ends are flush.

B. Cut the double top plates from 2 × 4 lumber. The double top plates must overlap the top plate joints, so that on through walls, the double plate is 3½" shorter on each end than the top plate; on butt walls, the double plate is 3½" longer on each end. Nail the double top plates to the top plates with 10d nails. Drive two nails at the ends of the plates that overlap intersecting walls, and one nail every 16" in between.

C. Use a handsaw or reciprocating saw to cut out the bottom plate in the door opening.

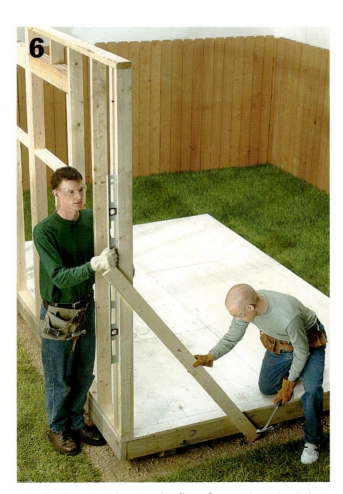

Nail the bottom plate to the floor frame, then plumb the wall and secure it with end braces.

Nail together the corner studs of intersecting walls (inset). Add the double top plates, overlapping the wall corners.

Manufactured trusses shown

Roof Framing

A roof frame is an important structure not only because it supports the roofing and helps keep the building dry, but because its style and shape have a great impact on the character of the building, the feel of the interior space, and the amount of storage space available.

There are four common roof types shown in this book. A gable roof is the classic, triangular design, with two sloped sides meeting at the peak, and flat ends (called gable ends). Gambrel roofs are like gable roofs with an extra joint on each side, resulting in two different slopes. A hip roof is structurally similar to a gable, but has no gable ends. Shed roofs are the simplest style, with only one sloped plane. They can be built with frames or, for small structures, a sheet of plywood.

All of these roof styles have a designated slope, which is the degree of angle of each side. The slope is expressed in a ratio that states the number of inches of vertical rise per 12" of horizontal run. For example, a roof that rises 6" for every 12" of run is said to have a slope of 6-in-12. Roof slope is indicated in drawings by a triangular symbol known as the roof-slope indicator. You'll use the roof slope to lay out rafters and fascia.

In standard roof framing, rafters are the principal structural members, rising from the walls to the ridge board at the peak of the roof. Rafters in outbuildings typically are made from 2 × 4s or 2 × 6s, are spaced 16" or 24" on center, and are installed perpendicular to the length of the building. To keep the roof planes from spreading apart, rafter ties, or collar ties, are nailed between opposing rafters to form a structural triangle. With shed-style roofs, the rafters span from wall-to-wall and no ridge board or ties are needed.

The key to successful roof framing is making accurate cuts on the rafters. Take your time to cut the first two rafters, making any necessary adjustments, then use one as a pattern for marking the rest.

As an alternative to rafter framing, you can take your plans to a truss manufacturer and have custom trusses built for your project. However, this will cost you more and probably will limit your storage space: the internal supports in truss frames leave little room for storage.

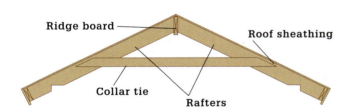

Ridge board

Roof sheathing

Collar tie

Rafters

Tools & Materials ▸

Circular saw
Framing square
4-ft. level

2× lumber
8d, 10d, and 16d
            common nails

Marking Angles with a Speed Square ▸

A speed square is a handy tool for marking angled cuts—using the degree of the cut or the roof slope. Set the square flange against the board edge and align the pivot point with the top of the cut. Pivot the square until the board edge is aligned with the desired degree marking or the rise of the roof slope, indicated in the row of common numbers. Mark along the right-angle edge of the square.

Pivot point

Common markings

Degree markings

How to Build a Roof Frame

Note: The following instructions are based on the sample rafter template shown here, which is designed for a 6-in-12 roof slope.

STEP 1: MARK THE PLUMB CUTS

A. Select a straight board to use for the pattern rafter. Mark the top plumb cut near one end of the board: Position a framing square with the 6" mark of the tongue (short part) and the 12" mark of the blade (wide part) on the top edge of the board. Draw a pencil line along the outside edge of the tongue.

B. Starting from the top of the plumb-cut mark, measure along the top edge of the board and mark the overall length of the rafter, then use the square to transfer this mark to the bottom edge of the board. Position the square so the tongue points down, and align the 6" mark of the tongue and the 12" mark of the blade with the bottom board edge, while aligning the tongue with the overall length mark. Draw a line along the tongue. If the bottom end cut of the rafter is square (perpendicular to the edges) rather than parallel to the top end, mark a square cut at the overall length mark.

STEP 2: MARK THE BIRD'S MOUTH CUTS

A. Measure from the bottom of the lower plumb cut and mark the plumb cut of the bird's mouth. Position the square as you did for the lower plumb cut and draw a line across the board face at the new mark.

B. Measure along the bird's mouth plumb cut and mark the bird's mouth level cut. Use the square to draw the level cut—it must be perpendicular to the bird's mouth plumb cut.

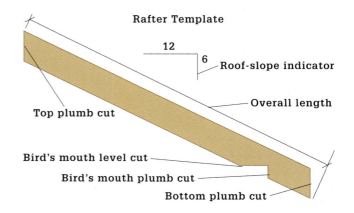

Rafter Template

12

6 — Roof-slope indicator

Top plumb cut

Overall length

Bird's mouth level cut

Bird's mouth plumb cut

Bottom plumb cut

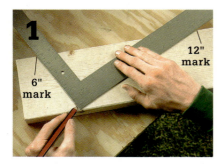

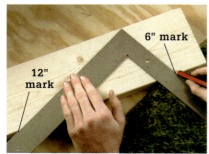

Position the framing square at the 6" and 12" marks to draw the top and bottom plumb-cut lines.

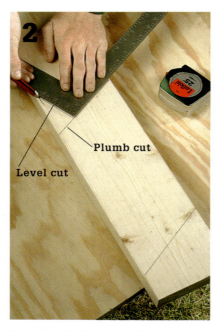

Mark the bird's mouth level cut by squaring off of the bird's mouth plumb cut.

Cut the bird's mouth by overcutting the lines just until the blade cuts entirely through the board.

Test-fit the pattern rafters, using a spacer made of 2× lumber to represent the ridge board.

Mark the rafter layout onto the wall plates and the ridge board, starting from the same end of the building for each.

STEP 3: MAKE THE CUTS

A. Cut the rafter ends at the plumb-cut lines, using a circular saw or power miter saw.

B. Set the base of a circular saw to cut at the maximum depth. Make the bird's mouth cuts, overcutting slightly to complete the cut through the thickness of the board. As an alternative to overcutting (for aesthetic reasons), you can stop the circular saw at the line intersections, then finish the cuts with a handsaw. It is not necessary to overcut 2 × 4 rafters with 8" or more overhang.

C. Select another straight board to use as a second pattern rafter. Use the original pattern rafter to trace the cutting lines onto the duplicate, then make the cuts.

STEP 4: TEST-FIT THE RAFTERS

A. Cut a 12"-long spacer block from 2 × 6 or 2 × 8 material.

B. With a helper or two, set the two rafters in place on top of the walls, holding the spacer block between the top rafter ends. Make sure the rafters are in line with each other (perpendicular to the walls) and are plumb.

C. Check the cuts for fit: The top-end plumb cuts should meet flush with the spacer block, and the bird's mouths should sit flush against the wall plates. Make sure the top ends are at the same elevation. Recut any angles that don't fit and test-fit the rafters again.

D. Write "PAT" on the pattern rafter, then use it to trace the cutting lines onto the remaining rafters. Before marking, check each rafter for crowning and mark the crowned edge; always install the crowned edge up. If your building has overhangs at the gable ends, mark the end cuts for the overhang rafters but not the bird's mouth cuts—overhang rafters don't have them. Also, if you have the fascia material on hand, use the pattern rafter to mark the angle for the top ends of the fascia boards (see page 48).

E. Cut the remaining rafters.

STEP 5: LAY OUT THE WALL PLATES & RIDGE BOARD

Note: Start the rafter layouts from the ends of the walls where you started the wall stud layouts. This ensures the rafters will fall above the studs. Install rafters aligned with the end studs but not the extra corner studs.

(continued)

6

Endnail the first rafter to the ridge, then toenail the second. Reinforce the bottom connection with a metal anchor (inset).

7

Angle-cut the ends of the collar ties to match the roof slope and facenail the ties to the rafters.

A. Make a mark on the top wall plate 1½" in from the end. Then, mark at 15¼" (for 16" on-center spacing) or 23¼" (for 24" on-center spacing)—measuring from this mark, make a mark every 16" (or 24") to the end of the wall. Make a mark 1½" in from the remaining end. Following your plan, draw an X next to each mark, designating to which side of the line the rafter goes.

B. Mark the wall on the other side of the building, starting from the same end.

C. Cut the ridge board to length, using the plan dimensions. Check the board for crowning, then lay it on top of the walls next to one of the marked plates, making sure it overhangs the end walls equally at both ends. Use a square to transfer the rafter layout onto both faces of the ridge board.

STEP 6: INSTALL THE RAFTERS

A. You'll need a couple of helpers and a long, straight 2 × 4 to get the rafters started. Lay the first two rafters on top of the wall, then nail the 2 × 4 to the far end of the ridge board to serve as a temporary support. Set up the rafters at the end of the walls and hold the free end of the ridge board in place between them. Have a helper tack

the rafters to the wall plates. Hold a level on the ridge board and make sure it's level, then have a helper tack the support to the far wall to keep the ridge level.

B. Slide one rafter a few inches to the side and endnail the other rafter through the ridge board with three 16d common nails (use two nails for 2 × 4 rafters). Slide the other rafter onto its layout mark and toenail it to the ridge with four 16d nails (three for 2 × 4s). Toenail the lower end of each rafter to the wall plate with two 16d nails, then reinforce the joint with a metal anchor, using the nails specified by the manufacturer.

C. Make sure the rafters are plumb and the ridge is level. Install the remaining rafters, checking for plumb and level periodically as you work.

STEP 7: INSTALL THE COLLAR TIES

A. Cut the collar ties (or rafter ties) to span between opposing rafters at the prescribed elevation, angle-cutting the ends to match the roof slope.

B. Position the collar tie ends against the rafter faces so the ends are about ½" from the rafters edges. Make sure the ties are level, then facenail them to the rafters with three 10d common nails at each end.

STEP 8: FRAME THE GABLE WALL

Note: Gable walls consist of top plates that attach to the undersides of the end rafters, and short studs set on top of the wall plates. They appear only on gable and gambrel roofs.

A. Cut the top plates to extend from the side of the ridge board to the wall plates. Angle-cut the ends so they meet flush with the ridge and wall plate. The top-end angle matches the rafter plumb cut; the bottom angle matches the level cut of the bird's mouth.

B. Fasten the plates to the rafters so the front plate edges are flush with the outside faces of the rafters; use 16d nails.

C. Mark the gable stud layout onto the wall plate, then use a level to transfer the layout to the gable plates. Cut the gable studs to fit, angle-cutting the ends to match the roof slope. Install the gable studs with 8d toenails. Also install a square-cut stud directly under the ridge board.

STEP 9: BUILD THE GABLE OVERHANG (GABLE & GAMBREL ROOFS)

Note: Gable overhangs are built with additional rafters installed at the gable ends. They are supported by the ridge board and blocks—called lookouts—attached to the end rafters.

A. Mark the layouts for the lookouts onto the end rafters, following the project plan. Cut the lookouts and toenail them to the rafters with 8d nails (or endnail them with 16d nails) so that the top edges of the blocks are flush with, and parallel to, the tops of the rafters.

B. Install the overhang rafters over the ends of the lookouts with 16d endnails.

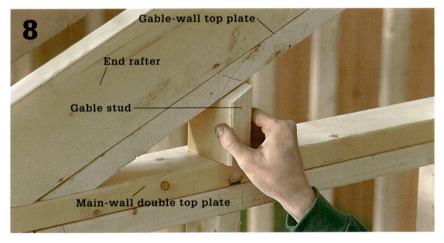

8

Gable-wall top plate

End rafter

Gable stud

Main-wall double top plate

Mark the gable stud layout onto the main-wall top plate and gable-wall top plate, then install the gable studs.

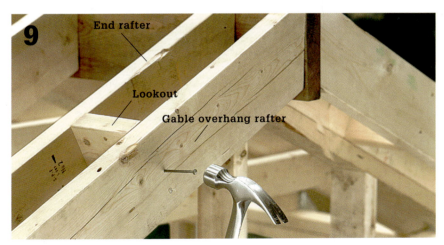

9

End rafter

Lookout

Gable overhang rafter

Nail the outer gable overhang rafters to the lookouts, making sure the top edges of the rafters are flush.

Roofing

The roofing phase typically follows the framing, for most building projects. As it's presented here, roofing includes installing the fascia board, the roof sheathing, and of course, the shingles or other material. You'll also see how to install roof vents.

Fascia board is 1× trim material, typically made of cedar, that covers the ends of the rafters. On gable and gambrel roofs, fascia also covers the end (or gable overhang) rafters. Sheathing is the structural deck of the roof. Depending on the type of roofing used, the sheathing may be plywood, tongue-&-groove decking boards, or spaced 1× or 2× lumber.

As for the roofing, deciding on a material is a matter of personal taste and practicality. Three common types used for outbuildings are covered here: asphalt shingles, cedar shingles, and metal roofing.

Asphalt shingles are the standard roofing material for outbuildings, just as they are for houses. For the money, asphalt shingles are the most durable and low-maintenance material available, and they come in a wide range of colors and styles.

Cedar shingles are a big step up in price from asphalt, but their visual appeal is undeniable. The type shown here is the factory-sawn shingle with flat, tapered sides. Cedar shingles are less expensive and easier to install than hand-split cedar shakes.

Metal roofing has been used for centuries on everything from chicken coops to cathedrals, and in recent years it has become increasingly popular in residential construction. Modern forms of metal roofing are extremely durable and easy to install, and they still make that nice sound when it rains.

Fascia & Sheathing

Fascia board and roof sheathing are always installed before the roofing, but which one you install first is up to you. Some buildings also have a 1× or 2× board installed behind the fascia, called subfascia. Made of rough lumber, the subfascia helps compensate for inconsistency in rafter length, ensuring the fascia will be straight. It also provides a continuous nailing surface for the fascia. To install subfascia, follow the same procedure used for installing fascia, but don't worry about mitering the ends—just overlap the boards at the corners.

The type of sheathing you use depends on the roof covering. Use CDX plywood (it's exterior-grade) for asphalt and cedar shingles. Depending on the building design, the fascia may be installed flush with the top of the sheathing, or the plywood may overlap the fascia. If you install the fascia first, cut spacers from the sheathing stock and use them when measuring and installing the fascia. Both shingle types must be installed over a layer of 15# building paper (also called tar paper or roofing felt), which goes on after the sheathing and fascia. The paper protects the sheathing from moisture and prevents the shingles from bonding to it.

As an alternative to plywood sheathing, you can use decking boards as a shingle underlayment. Typically sold in ¾ dimension (1¹⁄₁₆" thick), board sheathing creates an attractive "ceiling" for the inside of a building, and the nails won't show through as they do with plywood sheathing.

For metal roofing, install purlins—evenly spaced, parallel rows of 1× or 2× boards nailed perpendicular to the rafters. Install the fascia over the ends of the purlins, flush with the tops.

Tools & Materials ▸

Framing square	6d and 8d galvanized
Circular saw	finish nails
Stapler	CDX plywood
Fascia &	roof sheathing
trim material	8d box nails
	15# building paper

How to Install Fascia Board

STEP 1: CUT & FIT THE GABLE-END FASCIA

A. Mark a plumb cut on the top end of the first fascia board: If you didn't mark the fascia boards with the pattern rafter (page 48), use a framing square to mark the plumb cut, following the same method used for marking rafters (page 49). Make the cut with a circular saw or power miter saw.

B. Hold the cut end of the fascia against the end rafter. If the fascia will be flush with the top of the sheathing, use spacers set on the rafter and position the top edge of the fascia flush with the spacers.

C. Have a helper mark the lower end for length by tracing along the rafter end onto the back side of the fascia. Make the cut with a 45° bevel (miter). If you're using a circular saw, tilt the blade to 45° and follow the traced line; if you have a compound miter saw, rotate the blade to match the cutting line and tilt the blade to 45°.

Mark the bottom end of the gable fascia by tracing along the end of the rafter (or the subfascia). If the fascia will be installed flush with the sheathing, use a spacer for positioning.

(continued)

2

Fasten the fascia to the rafters (or subfascia) with 8d finish nails, then locknail the corner joints with 6d nails. Use scarf joints to join boards in long runs (inset).

D. Temporarily tack the fascia in place against the rafter with a couple of 8d galvanized finish nails. Repeat this process to mark, cut, and tack up the opposing fascia piece, then do the same at the other gable end.

STEP 2: INSTALL THE FASCIA ALONG THE EAVES

A. Cut a 45° bevel on the end of another fascia piece and fit it against one of the pieces on the gable end. If the board is long enough to span the building, mark the opposite end to length. If you'll need two pieces to complete the eave, mark the board about ¼" from the far edge of a rafter; cut that end with a 45° bevel, angled so the longer side of the board will be against the rafter. Cut the remaining piece with a 45°

bevel angled in the opposite direction. This is known as a scarf joint. Nail these with 8d galvanized finish nails and drill pilot holes to prevent splitting.

B. Make sure the corner joints fit well, then tack the fascia to the rafters.

C. Cut and tack up the fascia along the other eave. Make sure all of the joints fit well, then fasten the fascia permanently with 8d galvanized finish nails: drive three nails into each rafter end and a pair of nails every 16" along the gable ends.

D. Locknail each corner joint with three 6d galvanized finish nails. If necessary, drill pilot holes to prevent splitting.

E. Install any additional trim, such as 1 × 2, called for by the plan. Miter the ends for the best appearance.

How to Install Plywood Sheathing & Building Paper

STEP 1: INSTALL THE SHEATHING

A. Lay a full sheet of CDX plywood on top of the rafters at one of the lower corners of the roof. Position the edges of the sheet ⅛" from the fascia (or the outside edges of the rafters) and make sure the inside end of the sheet falls over the center of a rafter; trim the sheet, if necessary.

B. Fasten the sheet to the rafters with 8d box nails spaced every 6" along the edges and every 12" in the field of the sheet.

C. Cut and install the next sheet to complete the first row, leaving a ⅛" gap between the sheet ends.

D. Start the second row with a half-length sheet so the vertical joints will be staggered between rows. Measure from the top of the first row to the center of the ridge board, and rip the sheet to that dimension.

E. Install the first sheet of the second row, then cut and install the remaining sheet to complete the row.

F. Sheath the opposite side of the roof following the same process.

STEP 2: INSTALL THE BUILDING PAPER

Note: If you are installing asphalt shingles, add a drip edge along the eaves before laying the building paper.

A. Roll out 15# building paper across the roof along the eave edge. If you've installed a drip edge, hold the paper flush with the drip edge; if there's no drip edge, overhang the fascia on the eave by ⅜". Overhang the gable ends by 1 to 2". (On hip roofs, overhang the hip ridges by 6".)

B. Secure the paper with staples driven about every 12".

C. Apply the remaining rows, each overlapping the preceding row by at least 2". Overhang the ridge by 6". Overlap any vertical joints by at least 4".

D. Install the paper on the other roof side(s), again overlapping the ridge by 6".

E. Trim the paper flush with the fascia on the gable ends.

Install the plywood sheathing so the vertical joints are staggered between rows.

Apply building paper from the bottom up, so the lower paper is overlapped by the paper above it.

Asphalt Shingles

Asphalt shingles come in a variety of styles, but most are based on the standard three-tab system, in which each shingle strip has notches creating three equally sized tabs on the lower half of the strip. When installed, the tabs cover the solid portion of the shingle below it, giving the appearance of individual shingles.

For durability, use fiberglass-based shingles rather than organic-based. If you choose a specialty style, such as a decorative shingle or a type that is made to appear natural (similar to wood or slate), check with the manufacturer for specific installation instructions.

Prepare the roof for shingles by installing building paper and a metal drip edge along the roof perimeter. The drip edge covers the edges of the fascia and supports the shingle edges.

Tools & Materials ▸

Metal snips	Metal drip edge
Chalk line	Asphalt shingles
Utility knife	2d roofing nails
Straightedge	Roofing cement

How to Install Asphalt Shingles

STEP 1: INSTALL THE DRIP EDGE

Note: Install the drip edge along the eaves before applying building paper; install the drip edge along the gable ends on top of the paper.

A. Cut a 45° miter on the end of a drip-edge piece, using metal snips. Hold the end flush with the corner of the fascia, and fasten the flange of the drip edge to the sheathing with roofing nails driven every 12". To prevent corrosion, use galvanized nails with galvanized drip edge and aluminum nails with aluminum edge. Overlap vertical joints by 2".

B. Apply the building paper over the entire roof (see page 55). Install the drip edge along the gable ends, over the paper, cutting 45° miters to meet the ends of the eave drip edge. Overlap horizontal joints by 2", overlapping the higher piece on top of the lower. At the roof peak, trim the front flanges so the opposing edge pieces meet at a vertical joint.

STEP 2: INSTALL THE STARTER COURSE OF SHINGLES

A. Snap a chalk line 11½" up from the front edge of the drip edge (this will result in a ½" overlap for standard 12" shingles).

Install the drip edge along the eaves over the sheathing. Add the building paper, then install edging along the gable ends.

Trim 6" from the end tab to begin the starter row. Position the starter course shingles upside down so the tabs point up.

Stagger each course of shingles by ½ tab, repeating the pattern after overhanging the edge by 1½ tabs.

Divide the shingles into thirds, then trim the corners to create the shingle caps (inset). Install the caps at the ridge.

B. Trim off one-half (6") of the end tab of a shingle, using a utility knife and straightedge.

C. Position the shingle upside-down, so the tabs are on the chalk line and the half-tab overhangs the gable drip edge by ⅜". Fasten the shingle with four 2d roofing nails, about 3½" up from the bottom edge: drive one below each tab, one 2" in from the gable edge, and one 1" from the inside edge. Drive the nails straight and set the heads just flush to avoid tearing the shingle.

D. Use full shingles for the remainder of the course, placing them upside down and butting their edges together. Trim the last shingle so it overhangs the gable edge by ⅜".

STEP 3: INSTALL THE REMAINING COURSES

A. Install the first course of shingles, starting with a full shingle. Position the tabs down and align the shingle edges with those in the starter course. Drive four nails into each shingle: one ⅝" above each tab, and one 1" in from each end, at the same level. Trim the last shingle to match the starter course.

B. Snap a chalk line on the building paper, 17" up from the bottom edge of the first course; this will result in a 5" exposure for each course. Check your shingle dimensions and adjust measurements as necessary.

C. Begin the second course with a full shingle, but overhang the end of the first course by ½ of a tab. Begin the third course by overhanging a full tab, then 1½ tabs for the fourth course. Start the fifth course with a full shingle aligned with the first course, to repeat the staggered pattern. Snap a chalk line for each course, maintaining

a 5" exposure. After every few courses, measure from the ridge to the shingle edges to make sure the shingles are running parallel to the ridge. If necessary, make slight adjustments with each course until the shingles are parallel to the ridge.

D. Trim the top course of shingles at the ridge. If you are working on a hip roof (gazebo), trim the shingles at each hip ridge.

E. Repeat the procedure to shingle the remaining side(s) of the roof. Overlap the ridge with the top course of shingles and nail them to the other roof side; do not overlap more than 5". On a hip roof, trim the shingles along the hip ridge.

STEP 4: INSTALL THE RIDGE CAPS

A. Cut ridge caps from standard shingle tabs: taper each tab along the side edges, starting from the top of the slots and cutting up to the top edge. Cut three caps from each shingle—you'll need one cap for every 5" of ridge.

B. Snap a chalk line across the shingles, 6" from the ridge. Starting at the gable ends (for a gable roof) or the bottom edge (for a hip roof), install the caps by bending them over the ridge and aligning one side edge with the chalk line. Fasten each cap with one nail on each roof side, 5½" from the finished (exposed) edge and 1" from the side edge. Maintain a 5" exposure for each shingle. Fasten the last shingle with a nail at each corner, then cover the nail heads with roofing cement.

C. Trim the overhanging shingles along the gable ends: Snap chalk lines along the gable ends, ⅜" from the drip edges. Trim the shingles at the lines. Cover any exposed nails with roofing cement.

Cedar Shingles

Cedar shingles come in 16", 18", and 24" lengths and in random widths, generally between 3" and 10" wide. The exposure of the shingles depends on the slope of the roof and the length and quality of the shingles (check with the manufacturer). Because they're sold in a few different grades, make sure the shingles you get are good enough to be used as roofing. Also, be aware that galvanized nails may cause some staining or streaking on the shingles; if you can't accept that, use aluminum or stainless-steel nails.

The project shown here uses 18" shingles with a 5½" exposure installed on a gable roof. At the ridge, the shingles are covered with a 1× cedar ridge cap, which is easier to install than cap shingles. If you want to shingle a hip roof, consult a professional.

Tools & Materials ▸

Utility knife	2 × 4 lumber
Chalk line	1¼" and 2"
Circular saw	roofing nails
Table saw	6d galvanized nails
T-bevel	1 × 4 and 1 × 6 cedar
Cedar shingles	Caulk/Sealant

Installing Roof Vents ▸

Roof vents used in conjunction with soffit vents can help keep the air in your shed cooler and cleaner. Vents are rated by square inches of ventilation area; most sheds need only two roof vents and two to four soffit vents.

Install roof vents centered between two rafters, about 16" to 24" from the ridge board. Cut a hole through the roof sheathing, following the manufacturer's instructions (photo, far left).

After applying building paper (page 55), center the vent over the hole, and trace around its base flange.

Install shingles to a point at least 2" inside the bottom of the outline—don't cover the hole.

Apply roofing cement to the underside of the base flange, then install the vent over the shingles, using rubber-gasket roofing nails driven into all of the flange sides.

Shingle over the side and top vent flanges, leaving the bottom flange exposed; do not nail through the flanges with the shingle nails (photo, left).

How to Install Cedar Shingle Roofing

STEP 1: INSTALL THE STARTER COURSE
A. Apply building paper to the entire roof, overhanging the eaves by ⅜" (see page 55).
B. Position the first shingle in the starter course so it overhangs the gable edge by 1" and the eave edge by 1½". Tack or clamp a 2 × 4 spacer to the fascia to help set the overhang. Make sure the butt (thick) end of the shingle is pointing down. Fasten the shingle with two 1¼" roofing nails, driven 4" up from the butt end and at least 1" from the side edges. Drive the nails just flush with the surface—countersinking creates a cavity that collects water.
C. Install the remaining shingles in the starter course, maintaining a ¼" to ⅜" gap between shingles. If necessary, trim the last shingle to width.

STEP 2: INSTALL THE REMAINING COURSES
A. Set the first shingle in the first course so its butt and outside edges are flush with the shingles in the starter course and it overlaps the shingle gap

below by 1½". Fasten the shingle 1 to 2" above the exposure line and 1" from the side edges.

B. Install the remaining shingles in the first course, maintaining a ¼" to ⅜" gap between shingles.

C. Snap a chalk line across the shingles at the exposure line (5½" in this example). Install the second course, aligning the butt ends with the chalk line. Make sure shingle gaps are offset with the gaps in the first course by 1½".

D. Install the remaining courses, using chalk lines to set the exposure. Measure from the ridge periodically to make sure the courses are parallel to the ridge. Offset the shingle gaps by 1½" with the gaps in the preceding three courses—that is, any gaps that are aligned must be four courses apart. Add courses until the top (thin) ends of the shingles are within a few inches of the ridge.

E. Shingle the opposite side of the roof.

STEP 3: SHINGLE THE RIDGE

A. Cut a strip of building paper to 24" wide and as long as the ridge. Fold the paper in half and lay it over the ridge so it overlaps the shingles on both sides of the roof; tack it in place with staples.

B. Install another course of shingles on each side, trimming the top edges so they are flush with the ridge. Cut another strip of building paper 12" wide, fold it, and lay it over these shingles.

C. Install the final course on each side, trimming the ends flush with the ridge. Nail the shingles about 2½" from the ridge.

STEP 4: INSTALL THE RIDGE CAP

A. Find the angle of the ridge using a T-bevel and two scraps of 1× board: position the boards along the ridge with their edges butted together. Set the T-bevel to match the angle.

B. Transfer the angle to a table saw or circular saw and rip test pieces of 1×. Test-fit the pieces on the ridge, and adjust the angles as needed.

C. Cut the 1 × 6 and 1 × 4 cap boards to run the length of the ridge. Join the boards with sealant and 6d galvanized box nails. Attach the cap to the ridge with 2" roofing nails driven every 12".

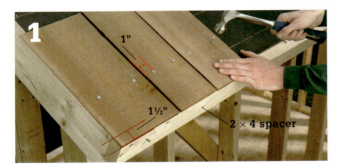

Install the starter row of shingles, overhanging the gable end by ⅜" and the eave by 1½".

Install the first course of shingles on top of the starter course, offsetting the shingle gaps 1½" between the courses.

Cover the ridge with 24" of building paper, then a course of trimmed shingles. Repeat with 12" of paper and shingles.

Use a T-bevel and scrap boards to find the ridge angles, then cut the 1 × 4 and 1 × 6 for the ridge cap.

Metal Roofing

Metal roofing panels typically are available in 3-ft.-wide panels, with most styles using some form of standing seam design, which adds strength and provides means for joining sheets. You can buy the roofing through metal roofing suppliers and at home centers, but the former typically offer more color options, and they'll custom-cut the panels to fit your project. Most manufacturers supply rubber-washered nails or screws for a watertight seal—use the recommended fasteners to prevent premature rusting due to galvanic action (caused by contact between dissimilar metals).

Install metal roofing over 1 × 4 or 2 × 4 purlins nailed perpendicular to the rafters at 12" to 24" on center—check with the manufacturer for purlin spacing and load requirements. Some roof panels require purlins with matching profiles. At the gable ends, add blocking between the purlins to provide a nailing surface for the end panels and the drip edge.

Tools & Materials ▸

Chalk line
Circular saw
Drill
1 × 4 or
  2 × 4 lumber

16d common nails
Metal roofing panels
  and preformed
  ridge cap,
  with fasteners

How to Install Metal Roofing

STEP 1: INSTALL THE PURLINS

A. Mark the purlin layout on the top edges of the the rafters, and snap a chalk line for each row. Fasten 2 × 4 purlins to the rafters with 16d common nails; use 8d nails for 1 × 4s. Make sure the upper-most purlins will support the roofing ridge cap.

B. On the gable ends, cut blocking to fit between the purlins, and install it so the outside edges are flush with the outer faces of the outer rafters.

Install the purlins across the rafters, then add blocking at the gable ends.

STEP 2: INSTALL THE ROOF PANELS

A. Set the first roof panel across the purlins so the finished side edge overhangs the gable-end fascia by 2" and the bottom end overhangs the eave by 2". Fasten the panel with self-tapping screws or roofing nails with rubber washers, following the manufacturer's directions for spacing.

B. Install the subsequent panels, overlapping each panel according to the manufacturer's directions.

C. Rotate the final panel 180° from the others, so the finished side edge is at the gable end. Overlap the preceding panel by as much as necessary so the finished edge overhangs the gable edge by 2". Fasten the final panel.

STEP 3: INSTALL THE RIDGE CAP

A. Center the preformed ridge cap over the peak so it overlaps the roofing panels. Make sure the cap overhangs the gable ends equally on both sides. *Note: Some products include ridge-cap sealing strips.*

B. Fasten the ridge cap to the top purlins.

Install the panels to the purlins using pole barn screws or other rubber-washer, self-tapping screws.

Add the ridge cap at the roof peak, covering the panels on both roof sides.

Siding & Trim

The siding and exterior trim not only provide an attractive skin for your building, they protect the structure from the weather. It's important to keep this function in mind as you install them: watch for areas where water can pool or trickle in, and make sure all unfinished edges and seams are covered or sealed with caulk.

Many siding manufacturers recommend staining or priming the back side of the siding (called backpriming) before installing it, which can help prevent the material from cupping or warping. Since conditions vary by region, ask your supplier about the best treatment for your siding, or contact the manufacturer.

The nails you use are another important consideration. All nails used outdoors must be corrosion-resistant, such as galvanized, aluminum, or stainless steel nails. Galvanized are the cheapest but can cause staining on unpainted cedar; aluminum will stain cedar less than galvanized, but the fasteners can be difficult to drive; stainless-steel nails are expensive but are strong and pretty much guaranteed to not stain cedar or ever corrode. Ring- or spiral-shank siding nails offer the greatest holding power.

Apply a protective finish—stain, paint, or varnish—to your siding and trim as soon as possible after installing them. Man-made products, although often factory-primed, are especially susceptible to water damage where hammer blows, nail holes, and cuts have marred the protective finish.

Wood siding is still the standard for building sheds, but as these photos show, not all wood siding looks alike.

Horizontal Siding

Common types of horizontal siding include clapboard (also called bevel or lap), which is installed to overlap the piece below it, and Dolly Varden, shiplap, and drop styles, which have grooved lower edges that receive the top edge of the board beneath. All types come in a variety of solid woods, and lap siding is also available in faux-textured hardboard—an inexpensive alternative to solid wood.

Install horizontal siding over plywood wall sheathing and 15# building paper. For most applications, it's easiest to install the exterior trim first then install the siding to fit between the trim boards. This means that the doors and windows will be in place, too.

The siding shown in this project is a hardboard lap siding installed with a 6" exposure. The boards have been primed on both sides, which protects the back side from moisture and saves time when painting the front side. Whichever siding you choose, check with the manufacturer regarding backpriming and moisture protection. Determine the overlap before starting. You can follow the manufacturer's minimum (typically 1"), or use more overlap so that the siding joints fall evenly at openings or along the tops of the walls.

Tools & Materials ▶

Circular saw	½" CDX plywood
Jigsaw	6d box nails
Stapler	15# building paper
Utility knife	Siding
Chalk line	8d siding nails
Level	Caulk

How to Install Horizontal Siding

STEP 1: INSTALL THE SHEATHING & BUILDING PAPER

A. Install ½" plywood sheathing (⅜" min. for 16" O.C.; ½" for 24" O.C.), starting at one corner of the building. Hold the side edge flush with the corner framing and the bottom edge flush with the bottom of the floor frame. Make sure the other side edge breaks on the center of a wall stud. The top edge should cover at least one of the wall plates. Nail the sheathing with 6d box nails, driven every 6" along the edges and 12" in the field of the sheet.

B. Install the remaining sheets, leaving a ⅛" gap between sheets. Overlap the sheathing at the corners. Sheath over window and door openings, then cut out the openings with a jigsaw or reciprocating saw.

C. Apply 15# building paper in horizontal strips over the entire wall surface, using staples driven about every 12". Overlap horizontal joints by 2", vertical joints by 6", and corners by 12". Hold or trim the paper flush with the bottom of the floor frame. Wrap door and window openings with paper.

D. Install all exterior trim, holding the corner and door trim ¾" below the floor framing. Install flashing over exposed doors and windows.

Install plywood sheathing over the entire frame, then staple building paper over the sheathing.

(continued)

STEP 2: INSTALL THE STARTER STRIP & FIRST COURSE

A. Cut 1"-wide starter strips of siding so there's enough to run the length of all of the walls. If the siding is beveled, cut only from the top edge of each piece, or use strips of plywood that match the thickness of the siding's top edge.

B. Position the starter strip along the bottom edge of the sheathing and fasten it to the framing with 8d siding nails.

C. Snap a chalk line above the bottom edge of the sheathing at a height equal to the width of the siding minus ¾". Mark the centers of the wall studs onto the building paper to facilitate nailing.

D. Cut the first course of siding to fit between the trim boards; make it snug but not so tight that you have to force the siding into place. Fasten the siding with one 8d siding nail driven at each stud location, about 1¼" from the bottom edge. If you need two boards to span the wall, center the inside ends over a stud, leaving a ⅛" gap between them; drive two nails at each end.

STEP 3: INSTALL THE REMAINING COURSES

A. Using the exposure dimension, measure from the top edge of the first course and snap a chalk line. Make sure the line is level; if it's not level, make slight adjustments over the next few courses.

B. Install the next course, aligning the top edge with the chalk line. Nail the siding just above the top edge of the course below, driving one nail at each stud. If the course has two boards, make sure the joint falls one or two studs away from the joint in the first course (stagger the joints for two more courses, then repeat the pattern at the original stud).

C. Snap chalk lines for the remaining courses, using the reveal dimension, and check the lines for level. Install the remaining courses. Mark angled cuts using a pattern made from scrap siding.

D. After completing one wall, use a level to transfer the siding layout onto the adjacent wall, so that the courses are aligned horizontally.

E. When all of the siding is installed, caulk all joints where siding meets trim or other pieces of siding.

Nail a starter strip along the edge of the sheathing, then snap a chalk line and install the first row of siding.

Drive siding nails into the studs, just above the preceding course (inset). Caulk all end joints after the installation.

Plywood Siding

Plywood siding is the least expensive and easiest to install of all the standard exterior finishes. It's available in 4 × 8-ft., 9-ft., and 10-ft. sheets; ⅜", ½", or ⅝" thicknesses; and in several styles, including striated, rough sawn, channel groove, and board-&-batten. The most common style, Texture 1-11 (shown here), is made to resemble vertical board siding and typically has ship-lap edges that form weather-proof vertical seams.

Another advantage of plywood siding is that the panels serve as bracing for framed walls, eliminating the need for sheathing. Plywood siding is exterior-grade, but the layered edges must be protected from moisture. For types with unmilled (square) edges, caulk the gap at vertical seams or install a 1 × 2 batten strip over the joint. All horizontal joints must have metal Z-flashing for moisture protection.

Tools & Materials ▸

Chalk line
Level
Circular saw
Plywood siding

8d galvanized finish nails
6d galvanized box nails
Galvanized or aluminum
    Z-flashing

How to Install Plywood Siding

STEP 1: INSTALL THE FIRST ROW OF SIDING

A. Snap a chalk line for the top edges of the siding, accounting for the overhang at the bottom edge: for wood floors, overhang the bottom of the floor frame by ¾" to 1"; for slabs, overhang the top of the slab by 1".

B. Position the first sheet—vertically—at a corner so one side edge is flush with the corner framing and the other breaks on the center of a stud; hold the top edge on the chalk line. Check with a level to make sure the sheet is plumb, then fasten it with 8d galvanized finish nails, driven every 6" along the perimeter and every 12" in the field of the sheet.

C. Install the remaining sheets, checking each one for plumb and leaving a ⅛" gap between sheets. (For ship-lap edges, first fit the sheets tight, then draw a pencil line along the upper sheet's edge. Slide over the upper sheet ⅛", using the mark as a gauge.) At the joints, do not nail through both sheets with one nail. Overlap the sheets at the corners, if desired (they will be covered by trim, in any case). Apply siding over door and window openings, but do not nail into the headers if you will install flashing (see page 73). If you start with a trimmed sheet, place the cut edge at the corner.

STEP 2: INSTALL THE FLASHING & SECOND ROW

A. Install Z-flashing along the top edge of the siding, using 6d galvanized box nails.

B. Install the upper row of siding, leaving a ⅛" gap above the flashing.

C. Cut out the door and window openings with a circular saw, jigsaw, or reciprocating saw.

D. Install trim over the flashed joints and at the building corners.

Install the plywood siding vertically. Plumb each sheet and fasten it to the framing with 6d nails.

Add galvanized metal flashing between rows of siding to prevent water from entering the seam.

Tongue & Groove Vertical Siding

Solid-wood, tongue-and-groove board siding has an attractive, natural look that is well-suited for outdoor buildings. Standard sizes of siding are 1 × 4, 1 × 6, and 1 × 8, available in cedar, redwood, pine, and other wood species. The type shown in this project is cedar 1 × 8 siding with V-grooves. Buy your siding long enough to run the full height of the building, because horizontal joints are difficult to make and they don't always look good.

Note: Unlike plywood siding, tongue-and-groove boards do not provide adequate bracing for the wall structure. Unless you use plywood sheathing as backing for tongue-and-groove siding, you must install 1 × 4 or 1 × 6 "let-in" bracing.

Siding that is 6" wide (nominal dimension) or narrower can be blindnailed with angled nails driven at the base of the tongue only, so the heads are hidden by the groove of the next piece (photo, right top); 8" or wider siding should be facenailed with two nails at each support (photo, right bottom).

If your building is stick-framed, add 2 × 4 blocking between the studs at 24" on center to support the siding.

Hidden nail pattern

Exposed nail pattern

Tools & Materials ▸

Circular saw	16d nails
Chalk line	Siding
Level	8d siding nails or
2 × 4 blocking	6d galvanized finish nails

How to Install Vertical Tongue & Groove Siding

Snap chalk lines at 24" intervals to guide the blocking placement. Endnail the blocking between the studs.

STEP 1: ADD BLOCKING (IF NEEDED)

A. Snap horizontal chalk lines across the studs, 24" apart, measuring from the floor.

B. Cut 2 × 4 blocks to fit between the studs. Endnail the blocks to the studs with 16d nails. Position alternate blocks below the chalk line to facilitate nailing.

STEP 2: INSTALL THE SIDING

A. If you are blindnailing the siding, position the first piece with the grooved edge flush with the corner framing; if you're facenailing, use either edge. Overhang the bottom of the board ¾" to 1" below the bottom of the floor framing (for wood floors) or 1" below the top of the slab (for concrete floors).

B. Hold a level along the leading edge to make sure the board is plumb, then fasten the board along the outside edge, every 16". For blindnailing, drive a 6d galvanized finish nail into each support along the tongue; for facenailing, drive two 8d siding nails at each support, 1½" to 2" from the side edges.

C. Install the next board, fitting together the tongue-and-groove joint. Nail at each support.

D. Install the remaining boards. Check every third or fourth board with the level to make sure it's plumb. Notch boards to fit flush around window and door openings; do not nail into the headers if you plan to install flashing (see page 73). To start a wall with a trimmed board, place the cut edge at the corner.

Plumb every third or fourth board with a level, making minor adjustments to the joints, if necessary.

Installing Trim

Trim includes the boards that conceal building seams, cover gaps around window and door frames, finish corners, and perform other decorative and weatherproofing functions. For sheds and outbuildings, simple trim details with 1 × 3, 1 × 4, or 1 × 6 cedar boards work well.

The type of siding you use will determine when to install the trim. For horizontal siding, install the trim first; for most other types, install the trim over the siding. If the trim is installed before the siding, make sure it's level and plumb—otherwise, you'll have to cut custom angles on the siding ends.

The simplest method for installing trim is to use butt joints. A slightly fancier alternative is to miter them. Trim joints are most noticeable on window and door trim (see photos, below), but you can miter corner trim, too.

To install window and door trim with butt joints, add the head trim first, then cut the two side pieces to fit. Install mitered trim pieces on opposing sides, (that is, top and bottom, then sides, or vice versa). Leave a ¼" reveal for all window and door trim. This adds interest and makes bowed jambs less noticeable. Exposed doors and windows must have flashing above the trim.

To install corner trim, cut two pieces to length, then nail them together at a right angle, using 6d or 8d galvanized box nails or finish nails. Set the trim on the corner, plumb it with a level, and nail it to the framing with 8d galvanized box or finish nails.

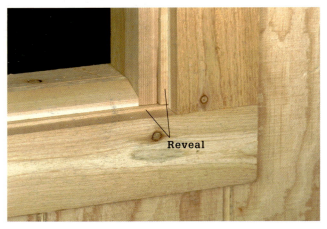

Window trim with butt joints

Window trim with miter joints

Nail corner trim pieces together before installing them.

Finishing Roof Overhangs ▸

A common method for finishing the underside of a roof overhang is to install soffit panels that enclose the rafter ends. Soffits can be attached directly to the rafters or to horizontal blocking that extends back to the wall. An alternative to soffitting is leaving the rafter ends exposed. With this application, the wall siding is notched to fit around the rafters.

A roof overhang should also include means for ventilating the building. With soffits, this can be achieved with soffit vents—metal grates (available in rectangular, plug, and strip styles) that cover holes cut into the soffit panels. Exposed overhangs are by nature ventilated but should have bug screen to seal the gaps between the walls and the roof sheathing. To increase ventilation, you can also install roof vents (see page 58).

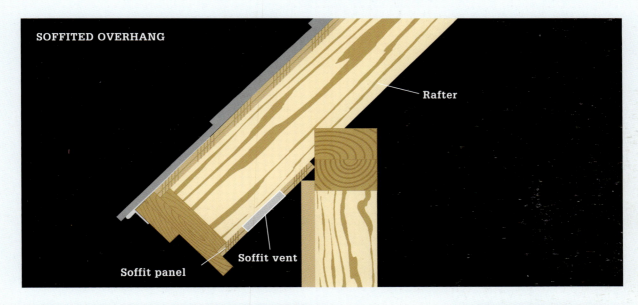

SOFFITED OVERHANG

Rafter

Soffit vent

Soffit panel

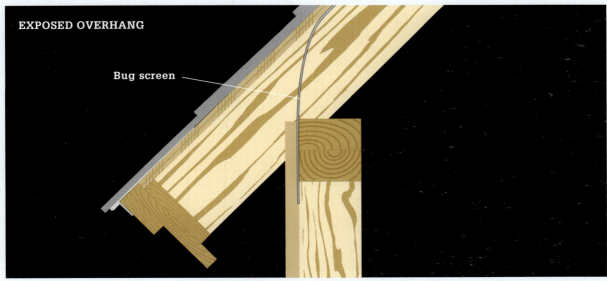

EXPOSED OVERHANG

Bug screen

Doors & Windows

Shed doors and windows can be either prehung (factory-built) or homemade. The shed projects in this book include plans for making your own doors and windows. They're simple designs using basic materials and can be built in an hour or two.

To keep water out, install flashing above the trim of any doors or windows that are exposed—that is, without a roof overhang above. If security is a concern, install a deadbolt for a pre-hung door or a hasp latch and padlock for a homemade door.

Prehung Doors & Windows

Prehung door and window units come in standard sizes, or they can be ordered in custom sizes, though at a higher price. Before framing the walls of your shed, select a door or window and confirm its exact dimensions before sizing the rough openings; be sure to use the outer dimensions of the unit's frame, not those of the door or window itself.

Most exterior doors have preattached trim, called brick molding, on the outsides of the jambs. You can remove this if you want to add your own trim.

Tools & Materials ▸

Level
Handsaw
Nail set
Door or window unit
Tapered cedar shims

Construction adhesive
16d galvanized casing
    nails (door) or
1¾" roofing nails
    (window)

How to Install a Prehung Window

1

Add pairs of tapered shims under the side window jambs and under the center of the sill.

Note: Window installations vary by product and manufacturer; follow the specific instructions provided for your window, including the steps for preparing the rough opening, shimming, flashing, etc. Shown here are the basic steps for installing a utility window with a nailing flange.

STEP 1: SET & SHIM THE WINDOW

A. Set the window into the rough opening and center it between the sides. Place pairs of tapered shims directly beneath the side jambs and at the center of the sill; position the shims so the tapered ends are opposed to form a flat surface.

B. From outside, drive one 1¾" roofing nail through the nailing flange at one of the lower corners of the window, but do not drive the nail completely.

STEP 2: LEVEL & FASTEN THE WINDOW

A. Place a level across the sill or top of the jamb, and adjust the shims until the window is perfectly level.

B. Drive one nail through the nailing flange at each corner of the window. Check the window operation to make sure it's smooth, then complete the nailing, following the manufacturer's instructions for spacing.

C. If the manufacturer recommends leaving the shims in place, trim the shims with a utility knife, then glue them in place with construction adhesive.

Level the window, then fasten the unit in place with roofing nails driven through the nailing flange on the exterior.

How to Install a Prehung Door

STEP 1: PLUMB & FASTEN THE HINGE JAMB

A. Cut out the bottom plate inside the rough opening, using a handsaw. Remove any bracing or nails installed to protect the door during shipping.

B. Set the door into the opening and center it between the sides. Push the brick molding flat against the sheathing or siding; if there's no molding, position the outside edge of the jamb flush with the siding or sheathing. Insert pairs of tapered shims (with the tapered ends opposed to form a flat surface) between the hinge jamb and the framing. Add shims at the top and bottom and at each hinge location.

C. Starting with the top shims, check the hinge jamb with a level to make sure it's plumb, and adjust the shims as needed. Nail through the jamb and shims and into the framing with one 16d casing nail. Repeat at the remaining shim locations.

STEP 2: SECURE THE LATCH & HEAD JAMBS

A. Standing inside the shed, close the door, and examine the gap between the door and latch jamb. Starting at the top of the latch jamb, install shims between the jamb and the framing. Check the gap to make sure you're not bowing the jamb. Fasten the jamb and shims with one 16d casing nail.

B. Shim and fasten the latch jamb at four more locations, level with the hinge-side shims, making sure the gap along the door remains consistent.

C. Shim and fasten the head jamb at two locations. For added support, you can replace one screw on each hinge with a 3½" screw, but be careful not to overtighten them and pull the frame out of square.

D. Nail through the brick molding and into the sheathing (or siding) and framing with 16d casing nails driven every 16".

E. Cut off the shims flush with the framing, using a utility knife. Set all nails with a nail set.

Plumb the door jamb, working from the top down. Fasten through the jamb and each shim pair with a casing nail.

Shim the latch jamb, using the gap between the door and the jamb as a gauge. Make sure the gap is consistent.

Homemade Doors & Windows

To make your own door or window, build and install the frame, measure the opening, then build and install the door to fit (or add the glass). Use 1× lumber for the frame, ripping it to width so it spans the wall section of the rough opening.

You can make a homemade door with almost any rigid board: siding, plywood, lumber, etc. Use the door plans provided in the shed project or create your own design.

For windows, you can use standard plate glass, tempered safety glass, Plexiglass™, or super-tough ¼" polycarbonate glazing (used in public structures such as bus stop shelters).

Installing a homemade door or window frame is similar to installing a prehung door: center the frame in the rough opening, shim between the jambs and framing, plumb and level the frame, and fasten it through the jamb and shims. Because a homemade door frame has no threshold to secure the bottom ends of the side jambs, install a temporary 1× spreader across the jambs to keep the frame square during installation.

To install a homemade door, mount the hinges to the door, then set the door in the frame and hold it against the stops. Insert shims underneath the door and between the door and latch jamb to set even gaps around the door. Mount the hinges to the wall with screws.

Flashing Above Doors & Windows ▶

Install metal flashing where siding meets trim to help divert water away from doors, windows, and their frames. When the siding is installed after the trim:

Nail the flashing to the sheathing so it laps over the trim, then install the siding over the vertical flange of the flashing.

When the siding is installed before the trim:

- Set the trim in place above the door or window, then trace along the top edge and ends of the trim (photo 1).
- Remove the trim and cut out the siding along the traced lines.
- Slip the flashing underneath the siding and fasten it with nails driven through the siding (complete the siding nailing).
- Reinstall the cut-out siding below the flashing—to serve as backing—then install the trim (photo 2).

Trace along the trim to mark the cutting lines for removing the siding.

Add the flashing, then install the siding cutout and the trim.

Ramps, Steps & Decks

Most of the sheds in this book with framed wood floors have a finished floor height that sits at least 10" above the ground. This makes for a fairly tall step up to the shed. On a sloping site, the approach to the shed may be considerably lower than the floor.

But not to worry—you can quickly build a custom ramp or set of steps for safe, easy access. As an alternative, you might add a large platform that serves as both a step and a sun porch.

Simple Ramp

A basic, sturdy ramp is a great convenience for moving heavy equipment in and out of your shed. Using the simple design shown here, you can make the slope of the ramp as gentle or as steep as you like (within reason). Of course, the gentler the slope, the easier it is roll things up the ramp. Construct your ramp from pressure-treated lumber rated for "ground contact." If desired, set the bottom end of the ramp on a bed of compacted gravel for added stability.

Tools & Materials ▸

Saw
Drill
Framing square
2 × 4 pressure-
    treated lumber

2 × 6 pressure-
    treated lumber
3" corrosion-
    resistant screws

How to Build a Shed Ramp

STEP 1: DETERMINE THE SLOPE & INSTALL THE LEDGER

A. Set a board onto the shed floor in front of the door opening with its end on the ground. Experiment with different placements until you find the best slope for your needs.

B. Mark where the end of the board meets the ground. Measure in toward the shed about 6" and make another mark—this represents the end of the ramp.

STEP 2: INSTALL THE LEDGER

A. Draw a level line onto the shed's floor frame 4⅝" below the shed's floor surface.

B. Cut a 2 × 4 ledger board to length so it equals the total width of the ramp. *Note: The ramp should be at least as wide as the door opening.*

C. Position the ledger on the level line so it is centered from side to side underneath the door.

Place a board between the ground and the shed floor to find the desired ramp slope.

(continued)

STEP 3: CUT THE FIRST STRINGER

A. To mark the angles for the stringer cuts, plot the layout of the ramp onto a sheet of plywood (or the shed floor). First, use a framing square to make two perpendicular lines representing the front of the shed and the ground. Measure the height of the shed floor, then subtract 1⅝". Transfer this dimension to one of the layout lines. Measure from the shed to the end-of-ramp mark on the ground, then transfer this dimension to the other layout line.

B. Place a 2 × 6 stringer board onto the layout lines so its top edge meets the two marks. Use the perpendicular lines to mark the angled end cuts on the stringer. Make the cuts.

C. Cut the upper end of the stringer to accept the ledger by making a 1½"-deep notch starting about 2¾" down from the top edge. The notch should be parallel to the end of the stringer.

Mark a level line 4⅝" below the floor to locate the top edge of the ledger.

Use perpendicular layout lines to mark the angled end cuts on the first stringer.

STEP 4: CUT & INSTALL
THE REMAINING STRINGERS

A. Test-fit the first stringer on the ledger. Make sure the 2 × 6 decking will not extend above the shed floor when installed. Make adjustments to the stringer cuts as needed.

B. Use the first stringer as a template to mark the cuts on the remaining stringers. You'll need one stringer for each end and every 12" to 16" in between. Cut the remaining stringers.

C. Fasten the stringers to the ledger and the shed's floor frame using 3" screws. The end stringers should be flush with the ends of the ledger.

D. Fasten the ledger to the floor framing with 3" corrosion-resistant screws.

STEP 5: INSTALL THE DECKING

A. Cut 2 × 6 decking boards to equal the width of the ramp.

B. Make sure the stringers are perpendicular to the shed, and then fasten the decking boards to the stringers with 3" screws. Leave a ¼" gap between boards to promote drainage and add traction on the ramp surface. *Note: If the top or bottom board will be narrower than 2", plan the decking layout so the first and last boards are roughly the same width.*

C. If desired, bevel the front edge of the board at the bottom of the ramp to ease the transition.

Make sure the first stringer fits well, then use it to mark the remaining stringers for cutting.

Fasten the decking to the stringers with 3" screws to complete the ramp.

Traditional Stairs

A small set of framed wooden stairs is usually called for when a shed floor stands at about 21" or more above the ground (for lower floors, you might prefer to build a couple of simple platforms for three easy steps into the shed; see page 82). But regardless of the floor height, notched-stringer stairs add a nice handmade, built-in look to an entrance. And it's fun to learn the geometry and carpentry skills behind traditional stair building.

When planning your project, bear in mind that stairs in general are strictly governed by building codes. Your local building department may impose specific design requirements for your project, or they may not get involved at all—just be sure to find out. In any case, here are some of the standard requirements for stairs:

- Minimum tread depth: 10"
- Maximum riser height: 7¾" (7¼" is a good standard height)
- Minimum stair width: 36" (make your staircase at least a few inches wider than the shed's door opening)
- A handrail is often required for stairs with more than one riser, but this may not apply for storage sheds and the like (check with the local building department)

Because stairs are easier and safer to use when starting from a flat landing area, it's a good idea to include a level pad of compacted gravel at the base of your stairs. This also provides stability for the staircase and eliminates the potential for a slippery, muddy patch forming at the landing area.

Calculating Step Size ▶

Properly built stairs have perfectly uniform treads (the part you step on) and risers (the vertical section of each step).

To determine the riser height, all you have to do is divide the total rise—the distance from the ground to the shed floor—and divide by the number of steps. If you end up with risers over 7¾", add another step.

Determining the tread depth is up to you. However, because shallow steps are hard to climb and easy to trip on, you should make your treads at least 10" deep, but preferably 11" or more. The tread depth multiplied by the number of steps gives you the total run—how far the steps extend in front of the shed. When cutting the stringers, you cut the first (bottom) riser shorter than the others to account for the thickness of the tread material.

Tools, Materials & Cutting List ▶

Framing square
Circular saw
Handsaw
Drill and bits
Sledgehammer

Compactible gravel
2 × 12 pressure-
    treated lumber
Corrosion resistant
    framing connectors

10d × 1½" galvanized nails
3" galvanized screws
2½" galvanized screws
2 × 4 pressure-
    treated lumber

2 16" lengths of
    #4 (½"-dia.)
    rebar
⁵⁄₄ × 6 pressure-
    treated lumber

STEP 1: LAY OUT THE FIRST STRINGER

A. Use a framing square to lay out the first stringer onto a straight piece of 2 × 12 lumber. Starting at one end of the board, position the square along the board's top edge. Align the 12" mark of the blade (long leg of the square) and the 6½" mark on the tongue (short leg of the square) with the edge of the board. Trace along the edges of the blade and tongue. The tongue mark represents the first riser.

B. Use the square to extend the blade marking across the full width of the board. Then, draw a parallel line 1" up from this line. The new line marks the bottom cut for the stringer (the 1" offset accounts for the thickness of the tread material).

C. Continue the step layout, starting at the point where the first riser meets the top of the board.

D. Mark the cutting line at the top end of the stringer by extending the third (top) tread marking across the full width of the board. From this line, make a perpendicular line 12" from the top riser: this is where you'll cut the edge of the stringer that fits against the shed.

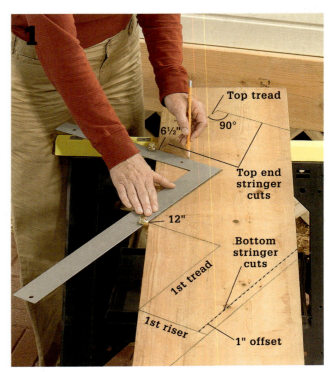

Use a framing square to mark the treads, risers, and end cuts on the stringer.

How to Build Notched-Stringer Stairs

STEP 2: CUT THE STRINGERS

A. Make the cuts on the first stringer using a circular saw set to full depth. Where treads and risers intersect, cut just up to the lines, then finish the cuts with a handsaw.

B. Test-fit the stringer on the shed. The top tread cut should be 1" below the shed floor. Make adjustments to the stringer cuts as needed.

C. Use the first stringer as a template to mark the remaining stringers. You'll need one stringer for each end and every 12" to 16" in between. Cut the remaining stringers.

STEP 3: INSTALL THE STRINGERS

A. Mark a level line onto the shed's floor frame, 1" below the finished floor surface. Onto the level line, mark the center and outsides of the stairs. Transfer the side markings to the ground using a square and straightedge.

B. Cut 2× blocking to carry the bottom ends of the stringers. Fasten the blocking to the ground using 16" pieces of #4 rebar driven through ½" holes. For concrete or masonry, use masonry screws or a powder-actuated nailer.

Cut out stringers with a circular saw, and finish the corners of the cuts with a handsaw.

Mount the top ends of the stringers to the shed using framing connectors (shown). Anchor the bottom ends to blocking.

C. Anchor the tops of the stringers to the floor frame with corrosion-resistant framing connectors, using 1½"-long 10d galvanized common nails. The tops of the stringers should be flush with the level line.

D. Anchor the bottom ends of the stringers with nails or screws.

STEP 4: ADD THE TREAD & RISER BOARDS

A. Cut the treads to length from ⁵⁄₄ × 8" pressure-treated decking lumber or two ⁵⁄₄ × 6" boards ripped to 4" each. You can cut the treads to fit flush with the outside stringers or overhang them by ½" or so for a different look.

B. On each step, position a full-width tread at the front with the desired overhang beyond the riser below. Fasten the tread to the stringers with 2½" galvanized screws. Rip the second tread to size and fasten it behind the first tread, leaving a ¼" gap between the boards. Install the remaining tread boards.

C. If desired, install 1 × 6 riser boards so the ends are flush with the outside stringers (no overhang). Or, you can omit the riser boards for open steps.

Trim the rear tread boards as needed to fit behind the front treads.

Option: Add riser boards to enclose each step.

Option: Leave off riser boards for an open staircase.

Platforms for Steps & Decking

This simple platform is a popular option for sheds because it's so easy to build and it provides a sturdy step for comfortable access. You can use the same basic design to make platforms of any size. A large platform can become an outdoor sitting area, while a stack of smaller platforms can create a set of steps that are accessible from three directions. For stability and longevity, set your platforms on top of solid concrete blocks—the same type used for block foundations. See page 30 for more information about buying concrete block.

Tools & Materials ▶

Shovel
Level
Saw
Drill
Compactible gravel
  (optional)

2× treated lumber
16d galvanized
  common nails
3" deck screws

How to Build a Basic Platform

STEP 1: BUILD THE PLATFORM FRAME

A. Cut two long side pieces from 2 × 6 lumber. These should equal the total length of the frame. Cut two end pieces to fit between the side pieces. For example, if your platform will measure 24 × 36", cut the sides at 36" and cut the ends at 23". Also cut an intermediate support for every 16" in between: make these the same length as the end pieces.

B. Fasten the end pieces between the sides with pairs of 16d galvanized common nails.

C. Fasten the intermediate support at the center of the frame or at 16" intervals.

STEP 2: INSTALL THE DECKING

A. Cut 2 × 6 decking boards to fit the long dimension of the platform frame (you can also use ⁵⁄₄ × 6 decking boards). *Option: For a finished look, cut the decking about 1" too long so it overhangs the frame structure.*

B. Measure the frame diagonally from corner to corner to make sure it is square.

C. Starting at the front edge of the frame, attach the decking to the framing pieces with pairs of 3" deck screws. Leave a ¼" gap between the boards. Rip the last board to width so that it overhangs the front edge of the frame by 1".

D. Set the platform in position on top of the block foundation. If desired, fasten the platform to the shed with 3" screws.

Assemble the frame pieces with pairs of 16d common nails.

Install the decking with screws, leaving a ¼" gap between boards.

Option: Building Stepped Platforms ▸

To stack platforms for a set of steps, build the upper platform at least 20" narrower and 10" shallower than the lower platform. This creates a 10"-deep step along the entire lower level. Fasten the platforms together with screws to keep the upper platform in place.

Shed Projects

It's time to roll out your cords, buckle on your tool belt, and start building. Each custom project features a complete materials list—use this as a shopping list for buying all the raw materials at your local home center or lumberyard. From the detailed drawings and how-to instructions you'll learn what length to cut each piece and where it goes in the finished product. The step-by-step instructions will walk you through the entire sequence, highlighting important and unique details along the way. If you choose to build a kit shed, keep in mind that the manufacturer of the kit you choose should provide detailed instructions. *Note: Making sheds larger than shown may require review of code/design criteria for lumber sizes, especially floor joists, roof joists, and headers.*

In This Chapter:

- Clerestory Studio
- Sunlight Garden Shed
- Lean-to Tool Bin
- Convenience Shed
- Gambrel Garage
- Simple Storage Shed
- Gothic Playhouse
- Timber-frame Shed
- Service Shed
- Metal & Wood Kit Sheds
- Shed with Firewood Bin

Clerestory Studio

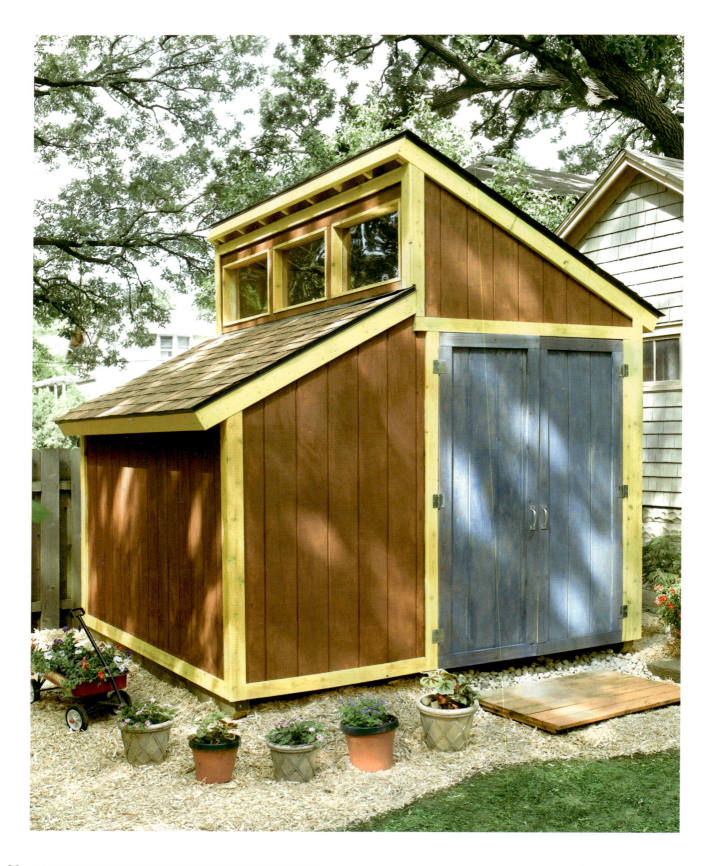

This easy-to-build shed is made distinctive by its three clerestory windows on the front side. In addition to their unique architectural effect, clerestory windows offer some practical advantages over standard windows. First, their position at the top of the building allows sunlight to spread downward over the interior space to maximize illumination. Most of the light is indirect, creating a soft glow without the harsh glare of direct sunlight. Clerestories also save on wall space and offer more privacy and security than windows at eye level. These characteristics make this shed design a great choice for a backyard office, artist's studio or even a remote spot for the musically inclined to get together and jam.

As shown, the Clerestory Studio has a 10 × 10-ft. floorplan. It can be outfitted with double doors that open up to a 5 ft.-wide opening, as seen here. But if you don't need a door that large, you can pick up about 2½ ft. of additional (and highly prized) wall space by framing the opening for a 30" wide door. The studio's striking roofline is created by two shed-style roof planes, which makes for deceptively easy construction.

The shed's walls and floor follow standard stick-frame construction. For simplicity, you can frame the square portions of the lower walls first, then piece in the framing for the four "rake," or angled, wall sections. To support the roof rafters, the clerestory wall has two large headers (beams) that run the full length of the building. These and the door header are all made with standard 2× lumber and a ½" plywood spacer.

You can increase the natural light in your studio—and add some passive solar heating—by including the two optional skylights. To prevent leaks, be sure to carefully seal around the glazing and the skylight frame. Flashing around the frame will provide an extra measure of protection.

Cutting List

Description	Quantity/Size	Material
Foundation		
Drainage material	1.5 cu. yd.	Compactible gravel
Skids	2 @ 10'	4 × 6 pressure-treated landscape timbers
Floor		
Rim joists	2 @ 10'	2 × 6 pressure-treated
Joists	9 @ 10'	2 × 6 pressure-treated
Floor sheathing	4 sheets, 4 × 8'	¾" tongue-&-groove ext.-grade plywood
Wall Framing		
Bottom plates	4 @ 10'	2 × 4
Top plates, front walls	5 @ 10'	2 × 4
Top plates, rear wall	2 @ 10'	2 × 4
Top plates, side walls	6 @ 10'	2 × 4
Studs, rear wall	11 @ 8'	2 × 4
Studs, front wall (& clerestory wall)	11 @ 8'	2 × 4
Studs, side walls	26 @ 8'	2 × 4
Header, above windows	2 @ 10'	2 × 6
Header, below windows	2 @ 10'	2 × 10
Header, door	2 @ 8'	2 × 6
Header & post spacers		See Sheathing, below
Roof Framing		
Rafters (& blocking)	20 @ 8'	2 × 6
Exterior Finishes		
Side wall fascia	4 @ 8'	2 × 6
Eave fascia	3 @ 12'	2 × 6
Fascia drip edge	8 @ 8'	1 × 2
Siding	10 sheets @ 4 × 8'	⅝" Texture 1-11 plywood siding
Corner trim	10 @ 8'	1 × 4 cedar
Bottom siding trim	5 @ 12'	1 × 4 cedar
Vents	8	2"-dia. round metal vents
Roofing		
Sheathing (& header/post spacers)	6 sheets @ 4 × 8'	½" exterior-grade plywood roof sheathing

Description	Quantity/Size	Material
15# building paper	1 roll	
Shingles	1⅔ squares	Asphalt shingles — 250# per sq. min.
Roof flashing	10'-6"	Aluminum
Windows		
Glazing	3 pieces @ 21 × 36"	¼"-thick acrylic or polycarbonate glazing
Window stops	5 @ 8'	1 × 2 cedar
Glazing tape	60 linear ft.	
Clear exterior caulk	1 tube	
Door		
Panels	2 sheets @ 4 × 8'	¾" exterior-grade plywood
Panel trim	8 @ 8'	1 × 4 cedar
Stops	3 @ 8'	1 × 2 cedar
Flashing	6 linear ft.	Aluminum
Skylights (optional)		
Glazing	2 pieces @ 13 × 22½"	¼"-thick plastic or polycarbonate glazing
Frame	2 @ 8'	1 × 4 cedar
Stops	2 @ 8'	1 × 2 cedar
Glazing tape	25 linear ft.	
Fasteners & Hardware		
16d galvanized common nails	4 lbs.	
16d common nails	16½ lbs.	
10d common nails	1 lb.	
8d galvanized common nails	3 lbs.	
8d box nails	3½ lbs.	
8d galvanized siding nails	7 lbs.	
1" galvanized roofing nails	5 lbs.	
8d galvanized casing nails	2 lbs.	
1¼" galvanized screws	1 lb.	
2" galvanized screws	1 lb.	
Door hinges with screws	6 @ 3½"	
Door handle	2	
Door lock (optional)	1	

10 × 10 FRONT ELEVATION

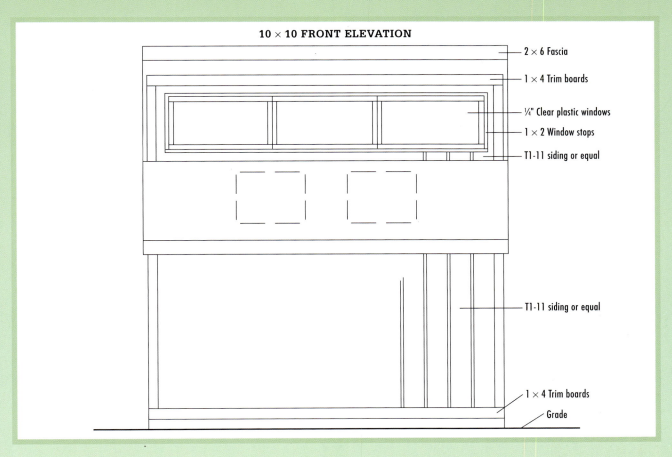

2 × 6 Fascia

1 × 4 Trim boards

¼" Clear plastic windows

1 × 2 Window stops

T1-11 siding or equal

T1-11 siding or equal

1 × 4 Trim boards

Grade

10 × 10 REAR ELEVATION

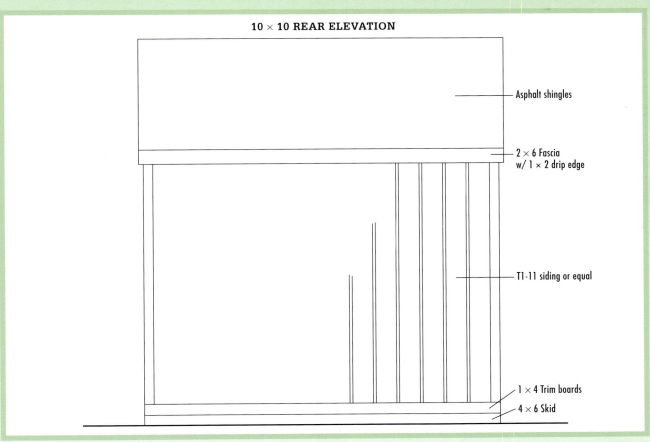

Asphalt shingles

2 × 6 Fascia
w/ 1 × 2 drip edge

T1-11 siding or equal

1 × 4 Trim boards

4 × 6 Skid

BUILDING SECTION

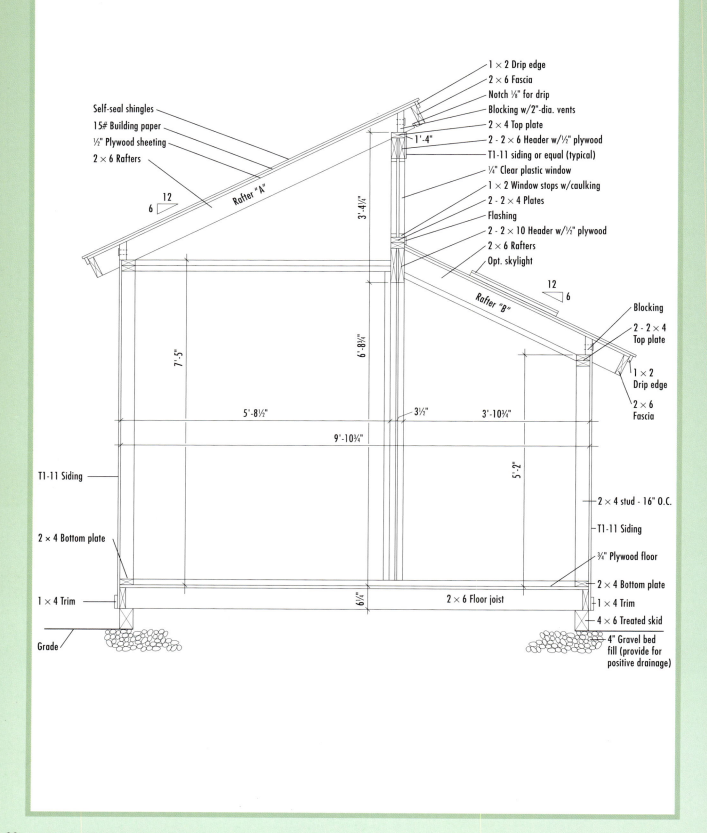

Self-seal shingles
15# Building paper
½" Plywood sheeting
2 × 6 Rafters

1 × 2 Drip edge
2 × 6 Fascia
Notch ⅛" for drip
Blocking w/2"-dia. vents
2 × 4 Top plate
2 - 2 × 6 Header w/½" plywood
T1-11 siding or equal (typical)
¼" Clear plastic window
1 × 2 Window stops w/caulking
2 - 2 × 4 Plates
Flashing
2 - 2 × 10 Header w/½" plywood
2 × 6 Rafters
Opt. skylight

Rafter "A"
Rafter "B"

12
6

12
6

3'-4¼"
6'-8¾"
7'-5"
5'-2"

Blocking
2 - 2 × 4 Top plate
1 × 2 Drip edge
2 × 6 Fascia

1'-4"

5'-8½"
3½"
3'-10¾"
9'-10¾"

T1-11 Siding

2 × 4 Bottom plate

1 × 4 Trim

Grade

6¼"
2 × 6 Floor joist

2 × 4 stud - 16" O.C.
T1-11 Siding
¾" Plywood floor
2 × 4 Bottom plate
1 × 4 Trim
4 × 6 Treated skid
4" Gravel bed fill (provide for positive drainage)

FRONT FRAMING

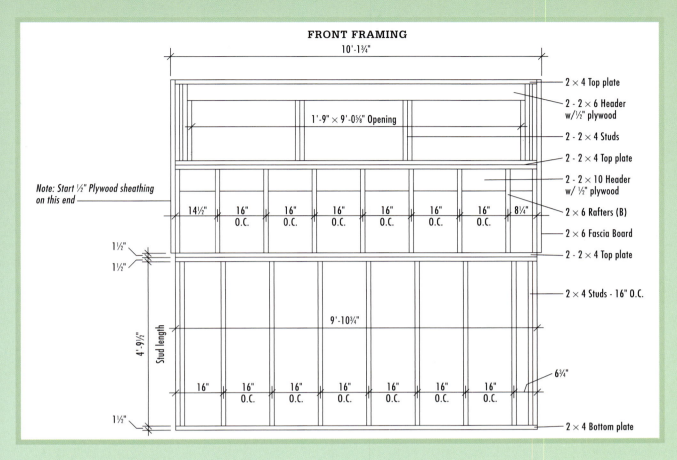

10'-1¾"

2 × 4 Top plate

2 - 2 × 6 Header w/ ½" plywood

1'-9" × 9'-0⅝" Opening

2 - 2 × 4 Studs

2 - 2 × 4 Top plate

2 - 2 × 10 Header w/ ½" plywood

Note: Start ½" Plywood sheathing on this end

14½"   16" O.C.   16" O.C.   16" O.C.   16" O.C.   16" O.C.   16" O.C.   8¼"

2 × 6 Rafters (B)

2 × 6 Fascia Board

2 - 2 × 4 Top plate

1½"

1½"

2 × 4 Studs - 16" O.C.

4'-9½"   Stud length

9'-10¾"

6¾"

16"   16"   16"   16"   16"   16"   16"
O.C.   O.C.   O.C.   O.C.   O.C.   O.C.   O.C.

1½"

2 × 4 Bottom plate

REAR FRAMING

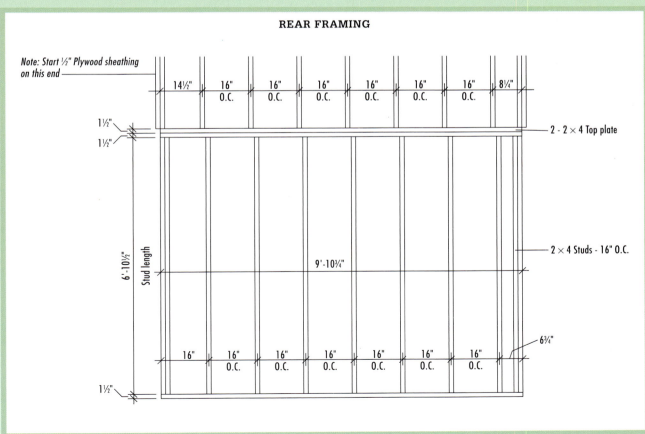

Note: Start ½" Plywood sheathing on this end

14½"   16" O.C.   16" O.C.   16" O.C.   16" O.C.   16" O.C.   16" O.C.   8¼"

1½"

1½"

2 - 2 × 4 Top plate

2 × 4 Studs - 16" O.C.

6'-10½"   Stud length

9'-10¾"

6¾"

16"   16"   16"   16"   16"   16"   16"
O.C.   O.C.   O.C.   O.C.   O.C.   O.C.   O.C.

1½"

LEFT SIDE WALL FRAMING

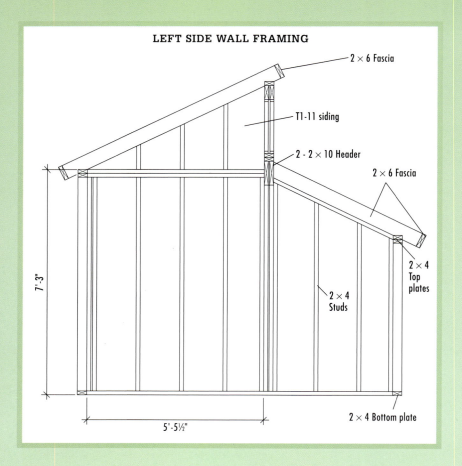

2 × 6 Fascia

T1-11 siding

2 - 2 × 10 Header

2 × 6 Fascia

2 × 4 Top plates

2 × 4 Studs

7'-3"

5'-5½"

2 × 4 Bottom plate

RAKE DETAIL

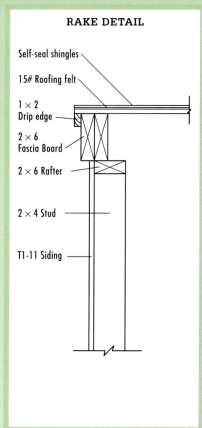

Self-seal shingles

15# Roofing felt

1 × 2 Drip edge

2 × 6 Fascia Board

2 × 6 Rafter

2 × 4 Stud

T1-11 Siding

DOOR DETAIL

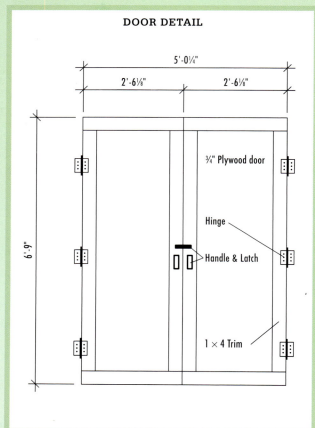

5'-0¼"

2'-6⅛"   2'-6⅛"

¾" Plywood door

Hinge

Handle & Latch

1 × 4 Trim

6'-9"

JAMB/CORNER DETAIL

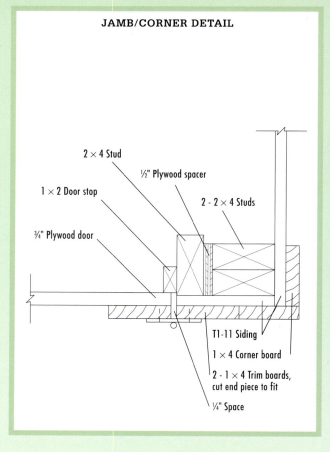

2 × 4 Stud

½" Plywood spacer

1 × 2 Door stop

2 - 2 × 4 Studs

¾" Plywood door

T1-11 Siding

1 × 4 Corner board

2 - 1 × 4 Trim boards, cut end piece to fit

¼" Space

RIGHT SIDE ELEVATION

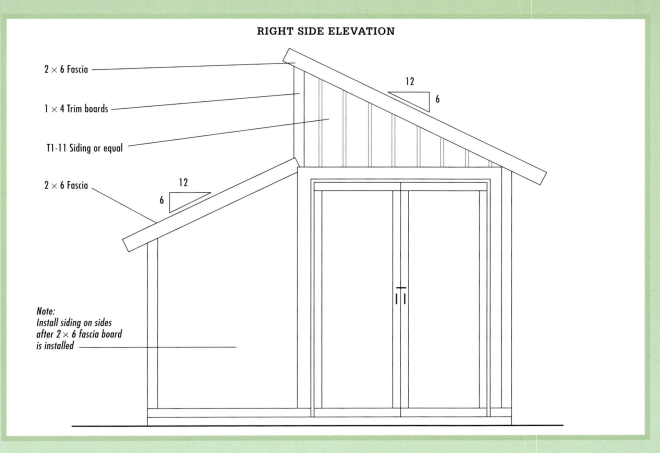

2 × 6 Fascia

1 × 4 Trim boards

T1-11 Siding or equal

2 × 6 Fascia

12

6

12

6

Note:
Install siding on sides
after 2 × 6 fascia board
is installed

FLOOR PLAN

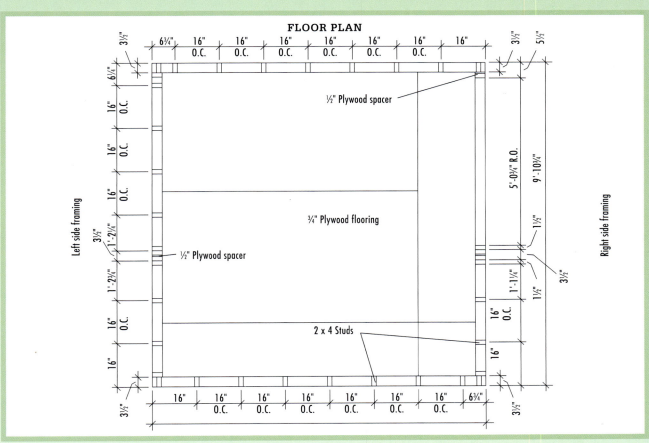

3½"

6¾" 16" 16" 16" 16" 16" 16" 16"
     O.C. O.C. O.C. O.C. O.C. O.C.

3½" 5½"

6¼"

16" O.C.

16" O.C.

16" O.C.

Left side framing

3½"
1'-2¼"

1'-2¾"

16" O.C.

16"

3½"

½" Plywood spacer

¾" Plywood flooring

½" Plywood spacer

2 x 4 Studs

5'-0¾" R.O.

9'-10¾"

1½"

1'-1¼"

1½"

3½"

16" O.C.

16"

Right side framing

16" 16" 16" 16" 16" 16" 16" 6¾"
O.C. O.C. O.C. O.C. O.C. O.C. O.C.

3½"

3½"

RAFTER TEMPLATE (A)

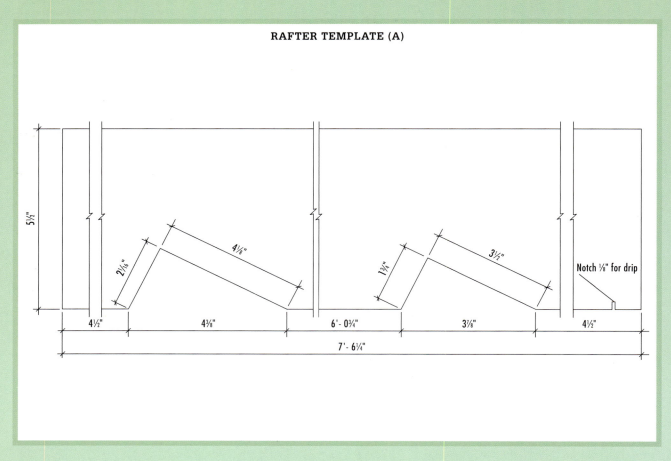

RAFTER TEMPLATE (B)

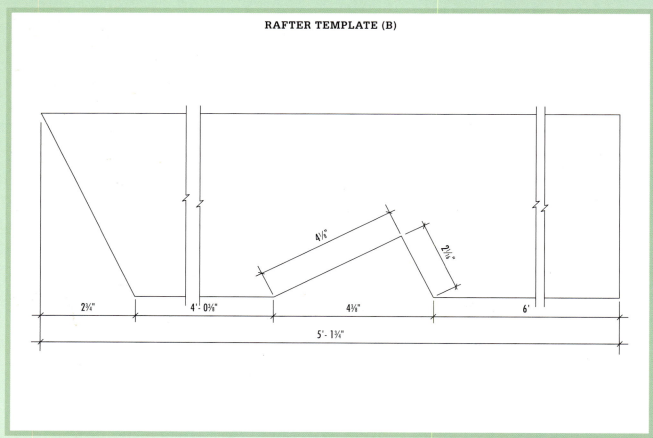

How to Build the Clerestory Studio

Prepare the foundation site with a 4"-deep layer of compacted gravel. Cut the two 4 × 6 timber skids at 118¾". Position the skids on the gravel bed so their outside edges are 118¾" apart, making sure they are level and parallel with one another.

Cut two 2 × 6 rim joists at 118¾". Cut nine 2 × 6 joists at 115¾". Build the floor frame on the skids and measure the diagonals to make sure the frame is square. Fasten the rim joists to the skids with 16d galvanized common nails driven toenail style through the joists and into the skids.

Install floor sheathing onto the floor frame, starting at the left rear corner of the shed, as shown in the FLOOR PLAN (page 93). Rip the two outer pieces and final corner piece so their outside edges are flush with the sides of the foundation skids.

Cut the studs and top and bottom plates for the front wall and nail together with 8d common nails. Position the wall on the floor deck and raise it. Fasten it by driving 16d common nails through the sole plate and into the floor deck and frame.

(continued)

Assemble the back wall framing with a bottom plate and double top plate at 118¾" and 82½" studs 16" O.C. Assemble the square portions of the left and right side walls. Attach the back wall and nail the side walls in place.

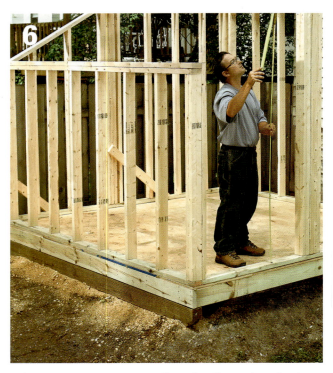

Take measurements to confirm the dimensions for the clerestory wall frame. Build the clerestory frame wall to match the dimensions.

Construct the sloped portions of the side walls. Install them by nailing them to the floor deck with 16d common nails. Also nail the corners to the front wall.

Create the headers by sandwiching a ½" plywood strip between two 2× dimensional framing members. Assemble the header with deck screws driven through both faces.

Set the main header on top of the sidewall posts and toenail it in place with 16d common nails. The main header ends should be flush with the outsides of the side walls.

Lift the clerestory wall frame onto the main header. Orient the wall so it is flush in front and on the ends and then attach it to the main header with 16d nails.

Install T1-11 siding on the front wall, starting at the left side (when facing the front of the shed). Cut the siding to length so it's flush with the top of the top plate and the bottom of the floor joists. Make sure any vertical seams fall at stud locations. Add strips of siding to cover the framing on the clerestory wall. Install siding on the rear wall, starting at the left side (when facing the rear side of the shed).

Cut one of each "A" and "B" pattern rafters from a single 16-ft. 2 × 6, using the RAFTER TEMPLATES (page 94). Both roof planes have a 6-in-12 slope. Test-fit the rafters and make any necessary adjustments, then use the patterns to cut eight more rafters of each type. Install the rafters as shown in the REAR FRAMING and FRONT FRAMING (page 91). Toenail the top ends of the "B" rafters to the main header.

(continued)

Frame each of the upper rake walls following the same technique used for gable walls (see page 51). Cut the top plate to fit between the clerestory header and the door header (on the right side wall) or the top plate (on the left side wall). Install four studs in each wall using 16" on-center spacing.

Install 2 × 6 fascia boards flush with the top edges and ends of the rafters. The upper roof gets fascia on all four sides; the lower roof on three sides. Miter the corner joints if desired. Install siding on the side walls, flush with the bottom of the fascia; see the RAKE DETAIL (page 92.)

Install ½" plywood roof sheathing, starting at the bottom left side of the roof on both sides of the shed. Run the sheathing to the outside edge of the fascia. Add 1 × 2 trim to serve as a drip edge along all fascia boards, flush with the top of the sheathing.

Fasten 1 × 2 stops inside the window rough openings, flush with the inside edges of the framing, using 2" screws. Set each window panel into its opening, using glazing tape as a sealant. Install the outer stops; see the BUILDING SECTION (page 90). Caulk around the windows and the bottom outside stops to prevent leaks. Add 2 × 6 blocking (and vents) or screen to enclose the rafter bays above the walls.

Add vertical trim at the wall corners. Trim and flash around the door opening and windows (also see sidebar: Flashing Above Doors & Windows, on page 73). Install flashing—and trim, if desired—along the joint where the lower roof plane meets the clerestory wall.

Add 15# building paper and install the asphalt shingle roofing. The shingles should overhang the fascia drip edge by ½" along the bottom of the roof and by ⅜" along the sides. Install 1 × 4 horizontal trim boards flush with the bottom of the siding on all four walls.

Cut out the bottom plate inside the door's rough opening. Cut the two door panels at 30⅛" × 81". Install 1 × 4 trim around the panels, as shown in the DOOR DETAIL (page 92), using exterior wood glue and 1¼" screws or nails. Add 1 × 2 stops at the sides and top of the rough opening; see the JAMB DETAIL (page 92). Also add a 1 × 4 stop to the back side of one of the doors. Hang the doors with galvanized hinges, leaving a ¼" gap all around.

Finish the interior to your desired level. If you will be occupying the shed for activities, adding some wall covering, such as paneling, makes the interior much more pleasant. If you add wiring and wall insulation, the Clerestory Studio can function as a 3-season studio in practically any climate.

Sunlight Garden Shed

This unique outbuilding is part greenhouse and part shed, making it perfect for a year-round garden space or backyard sunroom, or even an artist's studio. The front facade is dominated by windows—four 29 × 72" windows on the roof, plus four 29 × 18" windows on the front wall. When appointed as a greenhouse, two long planting tables inside the shed let you water and tend to plants without flooding the floor. If gardening isn't in your plans, you can omit the tables and cover the entire floor with plywood, or perhaps fill in between the floor timbers with pavers or stones.

Some other details that make this 10 × 12-ft. shed stand out are the homemade Dutch door, with top and bottom halves that you can open together or independently, and its traditional saltbox shape. The roof covering shown here consists of standard asphalt shingles, but cedar shingles make for a nice upgrade.

Because sunlight plays a central role in this shed design, consider the location and orientation carefully. To avoid shadows from nearby structures, maintain a distance between the shed and the structure that's at least 2½ times the height of the obstruction. With all of that sunlight, the temperature inside the shed is another important consideration. You may want to install some roof vents (see page 58) to release hot air and water vapor.

Building the Sunlight Garden Shed involves a few unconventional construction steps. First, the side walls are framed in two parts: You build the square portion of the end walls first, then move onto the roof framing. After the rafters are up, you complete the "rake," or angled, sections of the side walls. This makes it easy to measure for each wall stud, rather than having to calculate the lengths beforehand. Second, the shed's 4 × 4 floor structure also serves as its foundation. The plywood floor decking goes on after the walls are installed, rather than before.

Cutting List

Description	Quantity/Size	Material
Foundation/Floor		
Foundation base & interior drainage beds	5 cu. yds.	Compactible gravel
Floor joists & blocking	7 @ 10'	4 × 4 pressure-treated landscape timbers
4 × 4 blocking	1 @ 10' 1 @ 8'	4 × 4 pressure-treated landscape timbers
Box sills (rim joists)	2 @ 12'	2 × 4 pressure-treated
Nailing cleats & 2 × 4 blocking	2 @ 8'	2 × 4 pressure-treated
Floor sheathing	2 sheets @ 4 × 8'	¾" ext.-grade plywood
Wall Framing		
Bottom plates	2 @ 12', 2 @ 10'	2 × 4 pressure-treated
Top plates	4 @ 12', 2 @ 10'	2 × 4
Studs	43 @ 8'	2 × 4
Door header & jack studs	3 @ 8'	2 × 4
Rafter header	2 @ 12'	2 × 8
Roof Framing		
Rafters — A & C, & nailers	10 @ 12'	2 × 4
Rafters — B & lookouts	10 @ 10'	2 × 4
Ridge board	1 @ 14'	2 × 6
Exterior Finishes		
Rear fascia	1 @ 14'	1 × 6 cedar
Rear soffit	1 @ 14'	1 × 8 cedar
Gable fascia (rake board) & soffit	4 @ 16'	1 × 6 cedar
Siding	10 sheets @ 4 × 8'	⅝" Texture 1-11 plywood siding
Siding flashing	10 linear ft.	Metal Z-flashing
Trim*	4 @ 12' 1 @ 12'	1 × 4 cedar 1 × 2 cedar
Wall corner trim	6 @ 8'	1 × 4 cedar
Roofing		
Sheathing	5 sheets @ 4 × 8'	½" exterior-grade plywood roof sheathing
15# building paper	1 roll	
Drip edge	72 linear ft.	Metal drip edge

Description	Quantity/Size	Material
Shingles	2⅔ squares	Asphalt shingles — 250# per sq. min.
Windows		
Glazing	4 pieces @ 31¼ × 76½" 4 pieces @ 31¼ × 20¾"	¼"-thick clear plastic glazing
Window stops	12 @ 10'	2 × 4
Glazing tape	60 linear ft.	
Clear exterior caulk	5 tubes	
Door		
Trim & stops	3 @ 8'	1 × 2 cedar
Surround	4 @ 8'	2 × 2 cedar
Z-flashing	3 linear ft.	
Plant Tables (optional)		
Front table, top & trim	6 @ 12'	1 × 6 cedar or pressure-treated
Front table, plates & legs	4 @ 12'	2 × 4 pressure-treated
Rear table, top & trim	6 @ 8'	1 × 6 cedar or pressure-treated
Rear table, plates & legs	4 @ 8'	2 × 4 pressure-treated
Fasteners & Hardware		
16d galvanized common nails	5 lbs.	
16d common nails	16 lbs.	
10d common nails	1½ lbs.	
8d galvanized common nails	2 lbs.	
8d galvanized box nails	3 lbs.	
10d galvanized finish nails	2½ lbs.	
8d galvanized siding nails	8 lbs.	
1" galvanized roofing nails	7 lbs.	
8d galvanized casing nails	3 lbs.	
6d galvanized casing nails	2 lbs.	
Door hinges with screws	4 @ 3½"	Corrosion-resistant hinges
Door handle	1	
Sliding bolt latch	1	
Construction adhesive	1 tube	

Note: The 1 × 4 trim bevel at the bottom of the sloped windows can be steeper (45° or more) so the trim slopes away from the window if there is concern that the trim may capture water running down the glazing (see WINDOW DETAIL, page 108).

BUILDING SECTION

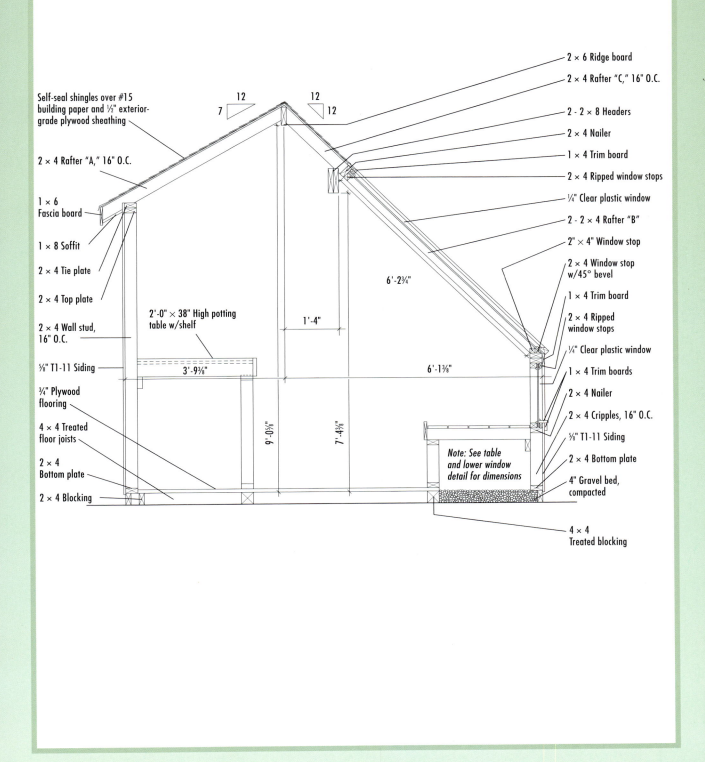

Self-seal shingles over #15 building paper and ½" exterior-grade plywood sheathing

2 × 4 Rafter "A," 16" O.C.

1 × 6 Fascia board

1 × 8 Soffit

2 × 4 Tie plate

2 × 4 Top plate

2 × 4 Wall stud, 16" O.C.

⅝" T1-11 Siding

¾" Plywood flooring

4 × 4 Treated floor joists

2 × 4 Bottom plate

2 × 4 Blocking

2'-0" × 38" High potting table w/shelf

3'-9⅜"

12 7

12 12

6'-2¾"

1'-4"

9'-0⅝"

7'-4⅜"

6'-1⅜"

Note: See table and lower window detail for dimensions

2 × 6 Ridge board

2 × 4 Rafter "C," 16" O.C.

2 - 2 × 8 Headers

2 × 4 Nailer

1 × 4 Trim board

2 × 4 Ripped window stops

¼" Clear plastic window

2 - 2 × 4 Rafter "B"

2" × 4" Window stop

2 × 4 Window stop w/45° bevel

1 × 4 Trim board

2 × 4 Ripped window stops

¼" Clear plastic window

1 × 4 Trim boards

2 × 4 Nailer

2 × 4 Cripples, 16" O.C.

⅝" T1-11 Siding

2 × 4 Bottom plate

4" Gravel bed, compacted

4 × 4 Treated blocking

FLOOR FRAMING PLAN

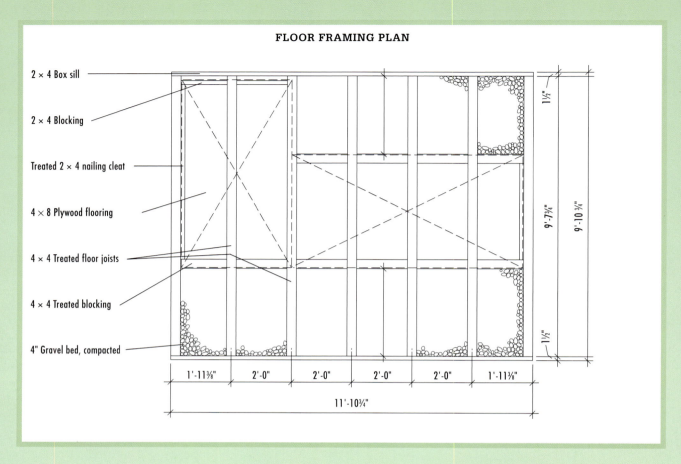

2 × 4 Box sill

2 × 4 Blocking

Treated 2 × 4 nailing cleat

4 × 8 Plywood flooring

4 × 4 Treated floor joists

4 × 4 Treated blocking

4" Gravel bed, compacted

1½"

9'-7¾"

9'-10¾"

1½"

1'-11⅜" 2'-0" 2'-0" 2'-0" 2'-0" 1'-11⅜"

11'-10¾"

LEFT SIDE FRAMING

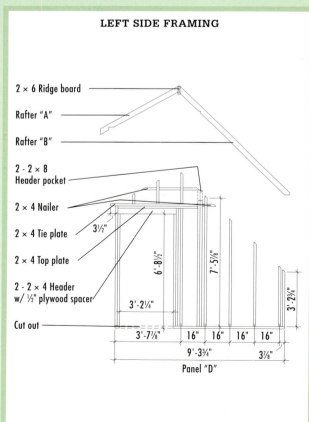

2 × 6 Ridge board

Rafter "A"

Rafter "B"

2 - 2 × 8
Header pocket

2 × 4 Nailer

2 × 4 Tie plate

2 × 4 Top plate

2 - 2 × 4 Header
w/ ½" plywood spacer

Cut out

3½"

6'-8½"

7'-5⅞"

3'-2¾"

3'-2¼"

3'-7⅞" 16" 16" 16" 16"

9'-3¾"

3⅞"

Panel "D"

RIGHT SIDE FRAMING

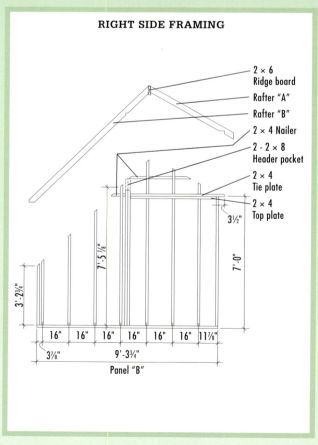

2 × 6
Ridge board

Rafter "A"

Rafter "B"

2 × 4 Nailer

2 - 2 × 8
Header pocket

2 × 4
Tie plate

2 × 4
Top plate

3½"

7'-5⅞"

7'-0"

3'-2¾"

16" 16" 16" 16" 16" 16" 11⅛"

3⅞"

9'-3¾"

Panel "B"

FRONT FRAMING

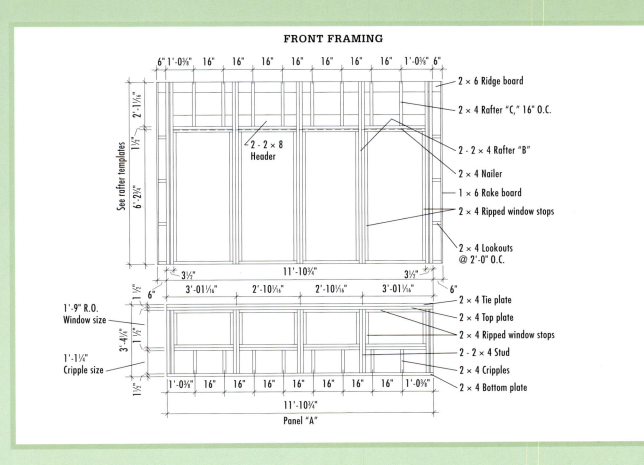

6" 1'-0⅜" 16" 16" 16" 16" 16" 16" 16" 1'-0⅜" 6"

2 × 6 Ridge board

2 × 4 Rafter "C," 16" O.C.

2 - 2 × 4 Rafter "B"

2 × 4 Nailer

1 × 6 Rake board

2 × 4 Ripped window stops

2 × 4 Lookouts @ 2'-0" O.C.

See rafter templates

2'-1¹⁄₁₆"

1½"

6'-2¾"

- 2 - 2 × 8 Header

3½"   11'-10¾"   3½"

1½" 6" 3'-01¹⁄₁₆"   2'-10¹⁄₁₆"   2'-10¹⁄₁₆"   3'-01¹⁄₁₆" 6"

2 × 4 Tie plate

2 × 4 Top plate

2 × 4 Ripped window stops

2 - 2 × 4 Stud

2 × 4 Cripples

2 × 4 Bottom plate

1'-9" R.O. Window size

3'-4¼"

1½"

1½"

1'-1¼" Cripple size

1½"

1'-0⅜" 16" 16" 16" 16" 16" 16" 16" 1'-0⅜"

11'-10¾"

Panel "A"

REAR FRAMING

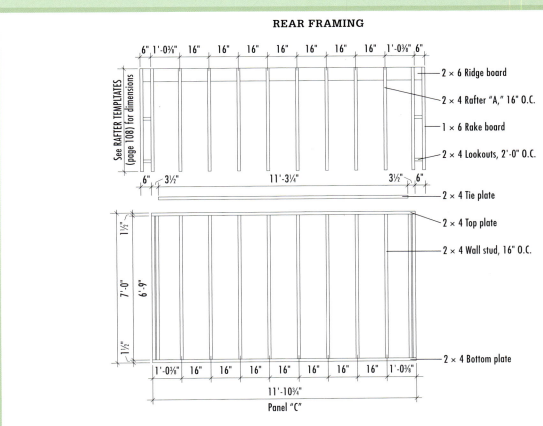

6" 1'-0⅜" 16" 16" 16" 16" 16" 16" 16" 1'-0⅜" 6"

2 × 6 Ridge board

2 × 4 Rafter "A," 16" O.C.

1 × 6 Rake board

2 × 4 Lookouts, 2'-0" O.C.

See RAFTER TEMPLATES (page 108) for dimensions

6" 3½"   11'-3¼"   3½" 6"

2 × 4 Tie plate

2 × 4 Top plate

2 × 4 Wall stud, 16" O.C.

7'-0"

6'-9"

1½"

1½"

2 × 4 Bottom plate

1'-0⅜" 16" 16" 16" 16" 16" 16" 16" 1'-0⅜"

11'-10¾"

Panel "C"

FRONT ELEVATION

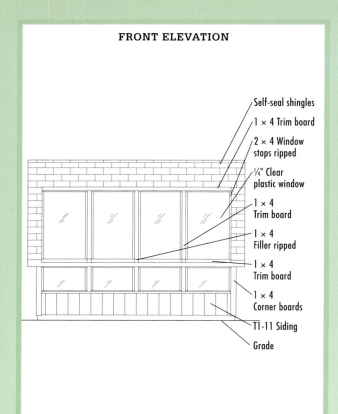

Self-seal shingles

1 × 4 Trim board

2 × 4 Window stops ripped

¼" Clear plastic window

1 × 4 Trim board

1 × 4 Filler ripped

1 × 4 Trim board

1 × 4 Corner boards

T1-11 Siding

Grade

REAR ELEVATION

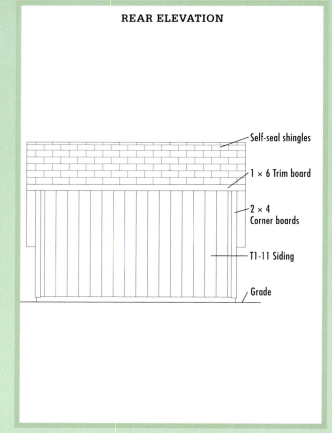

Self-seal shingles

1 × 6 Trim board

2 × 4 Corner boards

T1-11 Siding

Grade

RIGHT SIDE ELEVATION

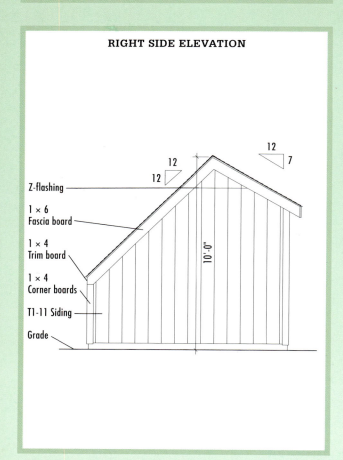

12
12

12
7

Z-flashing

1 × 6 Fascia board

1 × 4 Trim board

1 × 4 Corner boards

T1-11 Siding

Grade

10'-0"

SOFFIT DETAIL

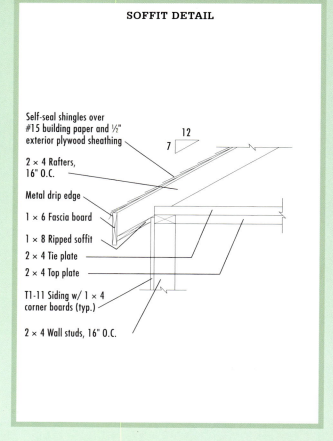

Self-seal shingles over #15 building paper and ½" exterior plywood sheathing

2 × 4 Rafters, 16" O.C.

Metal drip edge

1 × 6 Fascia board

1 × 8 Ripped soffit

2 × 4 Tie plate

2 × 4 Top plate

T1-11 Siding w/ 1 × 4 corner boards (typ.)

2 × 4 Wall studs, 16" O.C.

12
7

FRONT & SIDE DOOR CONSTRUCTION

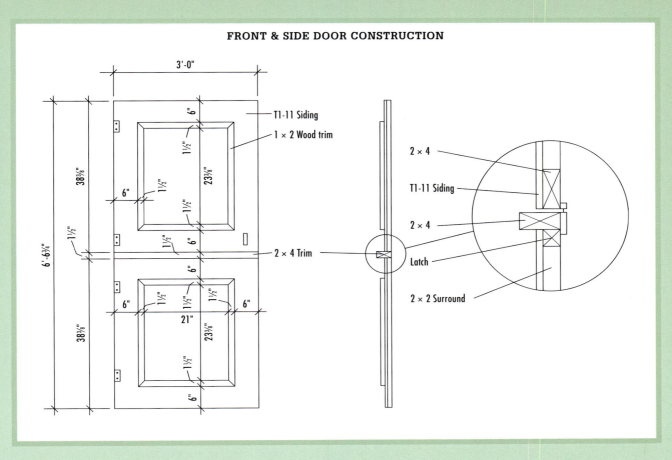

T1-11 Siding

1 × 2 Wood trim

2 × 4 Trim

3'-0"

6"

1½"

23⅜"

6"

1½"

6"

1½"

38⅜"

6'-6¾"

1½"

1½"

6"

6"

1½"

1½"

1½"

21"

23⅜"

1½"

38⅜"

6"

2 × 4

T1-11 Siding

2 × 4

Latch

2 × 2 Surround

FRONT & SIDE DOOR CONSTRUCTION (DOOR JAMB, REAR, DOOR HEADER)

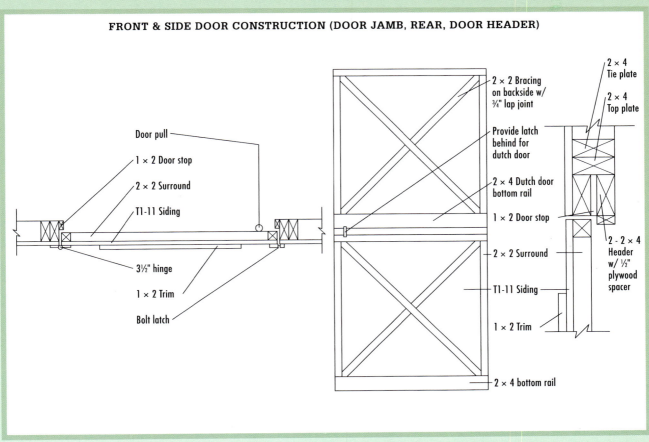

Door pull

1 × 2 Door stop

2 × 2 Surround

T1-11 Siding

3½" hinge

1 × 2 Trim

Bolt latch

2 × 2 Bracing on backside w/ ¾" lap joint

Provide latch behind for dutch door

2 × 4 Dutch door bottom rail

1 × 2 Door stop

2 × 2 Surround

T1-11 Siding

1 × 2 Trim

2 × 4 bottom rail

2 × 4 Tie plate

2 × 4 Top plate

2 - 2 × 4 Header w/ ½" plywood spacer

HEADER & WINDOW DETAIL

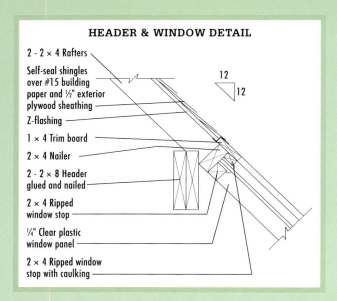

2 - 2 × 4 Rafters

Self-seal shingles over #15 building paper and ½" exterior plywood sheathing

Z-flashing

1 × 4 Trim board

2 × 4 Nailer

2 - 2 × 8 Header glued and nailed

2 × 4 Ripped window stop

¼" Clear plastic window panel

2 × 4 Ripped window stop with caulking

12
12

WINDOW SECTION

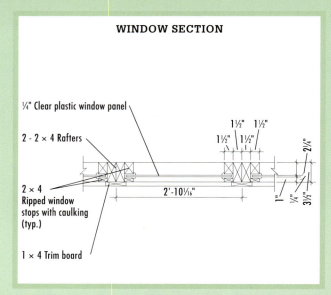

¼" Clear plastic window panel

2 - 2 × 4 Rafters

2 × 4 Ripped window stops with caulking (typ.)

1 × 4 Trim board

1½" 1½"
1½" 1½"
2¼"
2'-10¹⁵⁄₁₆"
1"
¼"
3½"

WINDOW DETAIL

¼" Clear plastic window panel

2 - 2 × 4 Rafters

2 × 4 Ripped window stop w/ 45° bevel and caulking

Caulking (typical)

2 × 2 Window stop with caulking

2 × 4 Tie plate

1 × 4 Trim board

2 × 4 Top plate

2 × 4 Ripped window stops with caulking (typical)

2 - 2 × 4 Wall stud

12
12

TABLE & LOWER WINDOW DETAIL

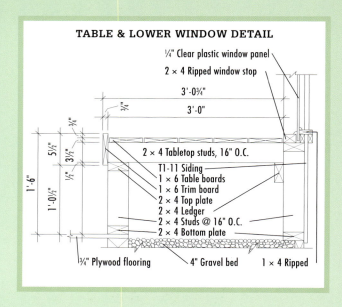

¼" Clear plastic window panel

2 × 4 Ripped window stop

3'-0¾"
3'-0"
¾"
¾"
5½"
3½"
½"
1'-6"
1'-0½"

2 × 4 Tabletop studs, 16" O.C.
T1-11 Siding
1 × 6 Table boards
1 × 6 Trim board
2 × 4 Top plate
2 × 4 Ledger
2 × 4 Studs @ 16" O.C.
2 × 4 Bottom plate

¾" Plywood flooring   4" Gravel bed   1 × 4 Ripped

RAFTER TEMPLATES

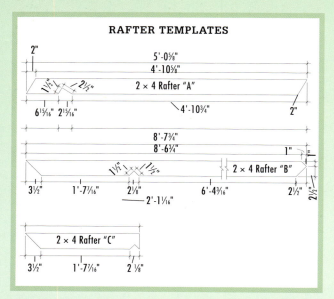

2"
5'-0⅝"
4'-10⅝"
2 × 4 Rafter "A"
1½"   2½"
4'-10¾"
2"
6¹⁵⁄₁₆" 2¹⁵⁄₁₆"

8'-7¾"
8'-6¾"
1"
1½"   1½"
2 × 4 Rafter "B"
1"
3½"   1'-7⁷⁄₁₆"   2⅛"   6'-4³⁄₁₆"   2½"
2½"
2'-1¹⁄₁₆"

2 × 4 Rafter "C"
3½"   1'-7⁷⁄₁₆"   2⅛"

RAKE BOARD DETAIL

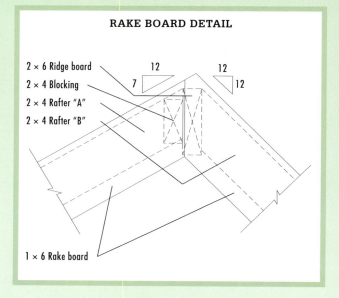

2 × 6 Ridge board
2 × 4 Blocking
2 × 4 Rafter "A"
2 × 4 Rafter "B"

12
7

12
12

1 × 6 Rake board

How to Build the Sunlight Garden Shed

Build the foundation, following the basic steps used for a wooden skid foundation (page 28). First, prepare a bed of compacted gravel. Make sure the bed is flat and level. Cut seven 4 × 4" × 10 ft. pressure-treated posts down to 115¾" to serve as floor joists. Position the joists as shown in the FLOOR FRAMING PLAN. Level each joist, and make sure all are level with one another and the ends are flush. Add rim joists and blocking: Cut two 12-ft. 2 × 4s (142¾") for rim joists. Fasten the rim joists to the ends of the 4 × 4 joists (see the FLOOR FRAMING PLAN) with 16d galvanized common nails.

Cut ten 4 × 4 blocks to fit between the joists. Install six blocks 34½" from the front rim joist, and install four blocks 31½" from the rear. Toenail the blocks to the joists. All blocks, joists, and sills must be flush at the top.

To frame the rear wall, cut one top plate and one pressure-treated bottom plate (142¾"). Cut twelve studs (81"). Assemble the wall following the layout in the REAR FRAMING (page 105). Raise the wall and fasten it to the rear rim joist and the intermediate joists, using 16d galvanized common nails. Brace the wall in position with 2 × 4 braces staked to the ground.

For the front wall, cut two top plates and one treated bottom plate (142¾"). Cut ten studs (35¾") and eight cripple studs (13¼"). Cut four 2 × 4 window sills (311⁄16"). Assemble the wall following the layout in the FRONT FRAMING (page 105). Add the double top plate, but do not install the window stops at this time. Raise, attach, and brace the front wall.

(continued)

Cut lumber for the right side wall: one top plate (54⅞"), one treated bottom plate (111¾"), four studs (81"), and two header post studs (86⅞"); and for the left side wall: top plate (54⅞"), bottom plate (111¾"), three studs (81"), two jack studs (77½"), two posts (86⅞"), and a built-up 2 × 4 header (39¼"). Assemble and install the walls as shown in the RIGHT SIDE FRAMING and LEFT SIDE FRAMING (page 104). Add the doubled top plates along the rear and side walls. Install treated 2 × 4 nailing cleats to the joists and blocking as shown in the FLOOR FRAMING PLAN (page 104) and BUILDING SECTION (page 103).

Trim two sheets of ¾" plywood as needed and install them over the joists and blocking as shown in the FLOOR FRAMING PLAN, leaving open cavities along the front of the shed and a portion of the rear. Fasten the sheets with 8d galvanized common nails driven every 6" along the edges and 8" in the field. Fill the exposed foundation cavities with 4" of gravel and compact it thoroughly.

Construct the rafter header from two 2 × 8s cut to 142¾". Join the pieces with construction adhesive and pairs of 10d common nails driven every 24" on both sides. Set the header on top of the side wall posts, and toenail it to the posts with four 16d common nails at each end.

Cut one of each "A" and "B" pattern rafters using the RAFTER TEMPLATES (page 108). Test-fit the rafters. The B rafter should rest squarely on the rafter header, and its bottom end should sit flush with outside of the front wall. Adjust the rafter cuts as needed, then use the pattern rafters to mark and cut the remaining A and B rafters.

Cut the 2 × 6 ridge board (154¾"). Mark the rafter layout onto the ridge and front and rear wall plates following the FRONT FRAMING and REAR FRAMING. Install the A and B rafters and ridge. Make sure the B rafters are spaced accurately so the windows will fit properly into their frames; see the WINDOW SECTION (page 108).

Cut a pattern "C" rafter, test-fit, and adjust as needed. Cut the remaining seven C rafters and install them. Measure and cut four 2 × 4 nailers (311⁄16") to fit between the sets of B rafters (as shown). Position the nailers as shown in the HEADER & WINDOW DETAIL (page 108) and toenail them to the rafters.

Complete the rake portions of each side wall. Mark the stud layouts onto the bottom plate, and onto the top plate of the square wall section; see the RIGHT and LEFT SIDE FRAMING. Use a plumb bob to transfer the layout to the rafters. Measure for each stud, cutting the top ends of the studs under the B rafters at 45° and those under the A rafters at 30°. Toenail the studs to the plates and rafters. Add horizontal 2 × 4 nailers as shown in the framing drawings.

Create the inner and outer window stops from 10-ft.-long 2 × 4s. For stops at the sides and tops of the roof windows and all sides of the front wall windows, rip the inner stops to 2¼" wide and the outer stops to 1" wide; see the WINDOW SECTION and WINDOW DETAIL (page 108). For the bottom of each roof window, rip the inner stop to 1½"; bevel the edge of the outer stop at 45°.

(continued)

Install each window as follows: Attach inner stops as shown in the drawings, using galvanized finish nails. Paint or varnish the rafters and stops for moisture protection. Apply a heavy bead of caulk at each location shown on the drawings (HEADER & WINDOW DETAIL, WINDOW SECTION/DETAIL, TABLE & LOWER WINDOW DETAIL). Set the glazing in place, add another bead of caulk, and attach the outer stops. Cover the rafters and stop edges with 1 × 4 trim.

Cover the walls with T1-11 siding, starting with the rear wall. Trim the sheets as needed so they extend from the bottom edges of the rafters down to at least 1" below the tops of the foundation timbers. On the side walls, add Z-flashing above the first row and continue the siding up to the rafters.

Install 1 × 6 fascia over the ends of the A rafters. Keep all fascia ½" above the rafters so it will be flush with the roof sheathing. Using scrap rafter material, cut the 2 × 4 lookouts (5¼"). On each outer B rafter, install one lookout at the bottom end and four more spaced 24" on center going up. On the A rafters, add a lookout at both ends and two spaced evenly in between. Install the 1 × 6 rake boards (fascia) as shown in the RAKE BOARD DETAIL (page 108).

Rip 1 × 6 boards to 5¼" width (some may come milled to 5¼" already) for the gable soffits. Fasten the soffits to the lookouts with siding nails. Rip a 1 × 8 board for the soffit along the rear eave, beveling the edges at 30° to match the A rafter ends. Install the soffit.

17

Deck the roof with ½" plywood sheathing, starting at the bottom ends of the rafters. Install metal drip edge, building paper, and asphalt shingles following the steps on page 56. If desired, add one or more roof vents during the shingle installation. Be sure to overlap shingles onto the 1 × 4 trim board above the roof windows, as shown in the HEADER & WINDOW DETAIL.

18

Construct the planting tables from 2 × 4 lumber and 1 × 6 boards, as shown in the TABLE & LOWER WINDOW DETAIL and BUILDING SECTION. The bottom plates of the table legs should be flush with the outside edges of the foundation blocking.

19

Build each of the two door panels using T1-11 siding, 2 × 2 bracing, a 2 × 4 bottom rail, and 1 × 2 trim on the front side; see the DOOR CONSTRUCTION drawings (page 107). The panels are identical except for a 2 × 4 sill added to the top of the lower panel. Install 1 × 2 stops at the sides and top of the door opening. Hang the doors with four hinges, leaving even gaps all around. Install a bolt latch for locking the two panels together.

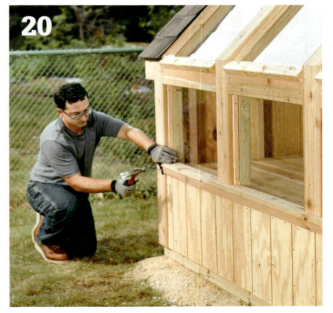

20

Complete the trim details with 1 × 4 vertical corner boards, 1 × 4 horizontal trim above the front wall windows, and ripped 1 × 4 trim and 1 × 2 trim at the bottom of the front wall windows (see the TABLE & LOWER WINDOW DETAIL). Paint the siding and trim, or coat with exterior wood finish.

Lean-to Tool Bin

The lean-to is a classic outbuilding intended as a supplementary structure for a larger building. Its simple shed-style roof helps it blend with the neighboring structure and directs water away and keeps leaves and debris from getting trapped between the two buildings. When built to a small shed scale, the lean-to (sometimes called a closet shed) is most useful as an easy-access storage locker that saves you extra trips into the garage for often-used lawn and garden tools and supplies.

This lean-to tool bin is not actually attached to the house, though it appears to be. It is designed as a freestanding building with a wooden skid foundation that makes it easy to move. With all four sides finished, the bin can be placed anywhere, but it works best when set next to a house or garage wall or a tall fence. If you locate the bin out in the open—where it won't be protected against wind and extreme weather—be sure to anchor it securely to the ground to prevent it from blowing over.

As shown here, the bin is finished with asphalt shingle roofing, T1-11 plywood siding, and 1× cedar trim, but you can substitute any type of finish to match or complement a neighboring structure. Its 65"-tall double doors provide easy access to its 18 square feet of floor space. The 8-ft.-tall rear wall can accommodate a set of shelves while leaving enough room below for long-handled tools.

Because the tool bin sits on the ground, in cold climates it will be subject to shifting with seasonal freeze-thaw cycles. Therefore, do not attach the tool bin to your house or any other building set on a frost-proof foundation.

Cutting List

Description	Quantity/Size	Material
Foundation		
Drainage material	0.5 cu. yd.	Compactible gravel
Skids	2 @ 6'	4 × 4 treated timbers
Floor framing		
Rim joists	2 @ 6'	2 × 6 pressure-treated
Joists	3 @ 8'	2 × 6 pressure-treated
Floor sheathing	1 sheet @ 4 × 8	¾" tongue-&-groove ext.-grade plywood
Joist clip angles	4	3 × 3 × 3" × 16-gauge galvanized
Wall Framing		
Bottom plates	1 @ 8', 2 @ 6'	2 × 4
Top plates	1 @ 8', 3 @ 6'	2 × 4
Studs	14 @ 8', 8 @ 6'	2 × 4
Header	2 @ 6'	2 × 6
Header spacer	1 piece @ 6'	½" plywood — 5" wide
Roof Framing		
Rafters	6 @ 6'	2 × 6
Ledger*	1 @ 6'	2 × 6
Roofing		
Roof sheathing	2 sheets @ 4 × 8'	½" ext.-grade plywood
Shingles	30 sq. ft.	250# per square min.
Roofing starter strip	7 linear ft.	
15# building paper	30 sq. ft.	
Metal drip edge	24 linear ft.	Galvanized metal
Roofing cement	1 tube	
Exterior Finishes		
Plywood siding	4 sheets @ 4 × 8'	⅝" Texture 1-11 plywood siding, grooves 8" O.C.

Description	Quantity/Size	Material
Door trim	2 @ 8'	1 × 10 S4S cedar
	2 @ 6'	1 × 8 S4S cedar
Corner trim	6 @ 8'	1 × 4 S4S cedar
Fascia	3 @ 6'	1 × 8 S4S cedar
	1 @ 6'	1 × 4 S4S cedar
Bug screen	8" × 6'	Fiberglass
Doors		
Frame	3 @ 6'	¾" × 3½" (actual) cedar
Stops	3 @ 6'	1 × 2 S4S cedar
Panel material	12 @ 6'	1 × 6 T&G V-joint S4S cedar
Z-braces	2 @ 10'	1 × 6 S4S cedar
Construction adhesive	1 tube	
Interior trim (optional)	3 @ 6'	1 × 3 S4S cedar
Strap hinges	6, with screws	
Fasteners		
16d galvanized common nails	3½ lbs.	
16d common nails	3½ lbs.	
10d common nails	12 nails	
10d galvanized casing nails	20 nails	
8d galvanized box nails	½ lb.	
8d galvanized finish nails	2 lbs.	
8d common nails	24 nails	
8d box nails	½ lb.	
1½" joist hanger nails	16 nails	
⅞" galvanized roofing nails	¼ lb.	
2½" deck screws	6 screws	
1¼" wood screws	60 screws	

*Note: 6-foot material is often unavailable at local lumber stores, so buy half as much of 12-foot material.

FLOOR FRAMING PLAN

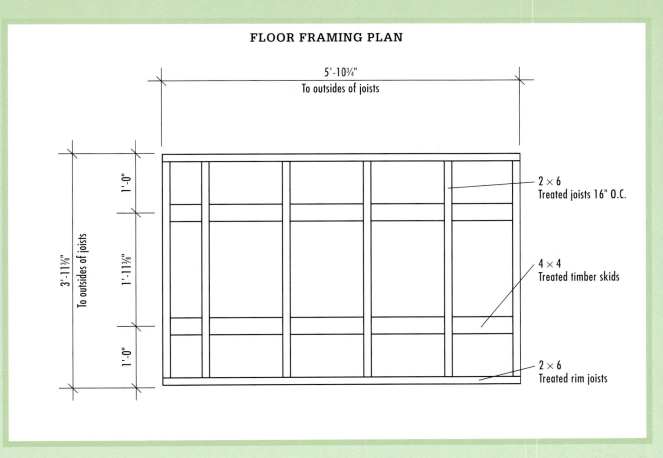

5'-10¾"
To outsides of joists

3'-11⅜"
To outsides of joists

1'-0"

1'-11⅜"

1'-0"

2 × 6
Treated joists 16" O.C.

4 × 4
Treated timber skids

2 × 6
Treated rim joists

ROOF FRAMING PLAN

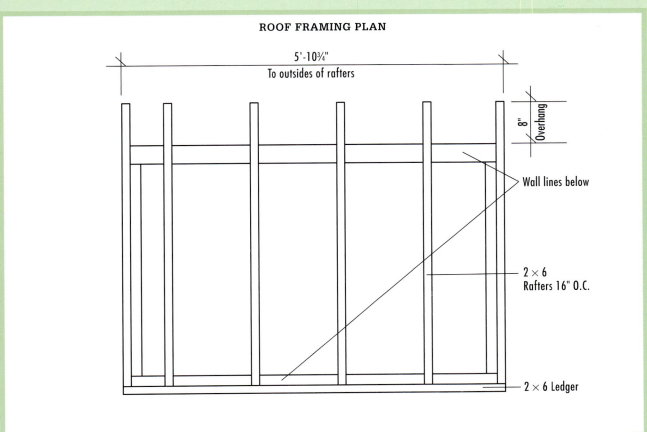

5'-10¾"
To outsides of rafters

8" Overhang

Wall lines below

2 × 6
Rafters 16" O.C.

2 × 6 Ledger

FRONT FRAMING ELEVATION

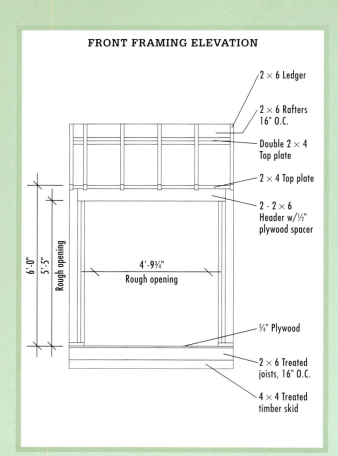

2 × 6 Ledger

2 × 6 Rafters 16" O.C.

Double 2 × 4 Top plate

2 × 4 Top plate

2 - 2 × 6 Header w/½" plywood spacer

6'-0"

5'-5" Rough opening

4'-9¾" Rough opening

¾" Plywood

2 × 6 Treated joists, 16" O.C.

4 × 4 Treated timber skid

LEFT FRAMING ELEVATION

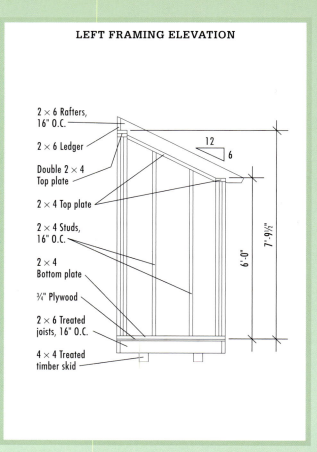

2 × 6 Rafters, 16" O.C.

2 × 6 Ledger

Double 2 × 4 Top plate

2 × 4 Top plate

2 × 4 Studs, 16" O.C.

2 × 4 Bottom plate

¾" Plywood

2 × 6 Treated joists, 16" O.C.

4 × 4 Treated timber skid

12

6

7'-9½"

6'-0"

REAR SIDE FRAMING ELEVATION

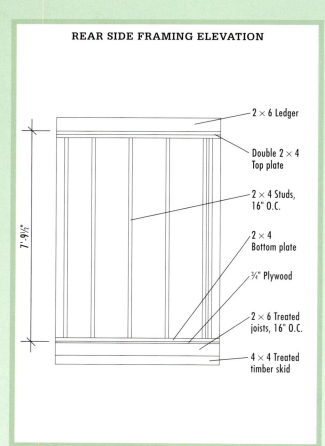

2 × 6 Ledger

Double 2 × 4 Top plate

2 × 4 Studs, 16" O.C.

2 × 4 Bottom plate

¾" Plywood

2 × 6 Treated joists, 16" O.C.

4 × 4 Treated timber skid

7'-9½"

RIGHT SIDE FRAMING ELEVATION

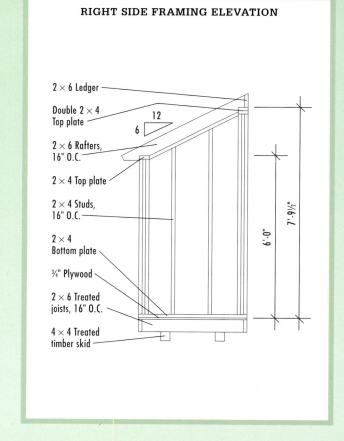

2 × 6 Ledger

Double 2 × 4 Top plate

12

6

2 × 6 Rafters, 16" O.C.

2 × 4 Top plate

2 × 4 Studs, 16" O.C.

2 × 4 Bottom plate

¾" Plywood

2 × 6 Treated joists, 16" O.C.

4 × 4 Treated timber skid

6'-0"

7'-9½"

BUILDING SECTION

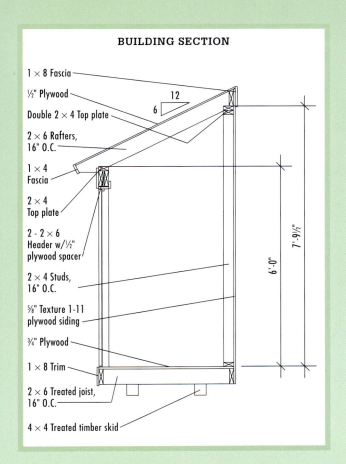

1 × 8 Fascia

½" Plywood

Double 2 × 4 Top plate

2 × 6 Rafters, 16" O.C.

1 × 4 Fascia

2 × 4 Top plate

2 - 2 × 6 Header w/½" plywood spacer

2 × 4 Studs, 16" O.C.

⅝" Texture 1-11 plywood siding

¾" Plywood

1 × 8 Trim

2 × 6 Treated joist, 16" O.C.

4 × 4 Treated timber skid

12 / 6

6'-0"

7'-9½"

SIDE ELEVATION

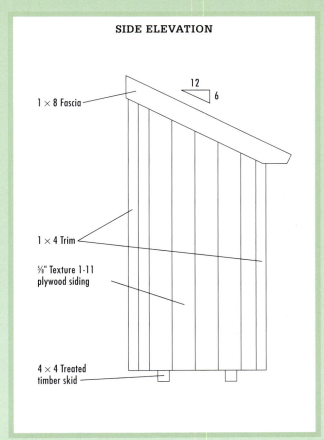

1 × 8 Fascia

12 / 6

1 × 4 Trim

⅝" Texture 1-11 plywood siding

4 × 4 Treated timber skid

FRONT ELEVATION

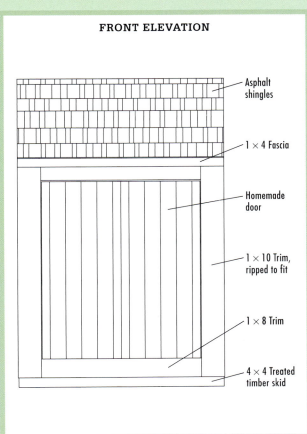

Asphalt shingles

1 × 4 Fascia

Homemade door

1 × 10 Trim, ripped to fit

1 × 8 Trim

4 × 4 Treated timber skid

REAR ELEVATION

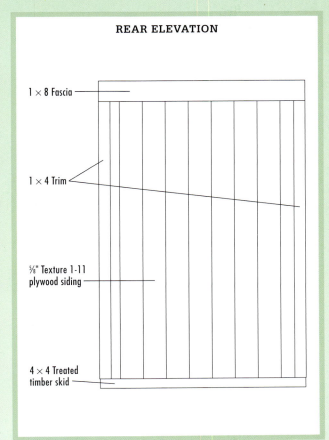

1 × 8 Fascia

1 × 4 Trim

⅝" Texture 1-11 plywood siding

4 × 4 Treated timber skid

WALL PLAN

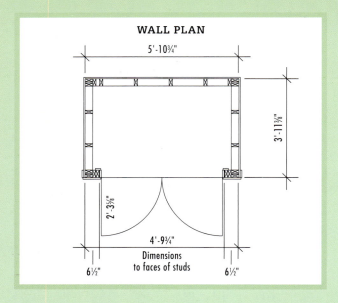

5'-10¾"

3'-11⅜"

2'-3⅜"

4'-9¾"

Dimensions
to faces of studs

6½" 6½"

RAFTER TEMPLATE

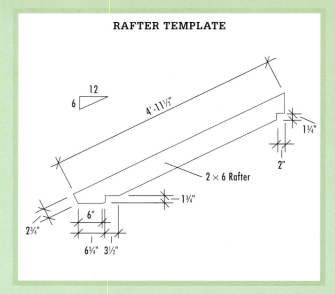

12
6

4'-11½"

2 × 6 Rafter

1¾"

2"

1¾"

6"

2¾"

6¾" 3½"

SIDE ROOF EDGE DETAIL

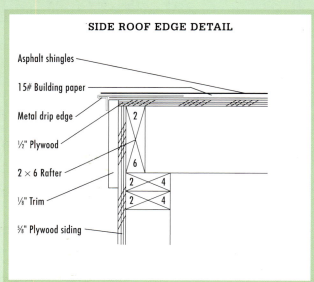

Asphalt shingles

15# Building paper

Metal drip edge

½" Plywood

2 × 6 Rafter

⅛" Trim

⅝" Plywood siding

2

6

2 4

2 4

OVERHANG DETAIL

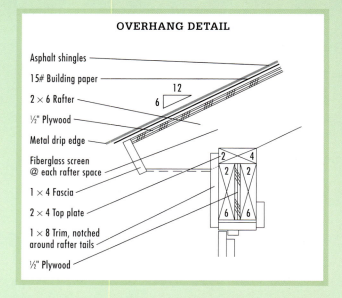

Asphalt shingles

15# Building paper

2 × 6 Rafter

½" Plywood

Metal drip edge

Fiberglass screen
@ each rafter space

1 × 4 Fascia

2 × 4 Top plate

1 × 8 Trim, notched
around rafter tails

½" Plywood

12
6

2 4

2 2

6 6

DOOR JAMB DETAIL

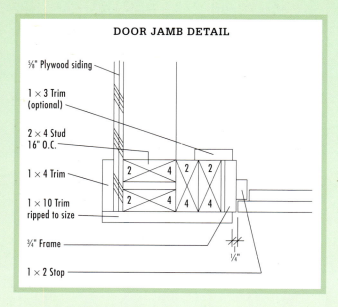

⅝" Plywood siding

1 × 3 Trim
(optional)

2 × 4 Stud
16" O.C.

1 × 4 Trim

1 × 10 Trim
ripped to size

¾" Frame

1 × 2 Stop

2 4 2 2

2 4 4 4

¼"

DOOR ELEVATION

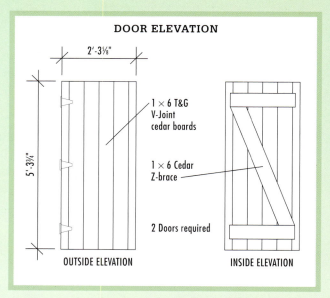

2'-3⅝"

5'-3¾"

1 × 6 T&G
V-Joint
cedar boards

1 × 6 Cedar
Z-brace

2 Doors required

OUTSIDE ELEVATION

INSIDE ELEVATION

How to Build the Lean-to Tool Bin

Prepare the site with a 4" layer of compacted gravel. Cut the two 4 × 4 skids at 70¾". Set and level the skids following FLOOR FRAMING PLAN (page 117). Cut two 2 × 6 rim joists at 70¾" and six joists at 44⅜". Assemble the floor and set it on the skids as shown in the FLOOR FRAMING PLAN. Check for square, and then anchor the frame to the skids with four joist clip angles (inset photo). Sheath the floor frame with ¾" plywood.

Cut plates and studs for the walls: Side walls—two bottom plates at 47⅜", four studs at 89", and four studs at 69"; Front wall—one bottom plate at 63¾", one top plate at 70¾", and four jacks studs at 63½". Rear wall—one bottom plate at 63¾", two top plates at 70¾", and six studs at 89". Mark the stud layouts onto the plates.

Fasten the four end studs of each side wall to the bottom plate. Install these assemblies. Construct the built-up 2 × 6 door header at 63¾". Frame and install the front and rear walls, leaving the top plates off at this time. Nail together the corner studs, making sure they are plumb. Install the rear top plates flush to the outsides of the side wall studs. Install the front top plate in the same fashion.

Cut the six 2 × 6 rafters following the RAFTER TEMPLATE (page 120). Cut the 2 × 6 ledger at 70¾" and bevel the top edge at 26.5° so the overall width is 4⁵⁄₁₆". Mark the rafter layout onto the wall plates and ledger, as shown in the ROOF FRAMING PLAN (page 117), then install the ledger flush with the back side of the rear wall. Install the rafters.

(continued)

Complete the side wall framing: Cut a top plate for each side to fit between the front and rear walls, mitering the ends at 26.5°. Install the plates flush with the outsides of the end rafters. Mark the stud layouts onto the side wall bottom plates, then use a plumb bob to transfer the marks to the top plate. Cut the two studs in each wall to fit, mitering the top ends at 26.5°. Install the studs.

Sheath the side walls and rear walls with plywood siding, keeping the bottom edges ½" below the floor frame and the top edges flush with the tops of the rafters. Overlap the siding at the rear corners, and stop it flush with the face of the front wall.

Add the 1 × 4 fascia over the bottom rafter ends as shown in the OVERHANG DETAIL (page 120). Install 1 × 8 fascia over the top rafter ends. Overhang the front and rear fascia to cover the ends of the side fascia, or plan to miter all fascia joints. Cut the 1 × 8 side fascia to length, and then clip the bottom front corners to meet the front fascia. Install the side fascia.

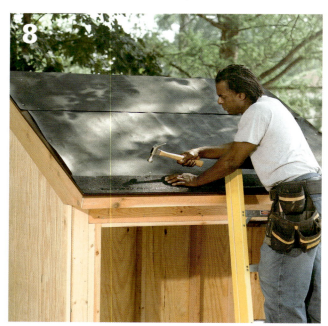

Install the ½" roof sheathing, starting with a full-width sheet at the bottom edge of the roof. Fasten metal drip edge along the front edge of the roof. Cover the roof with building paper, then add the drip edge along the sides and top of the roof. Shingle the roof, and finish the top edge with cut shingles or a solid starter strip.

9

Cut and remove the bottom plate inside the door opening. Cut the 1 × 4 head jamb for the door frame at 57⅛" and cut the side jambs at 64". Fasten the head jamb over the sides with 2½" deck screws. Install 1 × 2 door stops ¾" from the front edges of jambs, as shown in the DOOR JAMB DETAIL (page 120). Install the frame in the door opening, using shims and 10d casing nails.

10

For each door, cut six 1 × 6 tongue-and-groove boards at 63¾". Fit them together, then mark and trim the two end boards so the total width is 27⅝". Cut the 1 × 6 Z-brace boards following the DOOR ELEVATION (page 120). The ends of the horizontal braces should be 1" from the door edges. Attach the braces with construction adhesive and 1¼" screws. Install each door with three hinges.

11

Staple fiberglass insect mesh along the underside of the roof from each side 2 × 6 rafter. Cut and install the 1 × 8 trim above the door, overlapping the side door jambs about ¼" on each side (see the OVERHANG DETAIL, page 120).

12

Rip vertical and horizontal trim boards to width, then notch them to fit around the rafters, as shown in the DOOR JAMB DETAIL (page 120). Notch the top ends of the 1 × 10s to fit between the rafters and install them. Add 1 × 8 trim horizontally between the 1 × 10s below the door. Install the 1 × 4 corner trim, overlapping the pieces at the rear corners.

Convenience Shed

The Convenience Shed is so named for its exceptional versatility and ample storage space. This classic gabled outbuilding has a footprint that measures 12 × 16 ft. and it includes several features not found in most storage sheds. For starters, its 8-ft.-wide overhead garage door provides easy access for large equipment, supplies, projects or even a small automobile. The foundation and shed floor is a poured concrete slab, so it's ideal for heavy items like lawn tractors and stationary tools.

To the right of the garage door is a box bay window. This special architectural detail gives the building's facade a surprising house-like quality while filling the interior with natural light. And the bay's 33"-deep × 60"-wide sill platform is the perfect place for herb pots or an indoor flower box. The adjacent wall includes a second large window and a standard service door, making this end of the shed a pleasant, convenient space for all kinds of work or leisure.

Above the main space of the Convenience Shed is a fully framed attic built with 2 × 6 joists for supporting plenty of stored goods. The steep pitch of the roof allows for over 3 ft. of headroom under the peak. Access to the attic is provided by a drop-down staircase that folds up and out of the way, leaving the workspace clear below.

The garage door, service door, staircase, and both windows of the shed are pre-built factory units that you install following the manufacturers' instructions. Be sure to order all of the units before starting construction. This makes it easy to adjust the framed openings, if necessary, to match the precise sizing of each unit. Also consult your local building department to learn about design requirements for the concrete foundation. You may need to extend and/or reinforce the perimeter portion of the slab or include a footing that extends below the frost line. An extended apron (as seen in the Gambrel Garage, page 138) is very useful if you intend to house vehicles in the shed.

Cutting List

Description	Quantity/Size	Material
Foundation		
Drainage material	2.75 cu. yd.	Compactible gravel
Concrete slab	Field measure	3,000 psi concrete
Mesh	200 sq. ft.	6 × 6", W1.4 × W1.4 welded wire mesh
Reinforcing bar	As required by local code	As required by local code
Wall Framing		
Bottom plates	1 @ 16', 2 @ 12', 1 @ 10'	2 × 4 pressure-treated
Top plates	2 @ 14', 4 @ 12', 4 @ 10'	2 × 4
Standard wall studs	51 @ 8'* *may use 92⅝" precut studs	2 × 4
Diagonal bracing	5 @ 12'	1 × 4 (std. lumber)
Jack studs	5 @ 14'	2 × 4
Gable end studs	5 @ 8'	2 × 4
Header, overhead door	2 @ 10'	2 × 12
Header, windows	2 @ 10'	2 × 12
Header, service door	1 @ 8'	2 × 12
Header & stud spacers		See Sheathing, below
Box Bay Framing		
Half-wall bottom plate	1 @ 8'	2 × 4 pressure-treated
Half-wall top plate & studs	3 @ 8'	2 × 4
Joists	3 @ 8'	2 × 6
Window frame	4 @ 12'	2 × 4
Sill platform & top	1 sheet @ 4 × 8'	½" plywood
Rafter blocking	1 @ 8'	2 × 8
Roof Framing		
Rafters (& lookouts, blocking)	36 @ 10'	2 × 6
Ridge board	1 @ 18'	2 × 8
Attic		
Floor joists	16 @ 12'	2 × 6
Floor decking	6 sheets @ 4 × 8'	½" plywood
Staircase	1 unit for 22 × 48" rough opening	Disappearing attic stair unit
Exterior Finishes		
Eave fascia	2 @ 18'	2 × 8 cedar
Gable fascia	4 @ 10'	1 × 8 cedar

Description	Quantity/Size	Material
Drip edge & gable trim	160 linear ft.	1 × 2 cedar
Siding	15 sheets @ 4 × 8'	⅝" Texture 1-11 plywood siding w/ vertical grooves 8" on center (or similar)
Siding flashing	30 linear ft.	Metal Z-flashing
Overhead door jambs	1 @ 10', 2 @ 8'	1 × 6 cedar
Overhead door stops	3 @ 8'	Cedar door stop
Overhead door surround	1 @ 10', 2 @ 8'	2 × 6
Corner trim	8 @ 8'	1 × 4 cedar
Door & window trim	4 @ 8', 5 @ 10'	1 × 4 cedar
Box bay bottom trim	1 @ 8'	1 × 10 cedar
Roofing		
Sheathing (& header, stud spacers)	14 sheets @ 4 × 8'	½" exterior-grade plywood roof sheathing
15# building paper	2 rolls	
Shingles	4⅔ squares	Asphalt shingles — 250# per sq. min.
Roof flashing	10'6"	
Doors & Windows		
Overhead garage door w/hardware	1 @ ⁹⁄₀ × ⁷⁄₀	
Service door	1 unit for 38 × 72⅞" rough opening	Prehung exterior door unit
Window	2 units for 57 × 41⅜"	Casement mullion window unit — complete
Fasteners & Hardware		
J-bolts w/nuts & washers	14	½"-dia. × 12"
16d galvanized common nails	3 lbs.	
16d common nails	15 lbs.	
10d common nails	2½ lbs.	
8d box nails	16 lbs.	
8d common nails	5 lbs.	
8d galvanized siding nails	10 lbs.	
1" galvanized roofing nails	10 lbs.	
8d galvanized casing nails	3 lbs.	
Entry door lockset	1	

FOUNDATION PLAN

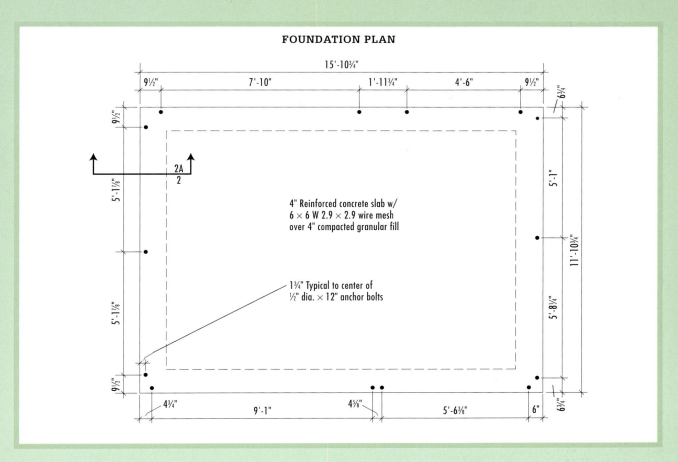

15'-10¾"

9½"   7'-10"   1'-11¾"   4'-6"   9½"   6¾"

9½"

5'-1⅞"

5'-1"

4" Reinforced concrete slab w/
6 × 6 W 2.9 × 2.9 wire mesh
over 4" compacted granular fill

11'-10¾"

5'-1⅞"

1¾" Typical to center of
½" dia. × 12" anchor bolts

5'-8¾"

9½"

2A
2

4¾"   9'-1"   4⅝"   5'-6⅜"   6"   6¾"

FOUNDATION DETAIL

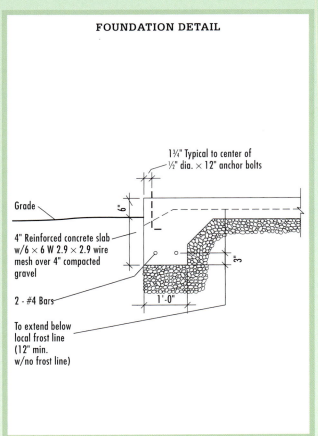

1¾" Typical to center of
½" dia. × 12" anchor bolts

Grade

6"

4" Reinforced concrete slab
w/6 × 6 W 2.9 × 2.9 wire
mesh over 4" compacted
gravel

3"

2 - #4 Bars

1'-0"

To extend below
local frost line
(12" min.
w/no frost line)

BUILDING SECTION

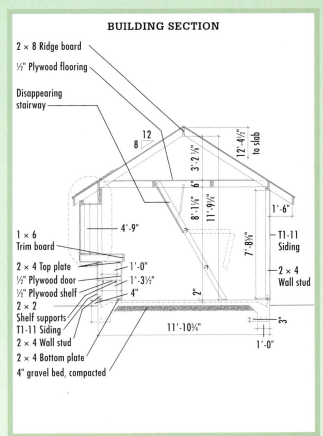

2 × 8 Ridge board

½" Plywood flooring

Disappearing
stairway

12
8

3'-2⅛"

12'-4½"
to slab

6"

8'-1⅛"

11'-9¾"

1'-6"

1 × 6
Trim board

4'-9"

7'-8⅝"

T1-11
Siding

2 × 4 Top plate

1'-0"

½" Plywood door

1'-3½"

½" Plywood shelf

4"

2 × 2
Shelf supports

2 × 4
Wall stud

T1-11 Siding

2"

2 × 4 Wall stud

2 × 4 Bottom plate

11'-10¾"

3"

4" gravel bed, compacted

1'-0"

FRONT ELEVATION

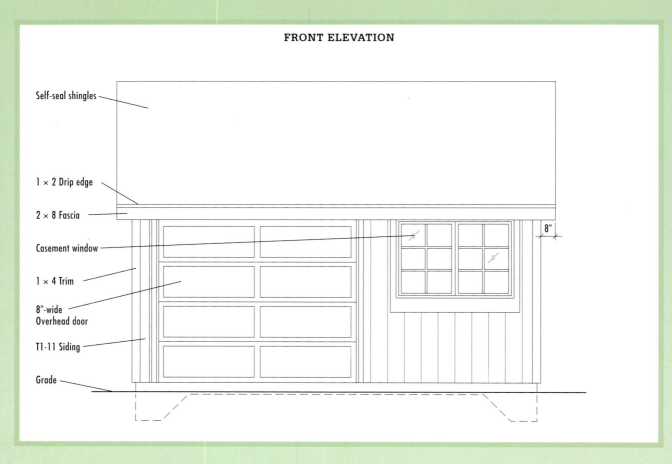

Self-seal shingles

1 × 2 Drip edge

2 × 8 Fascia

Casement window

1 × 4 Trim

8"-wide
Overhead door

T1-11 Siding

Grade

8"

RIGHT SIDE ELEVATION

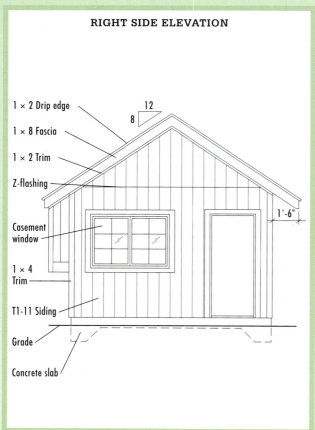

1 × 2 Drip edge

1 × 8 Fascia

1 × 2 Trim

Z-flashing

Casement
window

1 × 4
Trim

T1-11 Siding

Grade

Concrete slab

12
8

1'-6"

REAR ELEVATION

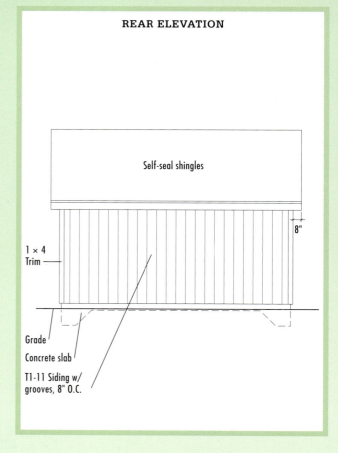

Self-seal shingles

1 × 4
Trim

Grade

Concrete slab

T1-11 Siding w/
grooves, 8" O.C.

8"

WALL FRAMING PLAN

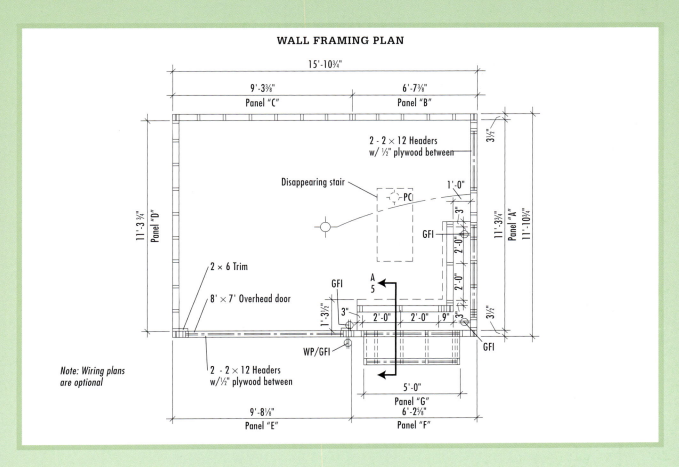

15'-10¾"

9'-3⅜"
Panel "C"

6'-7⅜"
Panel "B"

2 - 2 × 12 Headers
w/ ½" plywood between

Disappearing stair

PC

GFI

1'-0"

3"

11'-3¾"
Panel "A"
11'-10¾"

3½"

11'-3¾"
Panel "D"

2 × 6 Trim

8' × 7' Overhead door

GFI

A
5

2'-0"

2'-0"

1'-3½"
3"

2'-0"

2'-0"

9"

3"

3½"

GFI

WP/GFI

*Note: Wiring plans
are optional*

2 - 2 × 12 Headers
w/ ½" plywood between

5'-0"
Panel "G"
6'-2⅝"

9'-8⅛"
Panel "E"

Panel "F"

BACK SIDE FRAMING

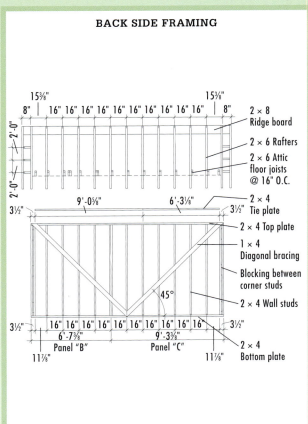

15⅜"   15⅜"
8" 16" 16" 16" 16" 16" 16" 16" 16" 16" 8"

2 × 8
Ridge board

2'-0"

2 × 6 Rafters

2 × 6 Attic
floor joists
@ 16" O.C.

2'-0"

3½"

9'-0⅝"   6'-3⅛"   3½"

2 × 4
Tie plate

2 × 4 Top plate

1 × 4
Diagonal bracing

Blocking between
corner studs

45°

2 × 4 Wall studs

3½"   16" 16" 16" 16" 16" 16" 16" 16" 16"   3½"

6'-7⅜"   9'-3⅜"

2 × 4
Bottom plate

11⅞"   Panel "B"   Panel "C"   11⅞"

LEFT SIDE FRAMING

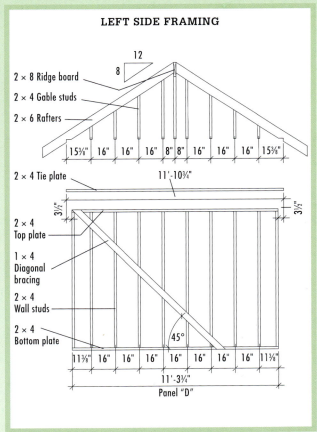

12
8

2 × 8 Ridge board

2 × 4 Gable studs

2 × 6 Rafters

15⅜" 16" 16" 16" 8" 8" 16" 16" 16" 15⅜"

2 × 4 Tie plate

11'-10¾"

3½"   3½"

2 × 4
Top plate

1 × 4
Diagonal
bracing

2 × 4
Wall studs

45°

2 × 4
Bottom plate

11⅜" 16" 16" 16" 16" 16" 16" 16" 11⅜"

11'-3¾"
Panel "D"

FRONT SIDE FRAMING

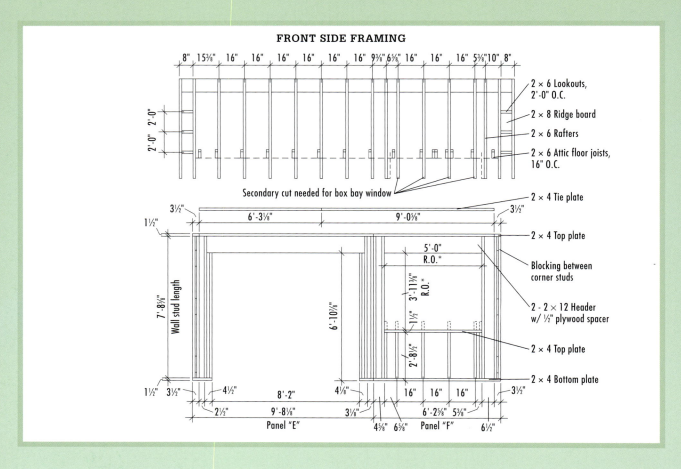

2 × 6 Lookouts, 2'-0" O.C.

2 × 8 Ridge board

2 × 6 Rafters

2 × 6 Attic floor joists, 16" O.C.

Secondary cut needed for box bay window

2 × 4 Tie plate

2 × 4 Top plate

Blocking between corner studs

2 - 2 × 12 Header w/ ½" plywood spacer

2 × 4 Top plate

2 × 4 Bottom plate

Panel "E" Panel "F"

Wall stud length

ATTIC FLOOR JOIST FRAMING

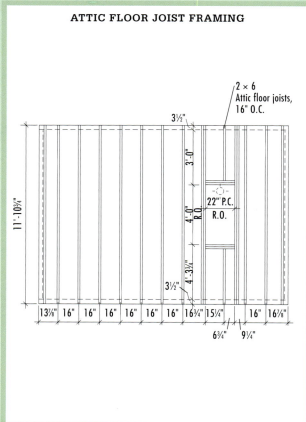

2 × 6 Attic floor joists, 16" O.C.

22" P.C. R.O.

BOX BAY WINDOW FRAMING

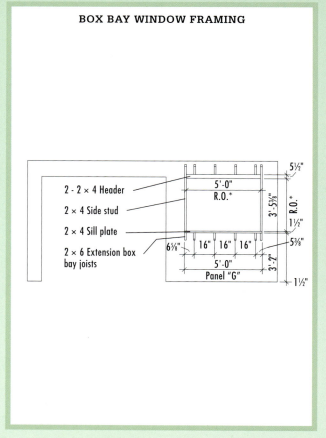

2 - 2 × 4 Header

2 × 4 Side stud

2 × 4 Sill plate

2 × 6 Extension box bay joists

Panel "G"

OVERHEAD DOOR HEADER DETAIL

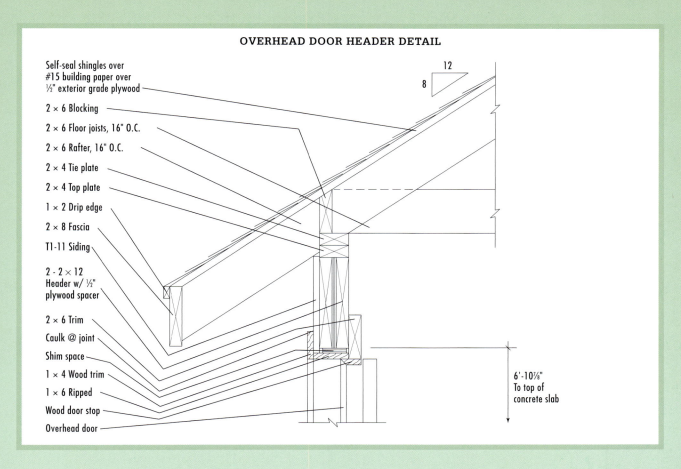

Self-seal shingles over
#15 building paper over
½" exterior grade plywood

2 × 6 Blocking

2 × 6 Floor joists, 16" O.C.

2 × 6 Rafter, 16" O.C.

2 × 4 Tie plate

2 × 4 Top plate

1 × 2 Drip edge

2 × 8 Fascia

T1-11 Siding

2 - 2 × 12
Header w/ ½"
plywood spacer

2 × 6 Trim

Caulk @ joint

Shim space

1 × 4 Wood trim

1 × 6 Ripped

Wood door stop

Overhead door

12
8

6'-10⅞"
To top of
concrete slab

OVERHEAD DOOR JAMB DETAIL

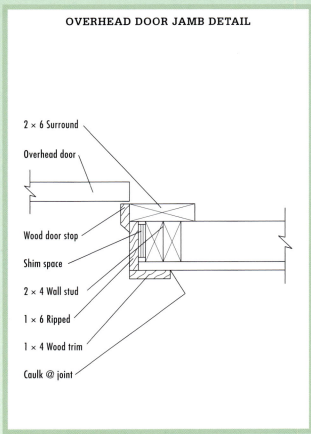

2 × 6 Surround

Overhead door

Wood door stop

Shim space

2 × 4 Wall stud

1 × 6 Ripped

1 × 4 Wood trim

Caulk @ joint

SERVICE DOOR HEADER/JAMB DETAIL

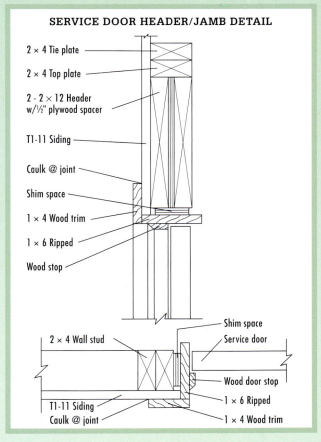

2 × 4 Tie plate

2 × 4 Top plate

2 - 2 × 12 Header
w/½" plywood spacer

T1-11 Siding

Caulk @ joint

Shim space

1 × 4 Wood trim

1 × 6 Ripped

Wood stop

2 × 4 Wall stud

T1-11 Siding

Caulk @ joint

Shim space

Service door

Wood door stop

1 × 6 Ripped

1 × 4 Wood trim

RAFTER TEMPLATE

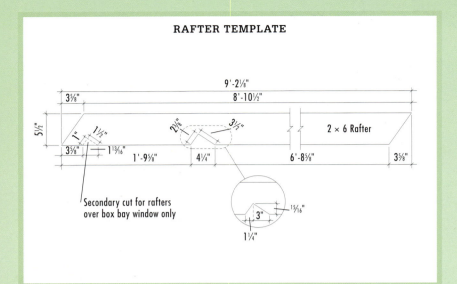

9'-2⅛"
8'-10½"
3⅝"
5½"
1" 1½"
3⅝" 1¹³⁄₁₆"
2⅞" 3½"
1'-9⅝" 4¼"
6'-8⅝" 3⅝"
2 × 6 Rafter

Secondary cut for rafters
over box bay window only

15⁄16"
3"
1¼"

CORNER DETAIL

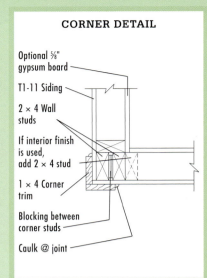

Optional ⅝"
gypsum board

T1-11 Siding

2 × 4 Wall
studs

If interior finish
is used,
add 2 × 4 stud

1 × 4 Corner
trim

Blocking between
corner studs

Caulk @ joint

BOX BAY WINDOW DETAIL

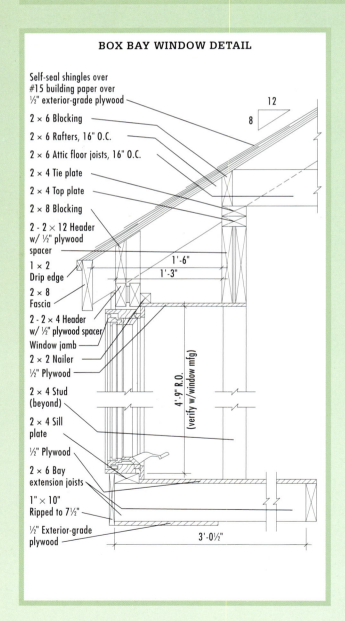

Self-seal shingles over
#15 building paper over
½" exterior-grade plywood

2 × 6 Blocking

2 × 6 Rafters, 16" O.C.

2 × 6 Attic floor joists, 16" O.C.

2 × 4 Tie plate

2 × 4 Top plate

2 × 8 Blocking

2 - 2 × 12 Header
w/ ½" plywood
spacer

1 × 2
Drip edge

2 × 8
Fascia

2 - 2 × 4 Header
w/ ½" plywood spacer

Window jamb

2 × 2 Nailer

½" Plywood

2 × 4 Stud
(beyond)

2 × 4 Sill
plate

½" Plywood

2 × 6 Bay
extension joists

1" × 10"
Ripped to 7½"

½" Exterior-grade
plywood

12
8

1'-6"
1'-3"

4'-9" R.O.
(verify w/window mfg)

3'-0½"

ISOMETRIC

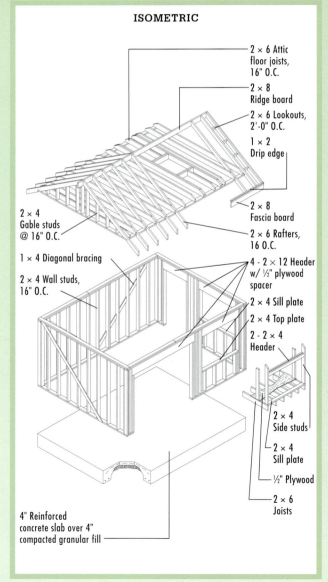

2 × 6 Attic
floor joists,
16" O.C.

2 × 8
Ridge board

2 × 6 Lookouts,
2'-0" O.C.

1 × 2
Drip edge

2 × 8
Fascia board

2 × 6 Rafters,
16 O.C.

4 - 2 × 12 Header
w/ ½" plywood
spacer

2 × 4 Sill plate

2 × 4 Top plate

2 - 2 × 4
Header

2 × 4
Side studs

2 × 4
Sill plate

½" Plywood

2 × 6
Joists

2 × 4
Gable studs
@ 16" O.C.

1 × 4 Diagonal bracing

2 × 4 Wall studs,
16" O.C.

4" Reinforced
concrete slab over 4"
compacted granular fill

How to Build the Convenience Shed

Build the concrete foundation using the specifications shown in the FOUNDATION DETAIL (page 127) and following the basic procedure on pages 36 to 39. The slab should measure 190¾" × 142¾". Set the 14 J-bolts into the concrete as shown in FOUNDATION PLAN (page 127). *Note: All slab specifications must comply with local building codes.*

Snap chalk lines for the bottom plates so they will be flush with the outside edges of the foundation. You can frame the walls in four continuous panels or break them up into panels "A" through "F", as shown in the WALL FRAMING PLAN (page 129). We completely assembled and squared all four walls before raising and anchoring them.

Frame the back wall(s) following the BACK SIDE FRAMING (page 129). Use pressure treated lumber for the bottom plate, and nail it to the studs with galvanized 16d common nails. All of the standard studs are 92⅝" long. Square the wall, then add 1 × 4 let-in bracing.

Raise the back wall and anchor it to the foundation J-bolts with washers and nuts. Brace the wall upright. Frame and raise the remaining walls one at a time, then tie all of the walls together with double top plates. Cover the outside of the walls with T1-11 siding.

(continued)

Cut fifteen 2 × 6 attic floor joists at 142¾". Cut the top corner at both ends of each joist: Mark 1⅞" along the top edge and ¹⁵⁄₁₆" down the end; connect the marks, then cut along the line. Clipping the corner prevents the joist from extending above the rafters.

Mark the joist layout onto the wall plates following the ATTIC FLOOR JOIST FRAMING (page 130). Leave 3½" between the outsides of the end walls and the outer joists. Toenail the joists to the plates with three 8d common nails at each end. Frame the rough opening for the staircase with doubled side joists and doubled headers; fasten doubled members together with pairs of 10d nails every 16". Install the drop-down staircase unit following the manufacturer's instructions.

Cover the attic floor with ½" plywood, fastening it to the joists with 8d nails.

Use the RAFTER TEMPLATE (page 132) to mark and cut two pattern rafters. Test-fit the rafters and adjust the cuts as needed. Cut all (24) standard rafters. Cut four special rafters with an extra bird's-mouth cut for the box bay. Cut four gable overhang rafters—these have no bird's-mouth cuts.

Cut the 2 × 8 ridge board at 206¾". Mark the rafter layout on the ridge and wall plates as shown in the FRONT SIDE FRAMING (page 130) and BACK SIDE FRAMING (page 129). Frame the roof following the steps on pages 48 to 51. Install 6½"-long lookouts 24" on center, then attach the overhang rafters. Fasten the attic joists to the rafters with three 10d nails at each end.

Mark the stud layout for the gable end walls onto the end wall plates following the SIDE FRAMING (page 129). Transfer the layout to the rafters, using a level. Cut each of the 2 × 4 studs to fit, mitering the top ends at 33.5°. Install the studs flush with the end walls.

Construct the 2 × 4 half-wall for the interior apron beneath the box bay: Cut two plates at 60" (pressure-treated lumber for bottom plate); cut five studs at 32½". Fasten one stud at each end, and space the remaining studs evenly in between. Mark a layout line 12" from the inside of the shed's front wall (see the BUILDING SECTION page 127). Anchor the half-wall to the slab using masonry screws or a powder-actuated nailer.

Cut six 2 × 6 joists at 36½". Toenail the joists to the inner and outer half-walls following the layout in the BOX BAY WINDOW FRAMING (page 130); the joists should extend 15" past the outer shed wall. Add a 60"-long 2 × 4 sill plate at the ends of the joists. Cut two 2 × 4 side studs to extend from the sill plate to the top edges of the rafters (angle top ends at 33.5°), and install them. Install a built-up 2 × 4 header between the side studs 41⅜" above the sill plate.

(continued)

Install a 2 × 2 nailer ½" up from the bottom of the 2 × 4 bay header. Cover the top and bottom of the bay with ½" plywood as shown in the BOX BAY WINDOW DETAIL. Cut a 2 × 4 stud to fit between the plywood panels at each end of the 2 × 4 shed wall header; fasten these to the studs supporting the studs and the header.

Bevel the side edge of the 2 × 6 blocking stock at 33.5°. Cut individual blocks to fit between the rafters and attic joists, and install them to seal off the rafter bays; see the OVERHEAD DOOR HEADER (page 131). The blocks should be flush with the tops of the rafters. Custom-cut 2 × 8 blocking to enclose the rafter bays above the box bay header; see the BOX BAY WINDOW DETAIL.

Add 2 × 8 fascia to the ends of the rafters along each eave so the top outer edge will be flush with the top of the roof sheathing. Cover the gable overhang rafters with 1 × 8 fascia. Add 1 × 2 trim to serve as a drip edge along the eaves and gable ends so it will be flush with the top of the roof sheathing.

Add Z-flashing above the first row of siding, then cut and fit T1-11 siding for the gable ends. Cover the horizontal seam with 1 × 4 trim snugged up against the flashing.

17

To complete the trim details, add 1 × 2 along the gable ends and sides of the box bay. Use 1 × 4 on all vertical corners and around the windows, service door, and overhead door. Rip down 1 × 10s for horizontal trim along the bottom of the box bay. Also cover underneath the bay joists with ½" exterior-grade plywood.

18

Rip-cut 1 × 6 boards to 4⅛" wide for the overhead door jambs. Install the jambs using the door manufacturer's dimensions for the opening. Shim behind the jambs if necessary. Make sure the jambs are flush with the inside of the wall framing and extend ⅝" beyond the outside of the framing. Install the 2 × 6 trim as shown in the OVERHEAD DOOR HEADER and OVERHEAD DOOR JAMB.

19

Install the two windows and the service door following the manufacturers' instructions. Position the jambs of the units so they will be flush with the siding, if applicable. Install the overhead door, then add stop molding along the top and side jambs; see the SERVICE DOOR HEADER/JAMB.

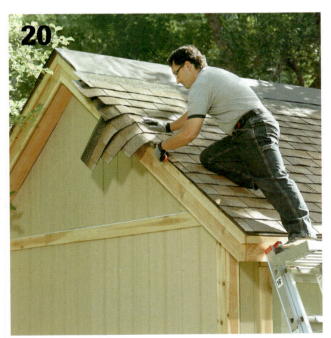

20

Install ½" plywood roof sheathing, starting at the bottom ends of the rafters. Add building paper and asphalt shingles following the steps on pages 55 to 57.

Gambrel Garage

Following classic barn designs, this 12 × 12-ft. garage-size storage shed has several features that make it a versatile storage shed or workshop. The garage's 144-square-foot floor is a poured concrete slab with a thickened edge that allows it to serve as the building's foundation. Designed for economy and durability, the floor can easily support heavy machinery, woodworking tools, and recreational vehicles.

The garage's sectional overhead door makes for quick access to equipment and supplies and provides plenty of air and natural light for working inside. The door opening is sized for an 8-ft.-wide × 7-ft.-tall door, but you can buy any size or style of door you like—just make your door selection before you start framing the garage.

Another important design feature of this building is its gambrel roof, which maximizes the usable interior space (see Sidebar next page). Beneath the roof is a sizeable storage attic with 315 cubic feet of space and its own double doors above the garage door. *Note: we added a patio section to the front of this shed. This optional slab will appear throughout the how-to photos.*

The Gambrel Roof ▸

The gambrel roof is the defining feature of two structures in American architecture: the barn and the Dutch Colonial house. Adopted from earlier English buildings, the gambrel style became popular in America during the early 17th century and was used on homes and farm buildings throughout the Atlantic region. Today, the gambrel roof remains a favorite detail for designers of sheds, garages, and carriage houses.

The basic gambrel shape has two flat planes on each side, with the lower plane sloped much more steeply than the upper. More elaborate versions incorporate a flared eave, known as a "Dutch kick," that was often extended to shelter the front and rear facades of the building. Barns typically feature an extended peak at the front, sheltering the doors of the hayloft. The main advantage of the gambrel roof is the increased space underneath the roof, providing additional headroom for upper floors in homes or extra storage space in outbuildings.

Cutting List

Description	Quantity/Size	Material
Foundation		
Drainage material	1.75 cu. yds.	Compactible gravel
Concrete slab	2.5 cu. yds.	3,000 psi concrete
Mesh	144 sq. ft.	6 × 6", W1.4 × W1.4 welded wire mesh
Wall Framing		
Bottom plates	4 @ 12'	2 × 4 pressure-treated
Top plates	8 @ 12'	2 × 4
Studs	47 @ 92⅝"	2 × 4
Headers	2 @ 10', 2 @ 6'	2 × 8
Header spacers	1 @ 9', 1 @ 6'	½" plywood — 7" wide
Angle braces	1 @ 4'	2 × 4
Gable Wall Framing		
Plates	2 @ 10'	2 × 4
Studs	7 @ 10'	2 × 4
Header	2 @ 6'	2 × 6
Header spacer	1 @ 5'	½" plywood — 5" wide
Attic Floor		
Joists	10 @ 12'	2 × 6
Floor sheathing	3 sheets @ 4 × 8'	¾" tongue-&-groove ext.-grade plywood
Kneewall Framing		
Bottom plates	2 @ 12'	2 × 4
Top plates	4 @ 12'	2 × 4
Studs	8 @ 10'	2 × 4
Nailers	2 @ 14'	2 × 8
Roof Framing		
Rafters	28 @ 10'	2 × 4
Metal anchors — rafters	20, with nails	Simpson H2.5
Collar ties	2 @ 6'	2 × 4
Ridge board	1 @ 14'	2 × 6
Lookouts	1 @ 10'	2 × 4
Soffit ledgers	2 @ 14'	2 × 4
Soffit blocking	6 @ 8'	2 × 4
Exterior Finishes		
Plywood siding	14 sheets @ 4 × 8'	⅝" Texture 1-11 plywood, grooves 8" O. C.
Z-flashing — siding	2 pieces @ 12'	Galvanized 18-gauge
Horizontal wall trim	2 @ 12'	1 × 4 cedar
Corner trim	8 @ 8'	1 × 4 cedar
Fascia	6 @ 10', 2 @ 8'	1 × 6 cedar
Subfascia	4 @ 8'	1 × 4 pine
Plywood soffits	1 sheet @ 10'	⅜" cedar or fir plywood
Soffit vents	4 @ 4 × 12"	Louver w/ bug screen
Z-flashing — garage door	1 @ 10'	Galvanized 18-gauge

Description	Quantity/Size	Material
Roofing		
Roof sheathing	12 sheets @ 4 × 8'	½" plywood
Shingles	3 squares	250# per square (min.)
15# building paper	300 sq. ft.	
Metal drip edge	2 @ 14', 2 @ 12'	Galvanized metal
Roof vents (optional)	2 units	
Window		
Frame	3 @ 6'	¾ × 4" (actual) S4S cedar
Stops	4 @ 8'	1 × 2 S4S cedar
Glazing tape	30 linear ft.	
Glass	1 piece — field measure	¼" clear, tempered
Exterior trim	3 @ 6'	1 × 4 S4S cedar
Interior trim (optional)	3 @ 6'	1 × 2 S4S cedar
Door		
Frame	3 @ 8'	1 × 6 S4S cedar
Door sill	1 @ 6'	1 × 6 S4S cedar
Stops	1 @ 8', 1 @ 6'	1 × 2 S4S cedar
Panel material	4 @ 8'	1 × 8 T&G V-joint S4S cedar
Door X-brace/panel trim	4 @ 6', 2 @ 8'	1 × 4 S4S cedar
Exterior trim	1 @ 8', 1 @ 6'	1 × 4 S4S cedar
Interior trim (optional)	1 @ 8', 1 @ 6'	1 × 2 S4S cedar
Strap hinges	4	
Garage Door		
Frame	3 @ 8'	1 × 8 S4S cedar
Door	1 @ 8' × 6' - 8"	Sectional flush door w/2" track
Rails	2 @ 8'	2 × 6
Trim	3 @ 8'	1 × 4 S4S cedar
Fasteners		
Anchor bolts	16	⅜" × 8", with washers & nuts, galvanized
16d galvanized common nails	2 lbs.	
16d common nails	17 lbs.	
10d common nails	2 lbs.	
10d galvanized casing nails	1 lb.	
8d common nails	3 lbs.	
8d galvanized finish nails	6 lbs.	
8d box nails	6 lbs.	
6d galvanized finish nails	20 nails	
3d galvanized box nails	½ lb.	
⅞" galvanized roofing nails	2½ lbs.	
2½" deck screws	24 screws	
1¼" wood screws	48 screws	
Construction adhesive	2 tubes	
Silicone-latex caulk	2 tubes	

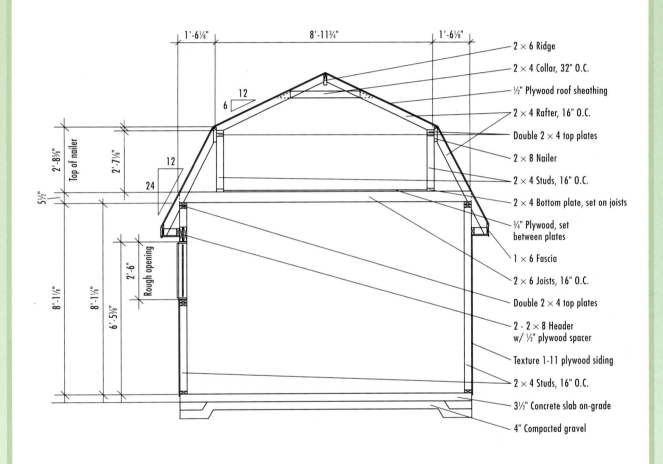

2 × 6 Ridge

2 × 4 Collar, 32" O.C.

½" Plywood roof sheathing

2 × 4 Rafter, 16" O.C.

Double 2 × 4 top plates

2 × 8 Nailer

2 × 4 Studs, 16" O.C.

2 × 4 Bottom plate, set on joists

¾" Plywood, set between plates

1 × 6 Fascia

2 × 6 Joists, 16" O.C.

Double 2 × 4 top plates

2 - 2 × 8 Header w/ ½" plywood spacer

Texture 1-11 plywood siding

2 × 4 Studs, 16" O.C.

3½" Concrete slab on-grade

4" Compacted gravel

1'-6⅛"   8'-11¾"   1'-6⅛"

12 / 6

12 / 24

2'-8⅝" Top of nailer

2'-7⅞"

5½"

8'-1⅛"

8'-1⅛"

6'-5⅞"

2'-6" Rough opening

FLOOR PLAN

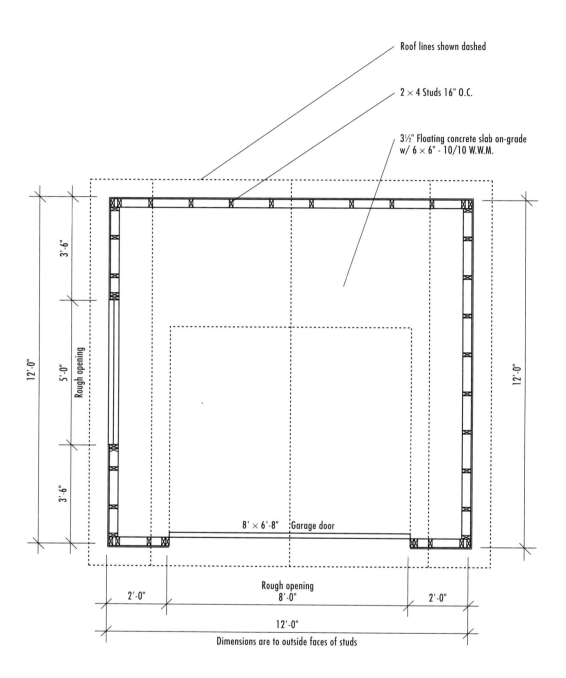

Roof lines shown dashed

2 × 4 Studs 16" O.C.

3½" Floating concrete slab on-grade
w/ 6 × 6" - 10/10 W.W.M.

12'-0"

3'-6"

5'-0"
Rough opening

3'-6"

12'-0"

8' × 6'-8" Garage door

Rough opening
8'-0"

2'-0"

2'-0"

12'-0"

Dimensions are to outside faces of studs

RAFTER TEMPLATES

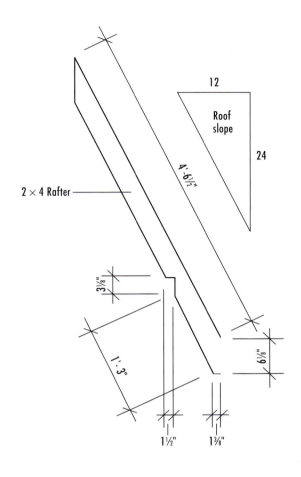

12

Roof slope

24

4'-6½"

2 × 4 Rafter

3⅛"

1'-3"

6⅛"

1½"

1⅜"

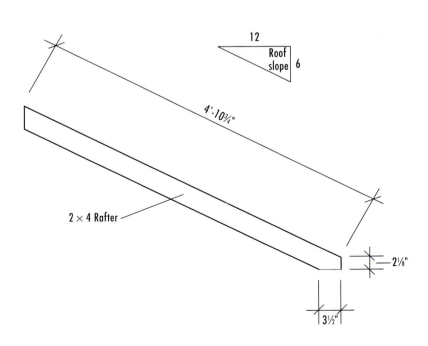

12

Roof slope

6

4'-10¾"

2 × 4 Rafter

2⅛"

3½"

FRONT ELEVATION

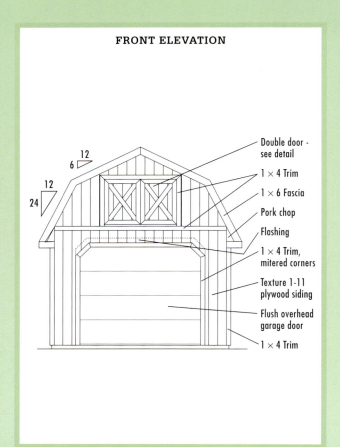

12
6

12
24

Double door - see detail

1 × 4 Trim

1 × 6 Fascia

Pork chop

Flashing

1 × 4 Trim, mitered corners

Texture 1-11 plywood siding

Flush overhead garage door

1 × 4 Trim

LEFT SIDE ELEVATION

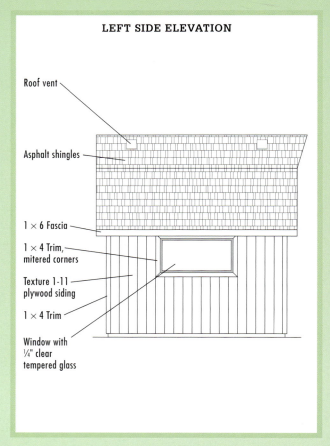

Roof vent

Asphalt shingles

1 × 6 Fascia

1 × 4 Trim, mitered corners

Texture 1-11 plywood siding

1 × 4 Trim

Window with ¼" clear tempered glass

REAR ELEVATION

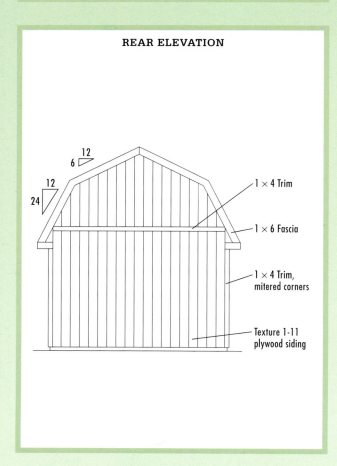

12
6

12
24

1 × 4 Trim

1 × 6 Fascia

1 × 4 Trim, mitered corners

Texture 1-11 plywood siding

RIGHT SIDE ELEVATION

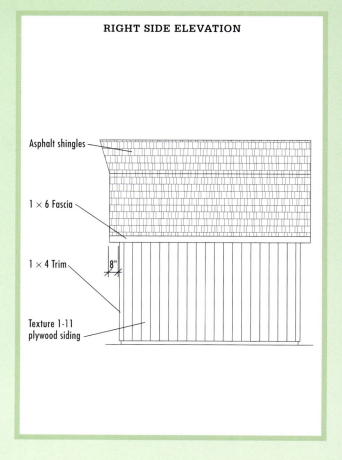

Asphalt shingles

1 × 6 Fascia

1 × 4 Trim

8"

Texture 1-11 plywood siding

GABLE OVERHANG DETAIL

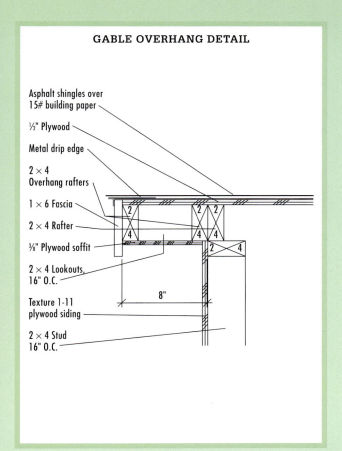

Asphalt shingles over
15# building paper

½" Plywood

Metal drip edge

2 × 4
Overhang rafters

1 × 6 Fascia

2 × 4 Rafter

⅜" Plywood soffit

2 × 4 Lookouts,
16" O.C.

Texture 1-11
plywood siding

2 × 4 Stud
16" O.C.

8"

GABLE OVERHANG RAFTER DETAILS

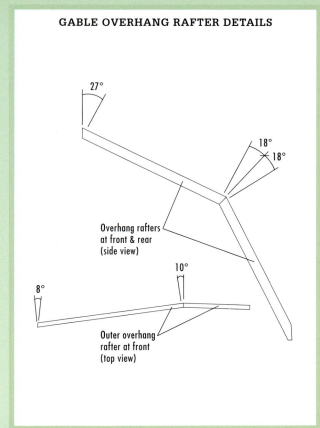

27°

18°
18°

Overhang rafters
at front & rear
(side view)

10°

8°

Outer overhang
rafter at front
(top view)

EAVE DETAIL

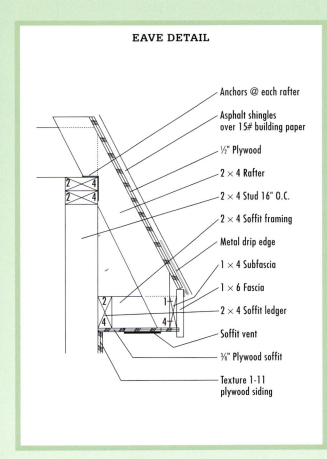

Anchors @ each rafter

Asphalt shingles
over 15# building paper

½" Plywood

2 × 4 Rafter

2 × 4 Stud 16" O.C.

2 × 4 Soffit framing

Metal drip edge

1 × 4 Subfascia

1 × 6 Fascia

2 × 4 Soffit ledger

Soffit vent

⅜" Plywood soffit

Texture 1-11
plywood siding

SILL DETAIL

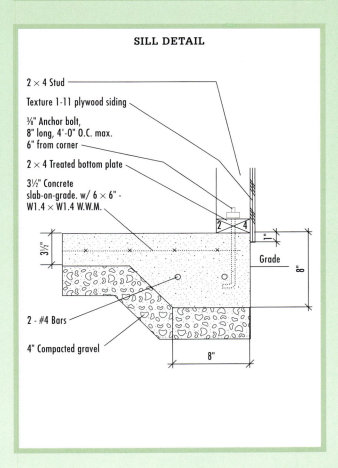

2 × 4 Stud

Texture 1-11 plywood siding

⅜" Anchor bolt,
8" long, 4'-0" O.C. max.
6" from corner

2 × 4 Treated bottom plate

3½" Concrete
slab-on-grade. w/ 6 × 6" -
W1.4 × W1.4 W.W.M.

3½"

2 × 4

Grade

1"

8"

2 - #4 Bars

4" Compacted gravel

8"

ATTIC DOOR ELEVATION

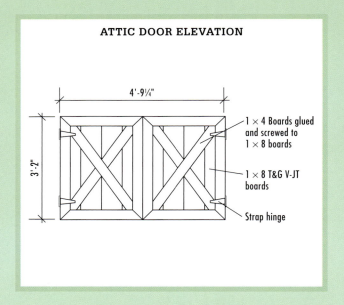

4'-9¼"

3'-2"

1 × 4 Boards glued and screwed to 1 × 8 boards

1 × 8 T&G V-JT boards

Strap hinge

ATTIC DOOR JAMB DETAIL

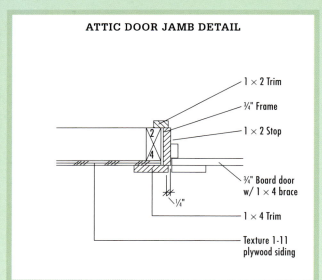

1 × 2 Trim

¾" Frame

1 × 2 Stop

¾" Board door w/ 1 × 4 brace

¼"

1 × 4 Trim

Texture 1-11 plywood siding

GARAGE DOOR TRIM DETAIL

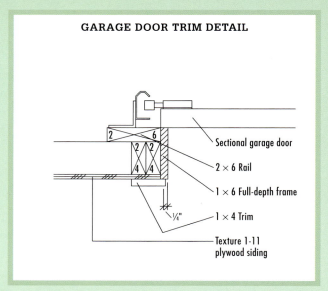

Sectional garage door

2 × 6 Rail

1 × 6 Full-depth frame

1 × 4 Trim

¼"

Texture 1-11 plywood siding

ATTIC DOOR SILL DETAIL

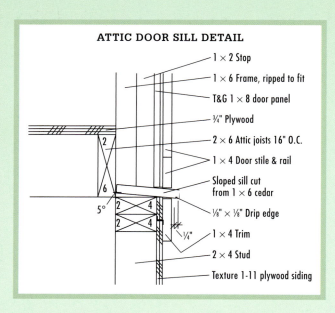

1 × 2 Stop

1 × 6 Frame, ripped to fit

T&G 1 × 8 door panel

¾" Plywood

2 × 6 Attic joists 16" O.C.

1 × 4 Door stile & rail

Sloped sill cut from 1 × 6 cedar

⅛" × ⅛" Drip edge

¼"

1 × 4 Trim

2 × 4 Stud

5°

Texture 1-11 plywood siding

WINDOW JAMB DETAIL

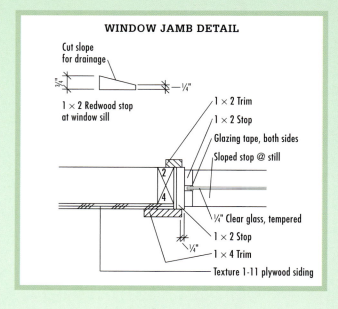

Cut slope for drainage

¾"

¼"

1 × 2 Redwood stop at window sill

1 × 2 Trim

1 × 2 Stop

Glazing tape, both sides

Sloped stop @ still

¼" Clear glass, tempered

1 × 2 Stop

¼"

1 × 4 Trim

Texture 1-11 plywood siding

FRONT FRAMING ELEVATION

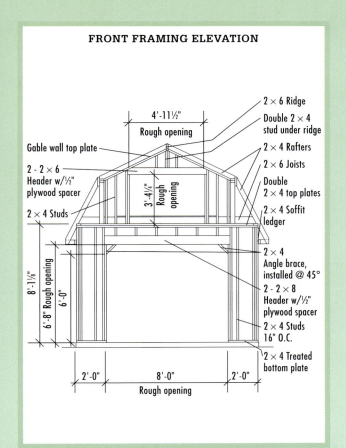

4'-11½"
Rough opening

2 × 6 Ridge

Double 2 × 4 stud under ridge

Gable wall top plate

2 × 4 Rafters

2 × 6 Joists

2 - 2 × 6 Header w/½" plywood spacer

Double 2 × 4 top plates

3'-4¼" Rough opening

2 × 4 Studs

2 × 4 Soffit ledger

2 × 4 Angle brace, installed @ 45°

2 - 2 × 8 Header w/½" plywood spacer

8'-1⅛"

6'-8" Rough opening

6'-0"

2 × 4 Studs 16" O.C.

2'-0"   8'-0"   2'-0"

2 × 4 Treated bottom plate

Rough opening

LEFT SIDE FRAMING ELEVATION

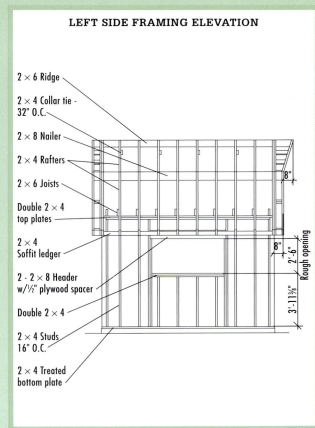

2 × 6 Ridge

2 × 4 Collar tie - 32" O.C.

2 × 8 Nailer

2 × 4 Rafters

2 × 6 Joists

Double 2 × 4 top plates

2 × 4 Soffit ledger

2 - 2 × 8 Header w/½" plywood spacer

Double 2 × 4

2 × 4 Studs 16" O.C.

2 × 4 Treated bottom plate

8"

8"

2'-6"

3'-11⅜" Rough opening

REAR FRAMING ELEVATION

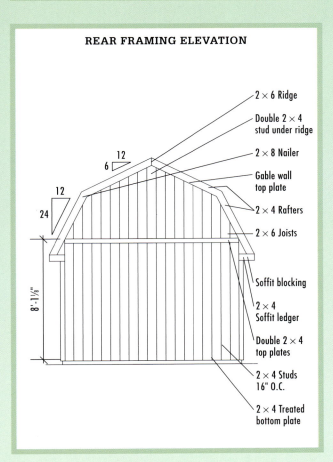

2 × 6 Ridge

Double 2 × 4 stud under ridge

2 × 8 Nailer

12
6

Gable wall top plate

12
24

2 × 4 Rafters

2 × 6 Joists

Soffit blocking

8'-1⅛"

2 × 4 Soffit ledger

Double 2 × 4 top plates

2 × 4 Studs 16" O.C.

2 × 4 Treated bottom plate

RIGHT SIDE FRAMING ELEVATION

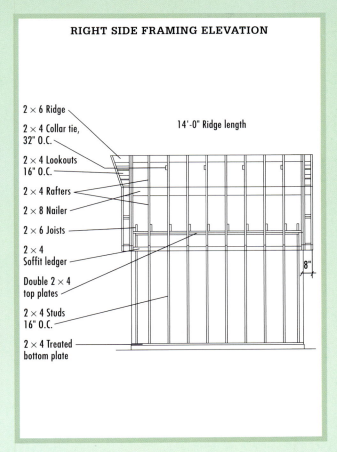

2 × 6 Ridge

14'-0" Ridge length

2 × 4 Collar tie, 32" O.C.

2 × 4 Lookouts 16" O.C.

2 × 4 Rafters

2 × 8 Nailer

2 × 6 Joists

2 × 4 Soffit ledger

Double 2 × 4 top plates

2 × 4 Studs 16" O.C.

2 × 4 Treated bottom plate

8"

How to Build the Gambrel Garage

Build the slab foundation at 144" × 144", following the steps on page 36. Set J-bolts into the concrete 1¾" from the outer edges and extending 2½" from the surface. Set a bolt 6" from each corner and every 48" in between (except in the door opening). Let the slab cure for at least three days before you begin construction.

Snap chalk lines on the slab for the wall plates. Cut two bottom plates and two top plates at 137" for the sidewalls. Cut two bottom and two top plates at 144" for the front and rear walls. Use pressure-treated lumber for all bottom plates. Cut 38 studs at 92⅝", plus two jack studs for the garage door at 78½" and two window studs at 75⅞". *Note: Add the optional slab now, as desired.*

Construct the built-up 2 × 8 headers at 99" (garage door) and 63" (window). Frame, install, and brace the walls with double top plates one at a time, following the FLOOR PLAN (page 142) and ELEVATION drawings (page 144). Use galvanized nails to attach the studs to the sole plates. Anchor the walls to the J-bolts in the slab with galvanized washers and nuts.

Build the attic floor. Cut ten 2 × 6 joists to 144" long, then clip each top corner with a 1½"-long, 45° cut. Install the joists as shown in the FRAMING ELEVATIONS, leaving a 3½" space at the front and rear walls for the gable wall studs. Fasten the joists with three 8d nails at each end.

Frame the attic kneewalls: Cut four top plates at 144" and two bottom plates at 137". Cut 20 studs at 26⅝" and four end studs at 33⅝". Lay out the plates so the studs fall over the attic joists. Frame the walls and install them 18⅛" from the ends of the joists, then add temporary bracing. *Option: You can begin building the roof frame by cutting two 2 × 8 nailers to 144" long. Fasten the nailers to the kneewalls so their top edges are 32⅝" above the attic joists.*

Cover the attic floor between the kneewalls with ¾" plywood. Run the sheets perpendicular to the joists, and stop them flush with the outer joists. Fasten the flooring with 8d ring-shank nails every 6" along the edges and every 12" in the field of the sheets.

Mark the rafter layouts onto the top and outside faces of the 2 × 8 nailers; see the FRAMING ELEVATIONS.

Cut the 2 × 6 ridge board at 168", mitering the front end at 16°. Mark the rafter layout onto the ridge. The outer common rafters should be 16" from the front end and 8" from the rear end of the ridge.

(continued)

Use the RAFTER TEMPLATES (page 143) to mark and cut two upper pattern rafters and one lower pattern rafter. Test-fit the rafters and make any needed adjustments. Use the patterns to mark and cut the remaining common rafters (20 total of each type). For the gable overhangs, cut an additional eight lower and six upper rafters following the GABLE OVERHANG RAFTER DETAILS (page 145).

Install the common rafters; then reinforce the joints at the knee walls with framing connectors. Also nail the attic joists to the sides of the floor rafters. Cut four 2 × 4 collar ties at 34", mitering the ends at 26.5°. Fasten them between pairs of upper rafters, as shown in the BUILDING SECTION (page 141) and FRAMING ELEVATIONS.

Snap a chalk line across the sidewall studs, level with the ends of the rafters. Cut two 2 × 4 soffit ledgers at 160" and fasten them to the studs on top of the chalk lines, with their ends overhanging the walls by 8". Cut 24 2 × 4 blocks to fit between the ledger and rafter ends, as shown in the EAVE DETAIL (page 145). Install the blocks.

Frame the gable overhangs. Cut 12 2 × 4 lookouts at 5" and nail them to the inner overhang rafters as shown in the LEFT and RIGHT SIDE FRAMING ELEVATIONS. Install the inner overhang rafters over the common rafters, using 10d nails. Cut the two front (angled) overhang rafters; see the GABLE OVERHANG RAFTER DETAILS. Install those rafters; then add two custom-cut lookouts for each rafter.

13

To complete the gable walls, cut top plates to fit between the ridge and the attic kneewalls. Install the plates flush with the outer common rafters. Mark the stud layout onto the walls and gable top plate; see the FRONT and REAR FRAMING ELEVATIONS. Cut the gable studs to fit and install them. Construct the built-up 2 × 6 attic door header at 62½"; then clip the top corners to match the roof slope. Install the header with jack studs cut at 40¼".

14

Install siding on the walls, holding it 1" below the top of the concrete slab. Add Z-flashing along the top edges, and then continue the siding up to the rafters. Below the attic door opening, stop the siding about ¼" below the top wall plate, as shown in the ATTIC DOOR SILL DETAIL (page 146). Don't nail the siding to the garage door header until the flashing is installed (Step 20).

15

Mill a ⅜"-wide × ¼"-deep groove into the 1 × 6 boards for the horizontal fascia along the eaves and gable ends (about 36 linear ft.); see the EAVE DETAIL. Use a router or table saw with a dado-head blade to mill the groove, and make the groove ⅞" above the bottom edge of the fascia.

16

Install the 1 × 4 subfascia along the eaves, keeping the bottom edge flush with the ends of the rafters and the ends flush with the outsides of the outer-most rafters; see the EAVE DETAIL. Add the milled fascia at the eaves, aligning the top of the groove with the bottom of the subfascia. Cut fascia to wrap around the overhangs at the gable ends but don't install them until Step 17.

(continued)

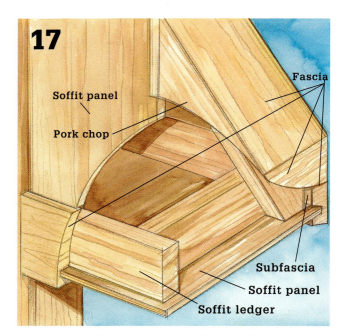

17

Soffit panel

Pork chop

Fascia

Subfascia

Soffit panel

Soffit ledger

Add fascia at the gable ends, holding it up ½" to be flush with the roof sheathing. Cut soffit panels to fit between the fascia and walls, and fasten them with 3d galvanized nails. Install the end and return fascia pieces at the gable overhangs. Enclose each overhang at the corners with a triangular piece of grooved fascia (called a pork chop) and a piece of soffit material. Install the soffit vents as shown in the EAVE DETAIL.

18

Sheath the roof, starting at one of the lower corners. Add metal drip edge along the eaves, followed by building paper; then add drip edge along the gable ends, over the paper. Install the asphalt shingles (see page 56). Plan the courses so the roof transition occurs midshingle, not between courses; the overlapping shingles will relax over time. If desired, add roof vents (page 58).

19

Cover the Z-flashing at the rear wall with horizontal 1 × 4 trim. Finish the four wall corners with overlapping vertical 1 × 4 trim. Install the 2 × 6 rails that will support the garage door tracks, following the door manufacturer's instructions to determine the sizing and placement; see the GARAGE DOOR TRIM DETAIL (page 146).

20

For the garage doorframe, rip 1 × 8 trim boards to width so they cover the front wall siding and 2 × 6 rails, as shown in the GARAGE DOOR TRIM DETAIL. Install the trim, mitering the pieces at 22.5°. Install the 1 × 4 trim around the outside of the opening, adding flashing along the top; see the FRONT ELEVATION (page 144).

Install the garage door in the door opening, following the manufacturer's directions.

Build the window frame, which should be ½" narrower and shorter than the rough opening. Install the frame using shims and 10d galvanized casing nails, as shown in the WINDOW JAMB DETAIL (page 146). Cut eight 1 × 2 stop pieces to fit the frame. Bevel the outer sill stop for drainage. Order glass to fit, or cut your own plastic panel. Install the glazing and stops, using glazing tape for a watertight seal. Add the window trim.

For the attic doorframe, rip 1 × 6s to match the depth of the opening and cut the head jamb and side jambs. Cut the sill from full-width 1 × 6 stock; then cut a kerf for a drip edge (see the ATTIC DOOR SILL DETAIL). Fasten the head jamb to the side jambs and install the sill at a 5° slope between the side jambs. Install the doorframe using shims and 10d casing nails. Add shims or cedar shingles along the length of the sill to provide support underneath. The front edge of the frame should be flush with the face of the siding. Add 1 × 2 stops at the frame sides and top, ¾" from the front edges.

Build the attic doors as shown in the ATTIC DOOR ELEVATION (page 146), using glue and 1¼" screws. Each door measures 28⅝" × 38", including the panel braces. Cut the 1 × 8 panel boards about ⅛" short along the bottom to compensate for the sloping sill. Install the door with two hinges each. Add 1 × 4 horizontal trim on the front wall, up against the doorsill; then trim around both sides of the doorframe. Prime and paint as desired.

Simple Storage Shed

The name of this practical outbuilding says it all. It's an easy-to-build, sturdy, 8 × 10-ft. shed with plenty of storage space. With no windows it also offers good security. The clean, symmetrical interior and centrally located double doors make for easy access to your stuff. The walls are ready to be lined with utility shelves, and you can quickly add a ramp to simplify parking the lawnmower, wheelbarrow, and other yard equipment.

This shed is indeed basic, but it's also a nicely proportioned building with architecturally appropriate features like overhanging eaves and just enough trim to give it a quality, hand-built appearance. Without getting too fancy—remember, simplicity is the central design idea—you might consider finishing the exterior walls and roof of the shed with the same materials used on your house. This easy modification visually integrates the shed with the rest of the property and provides a custom look that you can't get with kit buildings.

Inside the shed, you can maximize storage space by building an attic: Install full-length 2 × 4 or 2 × 6 joists (which also serve as rafter ties) and cover them with ½" plywood. Include one or more framed-in access openings that you can easily reach with a stepladder. This type of storage space is ideal for seldom-used household items—like winter clothing and holiday decorations—that you can stow in covered plastic bins.

The simplicity and economy of this shed design also make it a great choice for cabins, vacation homes, and other remote locations. A heavy-duty hasp latch and padlock on the door, along with head and foot slide bolts inside, will provide the security you need when you're away for long periods.

Cutting List

Description	Quantity/Size	Material
Foundation		
Drainage material	1.25 cu. yd.	Compactable gravel
Skids	2 @ 10'	4 × 6 pressure-treated landscape timbers
Floor		
Rim joists	2 @ 10'	2 × 8 pressure-treated, rated for ground contact
Joists	9 @ 8'	2 × 8 pressure-treated
Floor sheathing	3 sheets @ 4 × 8'	¾" tongue-&-groove ext.-grade plywood
Wall Framing		
Bottom plates	2 @ 10', 2 @ 8'	2 × 4
Top plates	4 @ 10', 4 @ 8'	2 × 4
Studs	36 @ 8'	2 × 4
Door header	1 @ 10'	2 × 6
Roof Framing		
Rafters	6 @ 12'	2 × 6
Rafter blocking	2 @ 10'	2 × 6
Ridge board	1 @ 10'	1 × 8
Collar ties	2 @ 12'	2 × 4
Exterior Finishes		
Siding	11 sheets @ 4 × 8'	½" Texture 1-11 plywood siding
Fascia	4 @ 12'	1 × 8
Corner trim	8 @ 8'	1 × 2
Gable wall trim	2 @ 8'	1 × 4
Siding flashing	16 linear ft.	Metal Z-flashing

Description	Quantity/Size	Material
Roofing		
Sheathing (& door header spacer)	5 sheets @ 4 × 8'	½" exterior-grade plywood roof sheathing
15# building paper	1 roll	
Shingles	1¼ squares	Asphalt shingles — 250# per sq. min.
Drip edge	45 linear ft.	Metal drip edge
Door		
Frames	7 @ 8'	2 × 4 pressure-treated
Panels	1 sheet @ 4 × 8'	½" Texture 1-11 plywood siding
Stops & overlap trim	4 @ 8'	1 × 2 pressure-treated
Fasteners & Hardware		
16d galvanized common nails	4 lbs.	
16d common nails	10 lbs.	
10d common nails	2 lb.	
8d galvanized common nails	3 lbs.	
8d box nails	3 lbs.	
8d galvanized siding or finish nails	9 lbs.	
1" galvanized roofing nails	5 lbs.	
Door hinges with screws	6 @ 3½"	Galvanized metal hinges
Door handle	1	
Door lock (optional)	1	
Door head bolt	1	
Door foot bolt	1	
Construction adhesive		

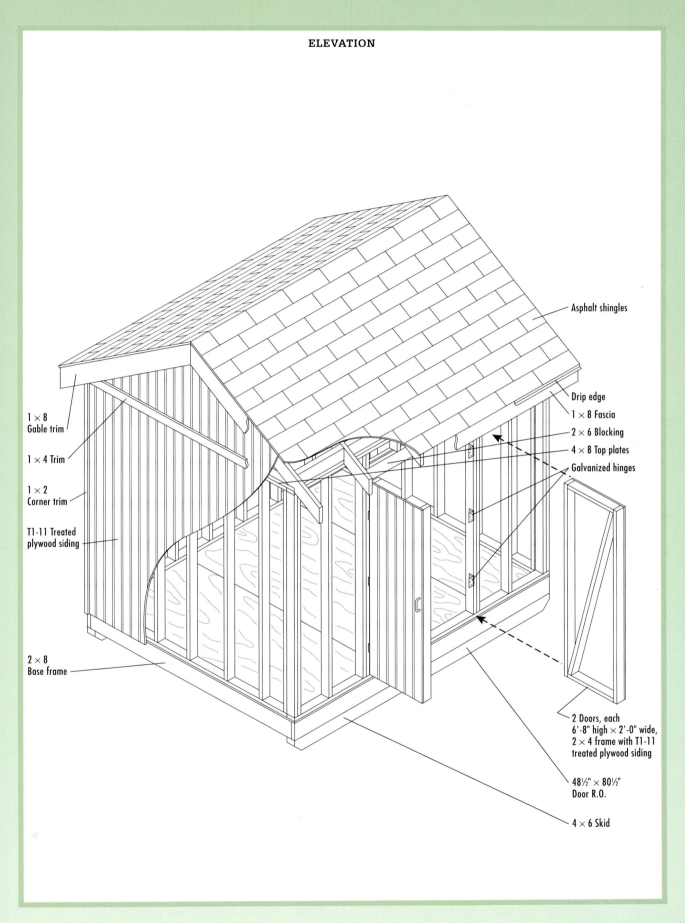

1 × 8
Gable trim

1 × 4 Trim

1 × 2
Corner trim

T1-11 Treated
plywood siding

2 × 8
Base frame

Asphalt shingles

Drip edge

1 × 8 Fascia

2 × 6 Blocking

4 × 8 Top plates

Galvanized hinges

2 Doors, each
6'-8" high × 2'-0" wide,
2 × 4 frame with T1-11
treated plywood siding

48½" × 80½"
Door R.O.

4 × 6 Skid

FRAMING ELEVATION

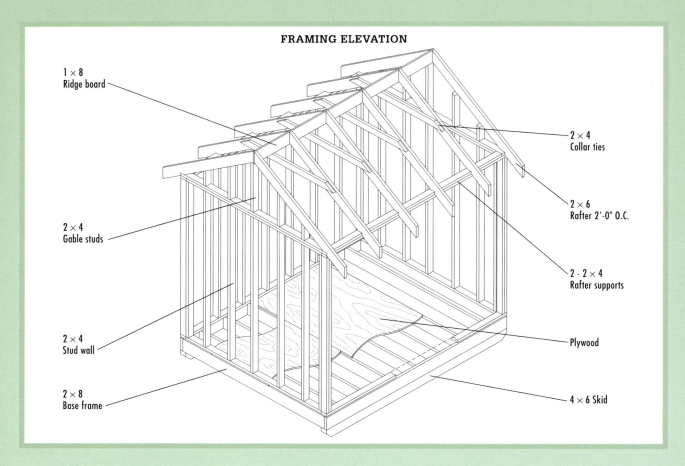

1 × 8
Ridge board

2 × 4
Collar ties

2 × 6
Rafter 2'-0" O.C.

2 × 4
Gable studs

2 - 2 × 4
Rafter supports

2 × 4
Stud wall

Plywood

2 × 8
Base frame

4 × 6 Skid

SIDE FRAMING

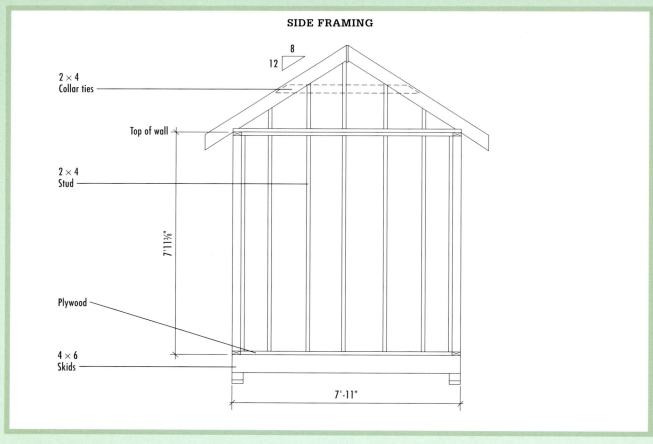

8
12

2 × 4
Collar ties

Top of wall

2 × 4
Stud

7'11 3/8"

Plywood

4 × 6
Skids

7'-11"

FLOOR FRAMING

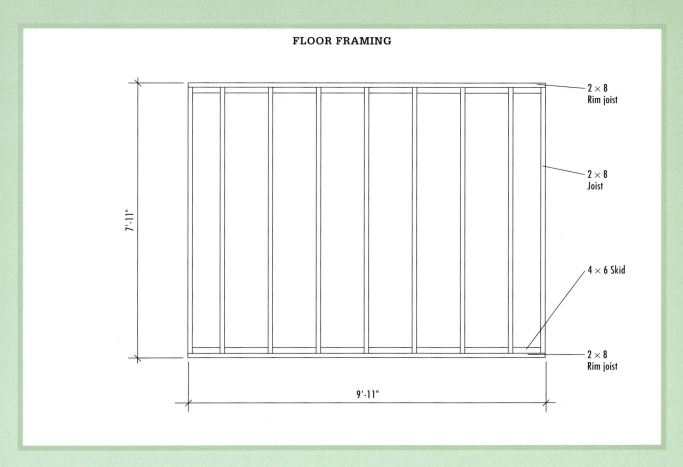

2 × 8
Rim joist

2 × 8
Joist

4 × 6 Skid

2 × 8
Rim joist

7'-11"

9'-11"

REAR FRAMING

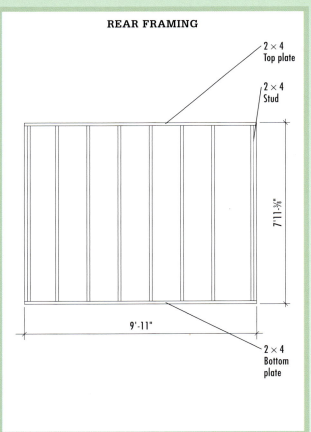

2 × 4
Top plate

2 × 4
Stud

7'11-3/8"

9'-11"

2 × 4
Bottom
plate

FRONT FRAMING

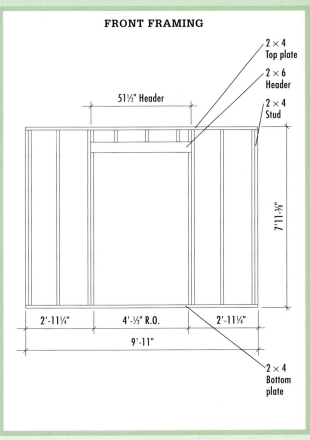

2 × 4
Top plate

2 × 6
Header

2 × 4
Stud

51½" Header

7'11-3/8"

2'-11¼"   4'-½" R.O.   2'-11¼"

9'-11"

2 × 4
Bottom
plate

ROOF PLAN

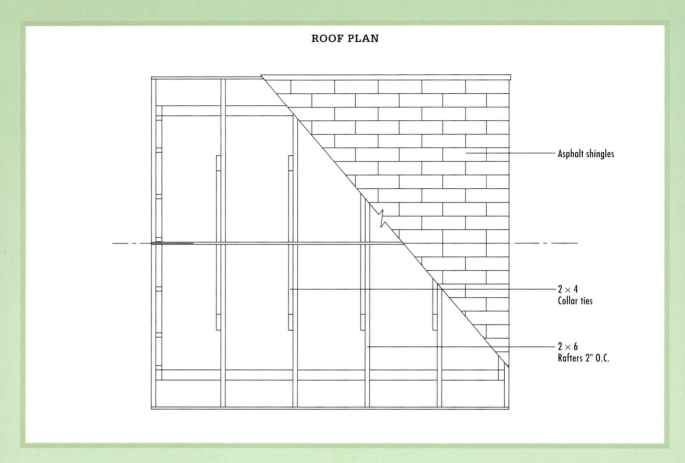

Asphalt shingles

2 × 4
Collar ties

2 × 6
Rafters 2" O.C.

FLOOR PLAN

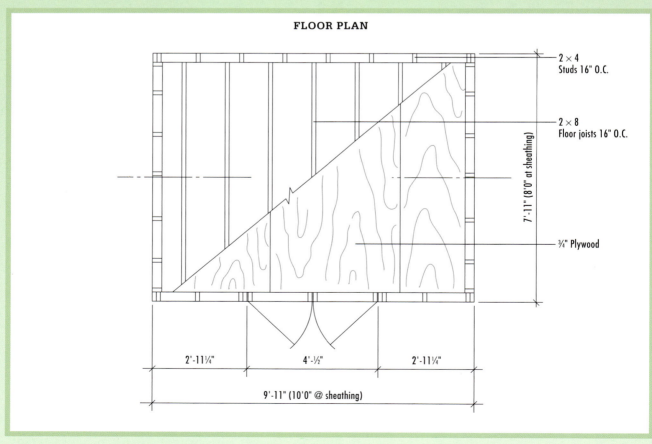

2 × 4
Studs 16" O.C.

2 × 8
Floor joists 16" O.C.

7'-11" (8'0" at sheathing)

¾" Plywood

2'-11¼"   4'-½"   2'-11¼"

9'-11" (10'0" @ sheathing)

RAFTER TEMPLATE

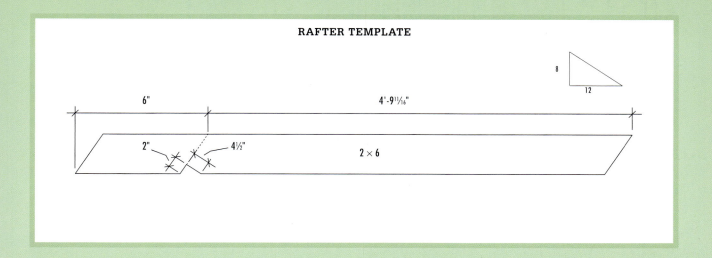

DOOR DETAIL

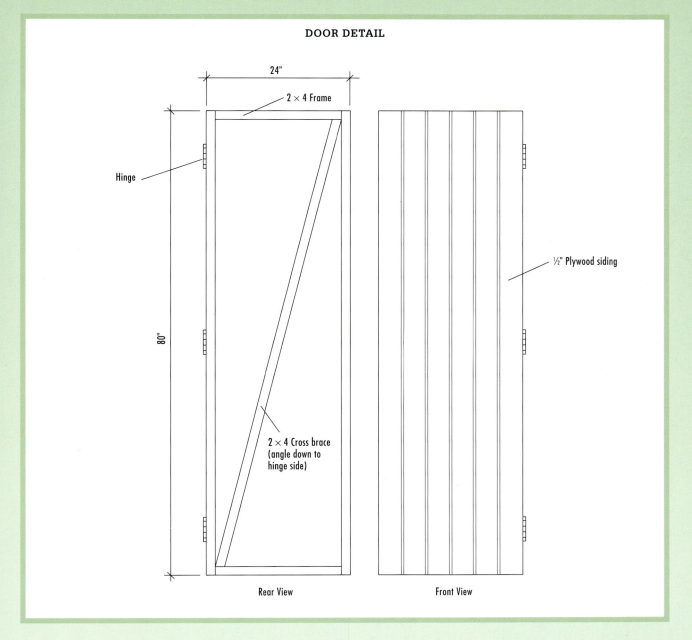

Rear View

Front View

How to Build the Simple Storage Shed

Prepare the foundation site with a 4" layer of compacted gravel where the skids will be located. Cut the two 4 × 6 timber skids at 119". Position the skids on the gravel beds so their outside edges are 95" apart, making sure they are level and parallel.

Cut two 2 × 8 rim joists at 119". Cut nine 2 × 8 joists at 92". Assemble the floor frame following the FLOOR FRAMING (page 159), then set it on the skids and measure the diagonals to make sure the frame is square. Fasten the joists to the skids with 16d galvanized common nails.

Attach tongue-and-groove plywood flooring to the floor frame, starting at the left front corner of the shed. Begin the second row of plywood with a full sheet in the right rear corner to stagger end joints. Make sure the tongues are fully seated in the mating grooves. Fasten the sheathing with 8d galvanized common nails.

Frame the rear wall: Cut one 2 × 4 bottom plate and one top plate at 119". Cut ten 2 × 4 studs at 92⅜". Assemble the wall using 16" on-center spacing, as shown in the REAR FRAMING (page 159). Raise the wall and fasten it flush to the rear edge of the floor, then brace the wall in position with 2 × 4 braces.

Build the side walls following the SIDE FRAMING (page 158). The two side walls are identical. Each has a bottom and top plate at 88" and seven studs at 92⅜". Assemble each wall, then install it and brace it in position.

Frame the front wall following the FRONT FRAMING (page 159): Cut two plates at 119", cut eight studs at 92⅜", and cut two jack studs at 79". Install the 2 × 6 built-up header (add a layer of ½" plywood as a spacer between the 2 × 6s), then add three cripple studs. Raise and fasten the front wall, then install the double top plates along all four walls.

Cut two 2 × 6 pattern rafters following the RAFTER TEMPLATE (page 161). Test-fit the rafters and make any necessary adjustments. Use one of the patterns to mark and cut the remaining 10 rafters. Cut the 1 × 8 ridge board at 119". Mark the rafter layout onto the ridge and the front and rear wall plates following the ROOF PLAN (page 160). *Note: Before installing the rafters on the long sides of the shed (door face and wall parallel to door), first install siding. The rafters overhang the siding on the long sides, therefore the siding (at least on those sides) needs to be in place before the rafters are installed.*

Cover the shed exterior with ½" siding, starting at the left end of the rear wall. Butt full sheets up against the rafters, letting the bottom edges overhang the floor frame by at least 1". Complete the front wall, and then the side walls, keeping the bottom edges even with the sheets on the front and side walls. Add Z-flashing, and continue the siding to the tops of the end rafters.

(continued)

Install the rafters and ridge board. Cut four 2 × 4 collar ties at 64", mitering the ends at 33.5°. Fasten the collar ties between each set of the four inner rafters, using 10d common nails. Make sure the ties are level and extend close to but not above the top edges of the rafters. *Note: Do not install collar ties if you're building an attic floor.*

Mark the gable wall stud layout onto the sidewall top plates. Use a level to transfer the marks to the end rafters. Cut each of the 10 2 × 4 studs to fit, mitering the top ends at 33.5°. Install the studs. *Note: The center stud on each wall is located to the rear side of the ridge board. If desired, frame in the attic floor at this time (see Adding an Attic, below).*

Adding an Attic ▸

To build an attic floor for storage, cut six 2 × 4 or 2 × 6 floor joists at 95" (use 2 × 6s if you plan to store heavy items in the attic). If necessary, clip the top corners of the joists so they won't extend above the tops of the rafters. Fasten the joists to the rafters and wall plates with 10d common nails (photo A). At the end rafters, install 2" blocking against the rafters, then attach the joists to the blocking and gable wall studs.

Frame access openings with two header joists spanning neighboring floor joists (photo B). For heavier storage, double up the floor joists on either side of the opening, then use doubled headers to frame the opening. Join doubled members with pairs of 10d common nails every 16". Cover the joists with ½" plywood fastened with 8d nails to complete the attic floor.

Enclose the rafter bays over the walls with 2 × 6 blocking. Bevel the top edge of the blocking at 33.5° so it will be flush with the rafters. Cut the blocks to fit snugly between pairs of rafters and install them. Install 1 × 8 fascia boards at the ends of the rafters along the eaves, and over the siding on the gable ends. Keep the fascia ½" above the tops of the rafters.

Apply ½" roof sheathing, starting at the bottom corner of either roof plane. The sheathing should be flush with the tops of the fascia boards. Add the metal drip edge, building paper, and asphalt shingle roofing following the steps on pages 55 to 57.

Construct the two doors from 2 × 4 bracing and ½" siding, as shown in the DOOR DETAIL (page 161). The doors are identical. Each measures 48½" × 80½". Mortise the butt hinges into the door brace and wall frame, and install the doors leaving a ¼" gap between the doors and along the top and bottom.

Trim the corners of the shed with 1 × 2s. Also add a piece of 1 × 2 trim on one of the doors to cover the gap between the doors. Install 1 × 4 trim horizontally to cover the Z-flashing at the side walls. Install door locks and hardware as desired.

Gothic Playhouse

Playhouses are all about stirring the imagination. Loaded with fancy American Gothic details, this charming little house makes a special play home for kids and an attractive backyard feature for adults. In addition to its architectural character (see Gothic Style, below), what makes this a great playhouse design is its size—the enclosed house measures 5 × 7½ ft. and includes a 5-ft.-tall door and plenty of headroom inside. This means your kids will likely "outgrow" the playhouse before they get too big for it. And you can always give the house a second life as a storage shed.

At the front of the house is a 30"-deep porch complete with real decking boards and a nicely decorated railing. Each side wall features a window and flower box, and the "foundation" has the look of stone created by wood blocks applied to the floor framing. All of these features are optional, but each one adds to the charm of this well-appointed playhouse.

As shown here, the floor of the playhouse is anchored to four 4 × 4 posts buried in the ground.

As an alternative, you can set the playhouse on 4 × 6 timber skids. Another custom variation you might consider is in the styling of the verge boards (the gingerbread gable trim). Instead of using the provided pattern, you can create a cardboard template of your own design. Architectural plan and pattern books from the Gothic period are full of inspiration for decorative ideas.

Gothic Style ▶

The architectural style known as American Gothic (also called Gothic Revival and Carpenter Gothic) dates back to the 1830s and essentially marks the beginning of the Victorian period in American home design. Adapted from a similar movement in England, Gothic style was inspired by the ornately decorated stone cathedrals found throughout Europe. The style quickly evolved in America as thrifty carpenters learned to re-create and reinterpret the original decorative motifs using wood instead of stone.

American Gothic's most characteristic feature is the steeply pitched roof with fancy scroll-cut bargeboards, or verge boards, which gave the style its popular nickname, "gingerbread." Other typical features found on Gothic homes (and the Gothic Playhouse) include board-and-batten siding, doors and windows shaped with Gothic arches, and spires or finials adorning roof peaks.

Cutting List

Description	Quantity/Size	Material
Foundation/Floor		
Drainage material	1 cu. yd.	Compactible gravel
Foundation posts	4 @ field measure	4 × 4 pressure-treated landscape timbers
Concrete	Field measure	3,000 psi concrete
Rim joists	3 @ 10', 1 @ 8'	2 × 12 pressure-treated, rated for ground contact
Floor joists	1 @ 10', 2 @ 8'	2 × 6 pressure-treated
Box sills (rim joists)	2 @ 12'	2 × 4 pressure-treated
Floor sheathing	2 sheets @ 4 × 8'	¾" ext.-grade plywood
Porch decking	5 @ 10'	1 × 6 pressure-treated decking
Foundation "stones"	7 @ 10'	⁵⁄₄ × 6" treated decking w/radius edge (R.E.D.), rated for ground contact
Framing		
Wall framing & railings	29 @ 12'	2 × 4
Rafters & spacers	7 @ 12'	2 × 4
Ridge board	1 @ 8'	1 × 6
Collar ties	1 @ 10'	1 × 4
Exterior Finishes		
Siding, window boxes & door trim	26 @ 10'	1 × 8 pressure-treated or cedar
Battens & trim	30 @ 8'	1 × 2 pressure-treated or cedar
Door panel, verge boards & fascia	10 @ 10'	1 × 6 pressure-treated or cedar
Door braces, trim & railing trim	2 @ 10'	1 × 4 pressure-treated or cedar
Railing balusters	4 @ 8'	2 × 2 pressure-treated or cedar
Window stops	2 @ 8'	⅜" pressure-treated or cedar quarter-round molding
Window glazing (optional)	4 @ 20 × 9½"	¼" plastic glazing
Spire		
Post	1 @ 8'	4 × 4 pressure-treated
Trim	1 @ 4'	1 × 2 pressure-treated
Molding	1 @ 4'	Cap molding, pressure-treated

Description	Quantity/Size	Material
Balls	2 @ 3"-dia.	Wooden sphere, pressure-treated
Roofing		
Sheathing	4 sheets @ 4 × 8'	½" exterior-grade plywood roof sheathing
15# building paper	1 roll	
Drip edge	40 linear ft.	Metal drip edge
Shingles	1 square	Asphalt shingles — 250# per sq. min.
Fasteners & Hardware		
16d galvanized common nails	3½ lbs.	
16d common nails	5 lbs.	
10d common nails (for double top plates)	½ lb.	
10d galvanized finish/casing nails	4 lbs.	
8d galvanized common nails	1 lb.	
8d box nails	2 lbs.	
8d galvanized siding nails	8 lbs.	
1" galvanized roofing nails	3 lbs.	
2" deck screws (for porch decking)	1 lb.	
6d galvanized finish nails	2 lbs.	
3½" galvanized wood screws	24 screws	
1¼" galvanized wood screws	12 screws	
Dowel screws (for spire)	3 screws	Galvanized dowel screws
Lag screws w/washers	2 @ 6"	½" galvanized lag screws
Door hinges w/screws	3	Corrosion-resistant hinges
Door handle/latch	1	
Exterior wood glue		
Clear exterior caulk (for optional window panes)		
Construction adhesive		

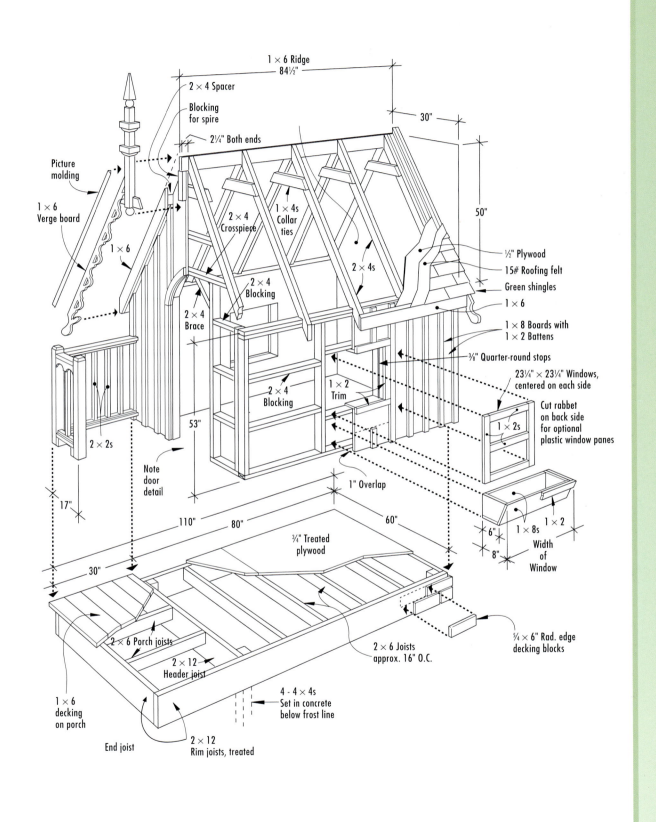

Picture molding

1 × 6 Verge board

1 × 6

1 × 6 Ridge
84½"

2 × 4 Spacer

Blocking for spire

2¼" Both ends

2 × 4 Crosspiece

1 × 4s Collar ties

2 × 4 Blocking

2 × 4 Brace

2 × 4 Blocking

1 × 2 Trim

2 × 2s

Note door detail

53"

17"

30"

110"

80"

60"

30"

2 × 4s

50"

½" Plywood

15# Roofing felt

Green shingles

1 × 6

1 × 8 Boards with 1 × 2 Battens

⅜" Quarter-round stops

23¼" × 23¼" Windows, centered on each side

Cut rabbet on back side for optional plastic window panes

1 × 2s

1" Overlap

6"

8"

1 × 8s   1 × 2

Width of Window

¾" Treated plywood

2 × 6 Porch joists

2 × 12 Header joist

2 × 6 Joists approx. 16" O.C.

5/4 × 6" Rad. edge decking blocks

1 × 6 decking on porch

End joist

2 × 12 Rim joists, treated

4 - 4 × 4s Set in concrete below frost line

FLOOR PLAN

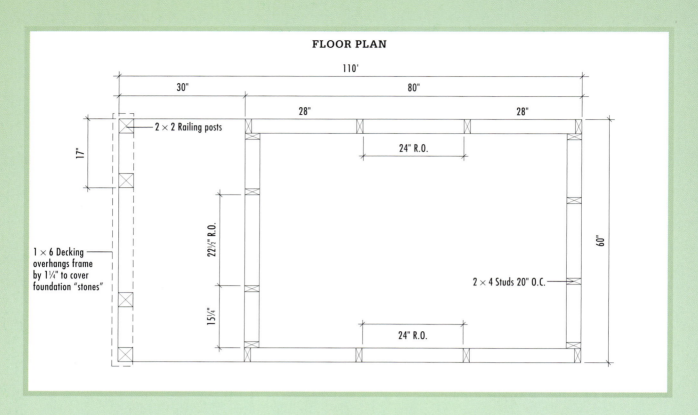

VERGE BOARD TEMPLATE

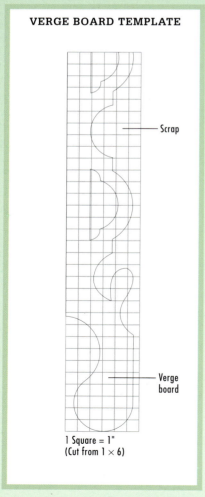

Scrap

Verge board

1 Square = 1"
(Cut from 1 × 6)

DECK RAILING DETAIL

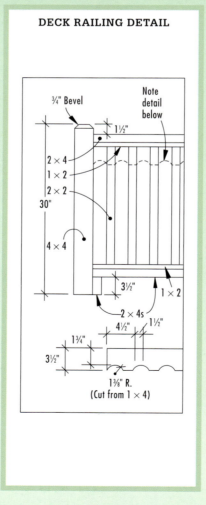

¾" Bevel

Note detail below

1½"

2 × 4
1 × 2
2 × 2

30"

4 × 4

3½"

1 × 2

2 × 4s

4½"   1½"

1¾"

3½"

1⅜" R.
(Cut from 1 × 4)

SPIRE DETAIL

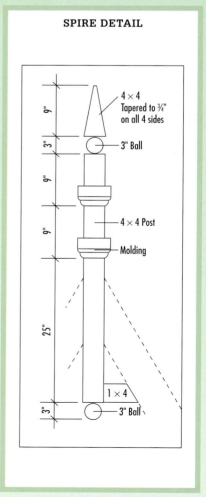

9"

4 × 4
Tapered to ¾"
on all 4 sides

3"

3" Ball

9"

4 × 4 Post

9"

Molding

25"

1 × 4

3"

3" Ball

DOOR DETAIL

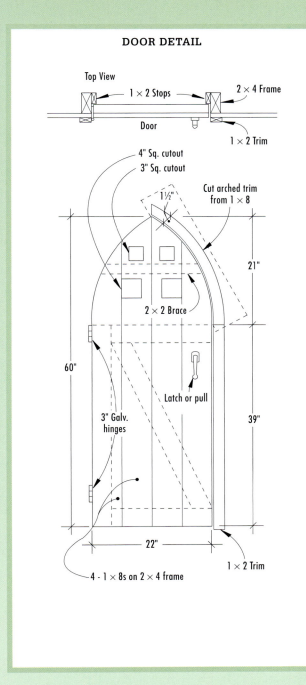

Top View

1 × 2 Stops
2 × 4 Frame
Door
1 × 2 Trim

4" Sq. cutout
3" Sq. cutout
Cut arched trim from 1 × 8
1½"

21"

2 × 2 Brace

Latch or pull

60"

3" Galv. hinges

39"

22"

1 × 2 Trim

4 - 1 × 8s on 2 × 4 frame

DOOR ARCH TEMPLATE

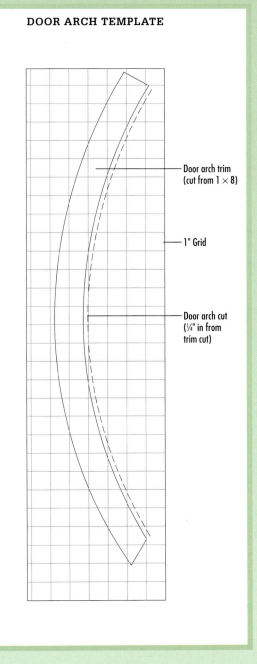

Door arch trim (cut from 1 × 8)

1" Grid

Door arch cut (¼" in from trim cut)

BOARD & BATTEN DETAIL

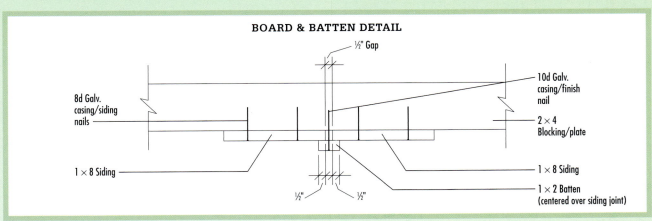

½" Gap

8d Galv. casing/siding nails

10d Galv. casing/finish nail

2 × 4 Blocking/plate

1 × 8 Siding

1 × 8 Siding

1 × 2 Batten (centered over siding joint)

½"   ½"

FRONT FRAMING

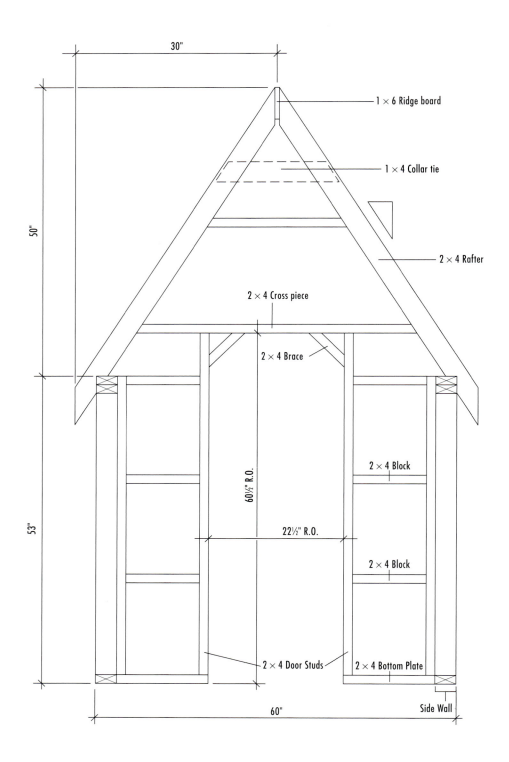

30"

1 × 6 Ridge board

1 × 4 Collar tie

2 × 4 Rafter

2 × 4 Cross piece

2 × 4 Brace

50"

60½" R.O.

2 × 4 Block

53"

22½" R.O.

2 × 4 Block

2 × 4 Door Studs

2 × 4 Bottom Plate

Side Wall

60"

FLOOR FRAMING PLAN

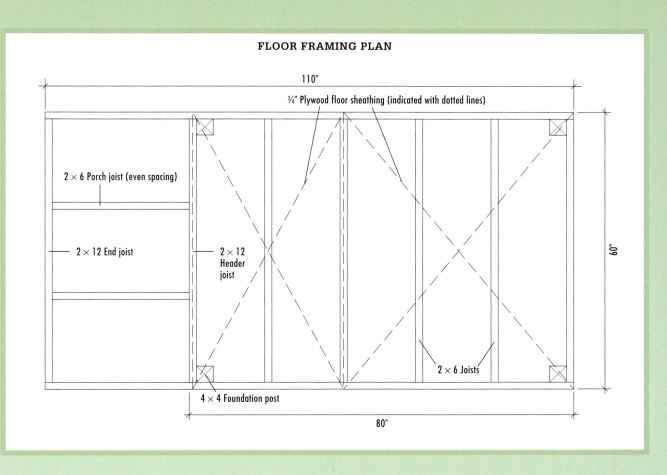

110"

¾" Plywood floor sheathing (indicated with dotted lines)

2 × 6 Porch joist (even spacing)

2 × 12 End joist

2 × 12 Header joist

60"

2 × 6 Joists

4 × 4 Foundation post

80"

SIDE FRAMING

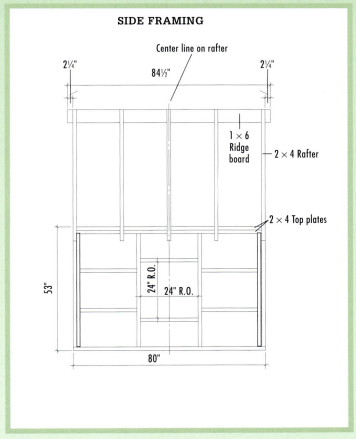

Center line on rafter

2¼"

84½"

2¼"

1 × 6 Ridge board

2 × 4 Rafter

2 × 4 Top plates

53"

24" R.O.

24" R.O.

80"

RAFTER TEMPLATE

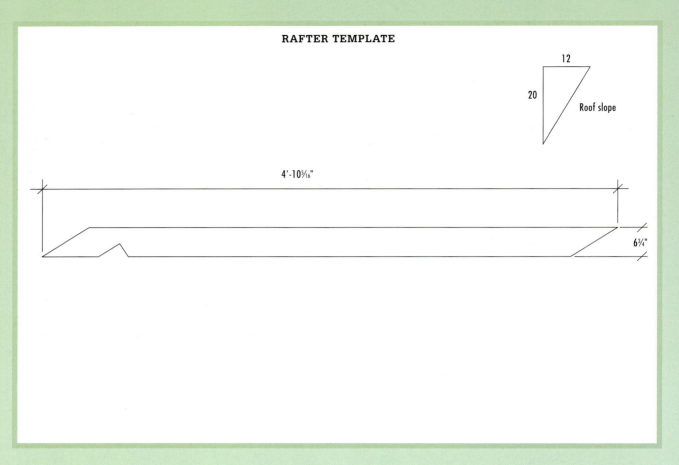

12

20

Roof slope

4'-10⁵⁄₁₆"

6¾"

WINDOW BOX DETAIL

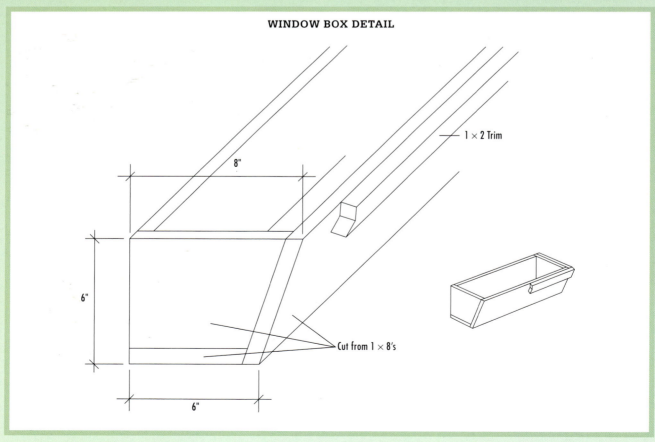

1 × 2 Trim

8"

6"

6"

Cut from 1 × 8's

How to Build the Gothic Playhouse

1

Set up perpendicular mason's lines and batter boards to plot out the excavation area and the post hole locations, as shown in FLOOR FRAMING PLAN (page 173). Excavate and grade the construction area, preparing for a 4"-thick gravel base. Dig 12"-dia. holes to a depth below the frost line, plus 4". Add 4" of gravel to each hole. Set the posts in concrete so they extend about 10" above the ground.

2

After the concrete dries (overnight) add compactable gravel and tamp it down so it is 4" thick and flat. Cut two 2 × 12 rim joists for the floor frame, two 2 × 12 end joists and one header joist. Cut four 2 × 6 joists at 57" and two porch joists at 27¾". Assemble the floor frame with 16d galvanized common nails following FLOOR FRAMING PLAN.

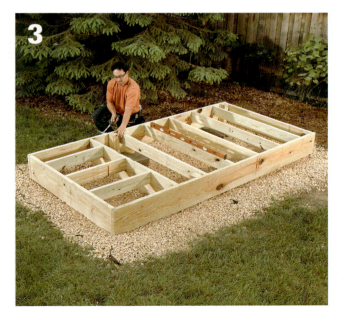

3

Make sure the frame is square and level (prop it up temporarily), and then fasten it to the posts with 16d galvanized common nails.

4

Cover the interior floor with plywood, starting at the rear end. Trim the second piece so it covers ½ of the header joist. Install the 1 × 6 porch decking starting at the front edge and leaving a ⅛" gap between boards. Extend the porch decking 1¼" beyond the front and sides of the floor frame.

(continued)

Frame the side walls as shown in the SIDE FRAMING (page 173) and FLOOR PLAN (page 170). Each wall has four 2 × 4 studs at 48½", a top and bottom plate at 80", and a 2 × 4 window header and sill at 24". Install the horizontal 2 × 4 blocking, spaced evenly between the plates. Install only one top plate per wall at this time.

Build the rear wall. Raise the side and rear walls, and fasten them to each other and to the floor frame. Add double top plates. Both sidewall top plates should stop flush with the end stud at the front of the wall.

To frame the front wall, cut two treated bottom plates at 15¼", two end studs at 51½" and two door studs at 59". Cut a 2 × 4 crosspiece and two braces, mitering the brace ends at 45°. Cut six 2 × 4 blocks at 12¼". Assemble the wall as shown in the FRONT FRAMING (page 172). Raise the front wall and fasten it to the floor and sidewall frames.

Cut one set of 2 × 4 pattern rafters following the RAFTER TEMPLATE (page 174). Test-fit the rafters and make any necessary adjustments. Use one of the pattern rafters to mark and cut the remaining eight rafters. Also cut four 2 × 4 spacers—these should match the rafters but have no bird's-mouth cuts.

Cut the ridge board to size and mark the rafter layout following the SIDE FRAMING, and then screw the rafters to the ridge. Cut five 1 × 4 collar ties, mitering the ends at 31°. Fasten the collar ties across each set of rafters so the ends of the ties are flush with the rafter edges. Fasten the 2 × 4 crosspiece above the door to the two end rafters. Install remaining cross-pieces as in the FRONT/REAR FRAMING.

Install the 1 × 8 siding boards so they overlap the floor frame by 1" at the bottom and extend to the tops of the side walls, and to the tops of the rafters on the front and rear walls. Gap the boards ½", and fasten them to the framing with pairs of 8d galvanized casing nails or siding nails. Install the four 2 × 4 spacers on top of the siding at the front and rear so they match the rafter placement.

Cut the arched sections of door trim from 1 × 8 lumber, following the arch template (page 171). Install the arched pieces and straight 1 × 2 side pieces flush with the inside of the door opening. Wrap the window openings with ripped 1 × 6 boards, and then frame the outsides of the openings with 1 × 2 trim. Install a 1 × 2 batten over each siding joint as shown in step 10.

Build the 1 × 2 window frames to fit snugly inside the trimmed openings. Assemble the parts with exterior wood glue and galvanized finish nails. If desired, cut a ¼" rabbet in the back side and install plastic windowpanes with silicone caulk. Secure the window frames in the openings with ⅜" quarter-round molding. Construct the window boxes as shown in the WINDOW BOX DETAIL (page 174). Install the boxes below the windows with 1¼" screws.

(continued)

To build the spire, start by drawing a line around a 4 × 4 post, 9" from one end. Draw cutting lines to taper each side down to ¾", as shown in the SPIRE DETAIL (page 170). Taper the end with a circular saw or handsaw, and then cut off the point at the 9" mark. Cut the post at 43". Add 1 × 2 trim and cap molding as shown in the detail, mitering the ends at the corners. Drill centered pilot holes into the post, balls, and point, and join the parts with dowel screws.

To cut the verge boards, enlarge the VERGE BOARD TEMPLATE (page 170) on a photocopier so the squares measure 1". Draw the pattern on a 1 × 6. Cut the board with a jigsaw. Test-fit the board and adjust as needed. Use the cut board as a pattern to mark and cut the remaining verge boards. Install the boards over the front and rear fascia, then add picture molding along the top edges.

Add a 1 × 2 block under the front end of the ridge board. Center the spire at the roof peak, drill pilot holes, and anchor the post with 6" lag screws. Cut and install the 1 × 6 front fascia to run from the spire to the rafter ends, keeping the fascia ½" above the tops of the rafters. Install the rear fascia so it covers the ridge board. Cut and install two 1 × 4 brackets to fit between the spire post and front fascia, as shown in the SPIRE DETAIL.

Cut the 1 × 6 eave fascia to fit between the verge boards, and install it so it will be flush with the top of the roof sheathing. Cut and install the roof sheathing. Add building paper, metal drip edge, and asphalt shingles, following the steps on page 56.

Mark the deck post locations 1¼" in from the ends and front edge of the porch decking, as shown in the FLOOR PLAN. Cut four 4 × 4 railing posts at 30". Bevel the top edges of the posts at 45°, as shown in DECK RAILING DETAIL (page 170). Fasten the posts to the decking and floor frame with 3½" screws. Cut six 2 × 4 treated blocks at 3½". Fasten these to the bottoms of the posts, on the sides that will receive the railings.

Assemble the railing sections following the DECK RAILING DETAIL. Each section has a 2 × 4 top and bottom rail, two 1 × 2 nailers, and 2 × 2 balusters spaced so the edges of the balusters are no more than 4" apart. You can build the sections completely and then fasten them to the posts and front wall, or you can construct them in place starting with the rails. Cut the shaped trim boards from 1 × 4 lumber, using a jigsaw. Notch the rails to fit around the house battens as needed.

Construct the door with 1 × 6 boards fastened to 2 × 4 Z-bracing, as shown in the DOOR DETAIL. Fasten the boards to the bracing with glue and 6d finish nails. Cut the square notches and the top of the door with a jigsaw. Add the 2 × 2 brace as shown. Install the door with two hinges, leaving a ¼" gap all around. Add a knob or latch as desired.

Make the foundation "stones" by cutting 116 6"-lengths of ⁵⁄₄ × 6 deck boards (the pieces in the top row must be ripped down 1"). Round over the cut edges of all pieces with a router. Attach the top row of stones using construction adhesive and 6d galvanized finish nails. Install the bottom row, starting with a half-piece to create a staggered joint pattern. If desired, finish the playhouse interior with plywood or tongue-and-groove siding.

Timber-frame Shed

Timber-framing is a traditional style of building that uses a simple framework of heavy timber posts and beams connected with hand-carved joints. From the outside, a timber-frame building looks like a standard stick-frame structure, but on the inside, the stout, rough-sawn framing members evoke the look and feel of an 18th-century workshop. This 8 × 10-ft. shed has the same basic design used in traditional timber-frame structures but with joints that are easy to make.

In addition to the framing, some notable features of this shed are its simplicity and proportions. It's a nicely symmetrical building with full-height walls and an attractively steep-pitched roof, something you seldom find on manufactured kit sheds. The clean styling gives it a traditional, rustic look, but also makes the shed ideal for adding custom details. Install a skylight or windows to brighten the interior, or perhaps cut a crescent moon into the door in the style of old-fashioned backyard privies.

The materials for this project were carefully chosen to enhance the traditional styling. The 1 × 8 tongue-and-groove siding and all exterior trim boards are made from rough-sawn cedar, giving the shed a natural, rustic quality. The door is hand-built from rough cedar boards and includes exposed Z-bracing, a classic outbuilding detail. As shown here, the roof frame is made with standard 2 × 4s, but if you're willing to pay a little more to improve the appearance, you can use rough-cut 2 × 4s or 4 × 4s for the roof framing.

Another option to consider is traditional spaced sheathing instead of plywood for the roof deck. Spaced sheathing consists of 1 × 4 boards nailed perpendicular to the roof frame, with a 1½" gap between boards. The roof shingles are nailed directly to the sheathing without building paper in between, creating an attractive ceiling of exposed boards and shingles inside the shed.

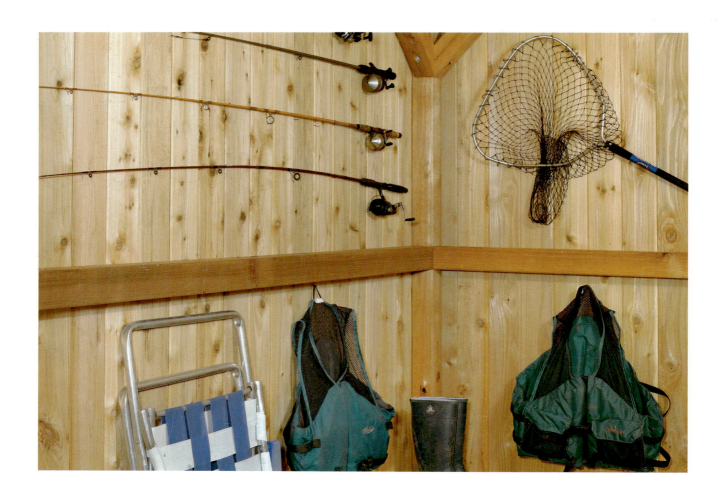

Cutting List

Description	Quantity/Size	Material
Foundation		
Drainage material	1 cu. yard	Compactible gravel
Skids	3 @ 10'	6 × 6 treated timbers
Floor Framing		
Rim joists	2 @ 10'	2 × 6 pressure-treated
Joists	9 @ 8'	2 × 6 pressure-treated
Joist clip angles	18	3 × 3 × 3" × 18-gauge galvanized
Floor sheathing	3 sheets @ 4 × 8'	¾" tongue-&-groove ext.-grade plywood
Wall Framing		
Posts	6 @ 8'	4 × 4 rough-sawn cedar
Window posts	2 @ 4'	4 × 4 rough-sawn cedar
Girts	2 @ 10' 2 @ 8'	4 × 4 rough-sawn cedar
Beams	2 @ 10' 2 @ 8'	4 × 6 rough-sawn cedar
Braces	8 @ 2'	4 × 4 rough-sawn cedar
Post bases	6, with nails	Simpson BC40
Post-beam connectors	8 pieces, with nails	Simpson LCE
L-connectors	4, with nails	Simpson A34
Additional posts	6 @ 8'	4 × 4 rough-sawn cedar
Roof Framing		
Rafters	12 @ 7'	2 × 4
Collar ties	2 @ 10'	2 × 4
Ridge board	1 @ 10'	2 × 6
Metal anchors — rafters	8, with nails	Simpson H1
Gable-end blocking	4 @ 7'	2 × 2
Exterior Finishes		
Siding	2 @ 14' 8 @ 12' 10 @ 10' 29 @ 9'	1 × 8 V-joint rough-sawn cedar
Corner trim	8 @ 9'	1 × 4 rough-sawn cedar
Fascia	4 @ 7' 2 @ 12'	1 × 6 rough-sawn cedar
Fascia trim	4 @ 7' 2 @ 12'	1 × 2 rough-sawn cedar
Subfascia	2 @ 12'	1 × 4 pine
Plywood soffits	1 sheet 4 × 8'	⅜" cedar or fir plywood

Description	Quantity/Size	Material
Soffit vents (optional)	4 @ 4 × 12"	Louver with bug screen
Flashing (door)	4 linear ft.	Galvanized — 18 gauge
Roofing		
Roof sheathing	6 sheets @ 4 × 8'	½" ext.-grade plywood
Cedar shingles	1.7 squares	
15# building paper	140 sq. ft.	
Roof vents (optional)	2 units	
Door		
Frame	2 @ 7' 1 @ 4'	¾ × 4¼" (actual) S4S cedar
Stops	2 @ 7' 1 @ 4'	1 × 2 S4S cedar
Panel material	7 @ 7'	1 × 6 T&G V-joint rough-sawn cedar
Z-brace	1 @ 8' to 2 @ 8'	1 × 6 rough-sawn cedar
Strap hinges	3	
Trim	5 @ 7'	1 × 3 rough-sawn cedar
Flashing	42" metal flashing	
Fasteners		
60d common nails	16 nails	
20d common nails	32 nails	
16d galvanized common nails	3½ lbs.	
10d common nails	1 lb.	
10d galvanized casing nails	½ lb.	
8d galvanized box nails	1½ lbs.	
8d galvanized finish nails	7 lbs.	
8d box nails	¼ lb.	
6d galvanized finish nails	40 nails	
3d galvanized finish nails	50 nails	
1½" joist hanger nails	72 nails	
2½" deck screws	25 screws	
1½" wood screws	50 screws	
⅞" galvanized roofing nails	2 lbs.	
⅜" × 6" lag screws, w/washers	16 screws	
¼" × 6" lag screws, w/washers		
Construction adhesive	4 tubes	

Note: Additional posts may be added as a safety precaution to prevent eave beam deflection.

FRONT FRAMING ELEVATION

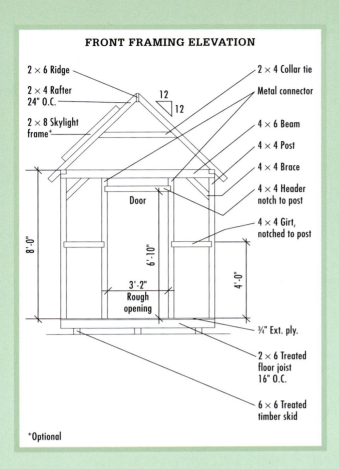

2 × 6 Ridge

2 × 4 Rafter
24" O.C.

2 × 8 Skylight
frame*

Door

8'-0"

6'-10"

3'-2"
Rough
opening

2 × 4 Collar tie

Metal connector

4 × 6 Beam

4 × 4 Post

4 × 4 Brace

4 × 4 Header
notch to post

4 × 4 Girt,
notched to post

4'-0"

¾" Ext. ply.

2 × 6 Treated
floor joist
16" O.C.

6 × 6 Treated
timber skid

*Optional

LEFT SIDE FRAMING ELEVATION

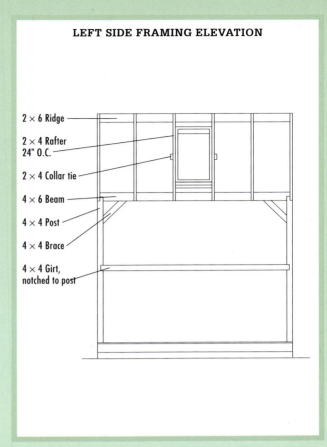

2 × 6 Ridge

2 × 4 Rafter
24" O.C.

2 × 4 Collar tie

4 × 6 Beam

4 × 4 Post

4 × 4 Brace

4 × 4 Girt,
notched to post

REAR FRAMING ELEVATION

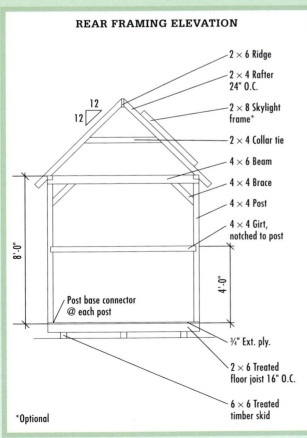

2 × 6 Ridge

2 × 4 Rafter
24" O.C.

2 × 8 Skylight
frame*

2 × 4 Collar tie

4 × 6 Beam

4 × 4 Brace

4 × 4 Post

4 × 4 Girt,
notched to post

8'-0"

4'-0"

Post base connector
@ each post

¾" Ext. ply.

2 × 6 Treated
floor joist 16" O.C.

6 × 6 Treated
timber skid

*Optional

RIGHT SIDE FRAMING ELEVATION

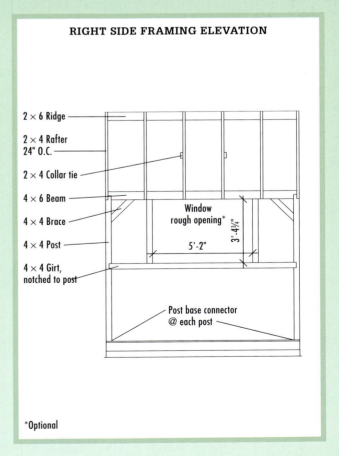

2 × 6 Ridge

2 × 4 Rafter
24" O.C.

2 × 4 Collar tie

4 × 6 Beam

4 × 4 Brace

4 × 4 Post

4 × 4 Girt,
notched to post

Window
rough opening*

5'-2"

3'-4¾"

Post base connector
@ each post

*Optional

BUILDING SECTION

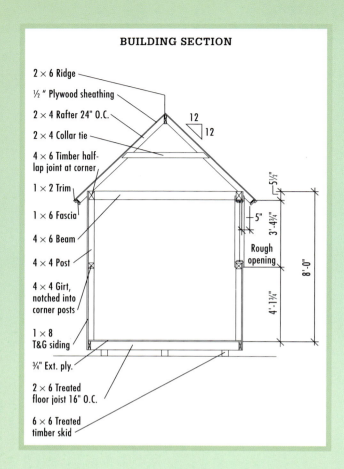

2 × 6 Ridge
½ " Plywood sheathing
2 × 4 Rafter 24" O.C.
2 × 4 Collar tie
4 × 6 Timber half-lap joint at corner
1 × 2 Trim
1 × 6 Fascia
4 × 6 Beam
4 × 4 Post
4 × 4 Girt, notched into corner posts
1 × 8 T&G siding
¾" Ext. ply.
2 × 6 Treated floor joist 16" O.C.
6 × 6 Treated timber skid

12
12

5½"
5"
3'-4¾"
Rough opening
8'-0"
4'-1¾"

RAFTER TEMPLATE

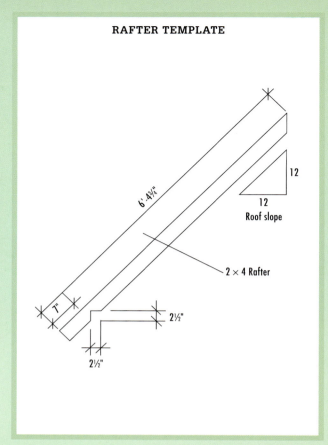

6'-4¾"
2 × 4 Rafter
12
12
Roof slope
7"
2½"
2½"

FLOOR FRAMING PLAN

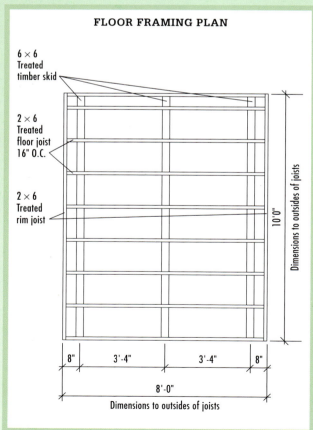

6 × 6 Treated timber skid
2 × 6 Treated floor joist 16" O.C.
2 × 6 Treated rim joist

Dimensions to outsides of joists
10'-0"

8"   3'-4"   3'-4"   8"
8'-0"
Dimensions to outsides of joists

FLOOR PLAN

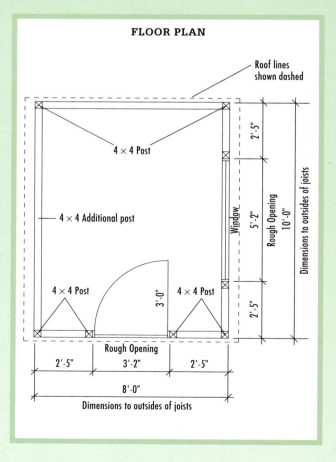

Roof lines shown dashed
4 × 4 Post
4 × 4 Additional post
Window
4 × 4 Post
3'-0"
4 × 4 Post
Rough Opening

2'-5"
5'-2" Rough Opening
2'-5"
10'-0" Dimensions to outsides of joists

2'-5"   3'-2"   2'-5"
8'-0"
Dimensions to outsides of joists

FRONT ELEVATION

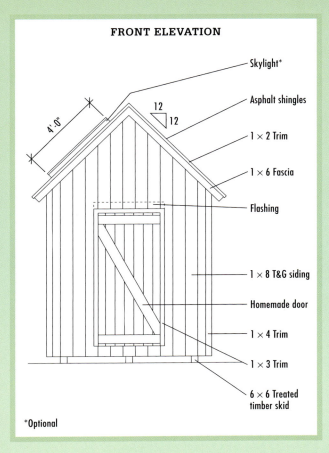

Skylight*

Asphalt shingles

1 × 2 Trim

1 × 6 Fascia

Flashing

1 × 8 T&G siding

Homemade door

1 × 4 Trim

1 × 3 Trim

6 × 6 Treated timber skid

4'-0"

12 / 12

*Optional

LEFT SIDE ELEVATION

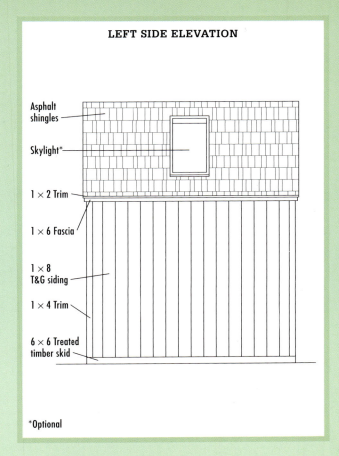

Asphalt shingles

Skylight*

1 × 2 Trim

1 × 6 Fascia

1 × 8 T&G siding

1 × 4 Trim

6 × 6 Treated timber skid

*Optional

REAR ELEVATION

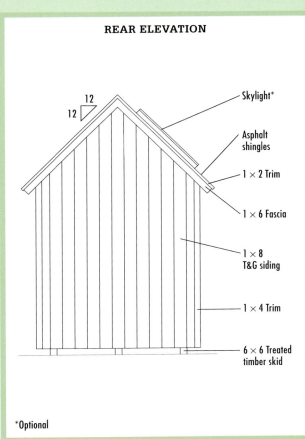

Skylight*

Asphalt shingles

1 × 2 Trim

1 × 6 Fascia

1 × 8 T&G siding

1 × 4 Trim

6 × 6 Treated timber skid

12 / 12

*Optional

RIGHT SIDE ELEVATION

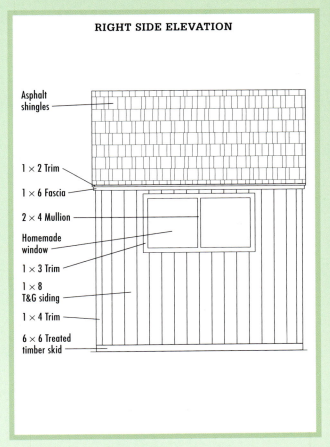

Asphalt shingles

1 × 2 Trim

1 × 6 Fascia

2 × 4 Mullion

Homemade window

1 × 3 Trim

1 × 8 T&G siding

1 × 4 Trim

6 × 6 Treated timber skid

GABLE OVERHANG DETAIL

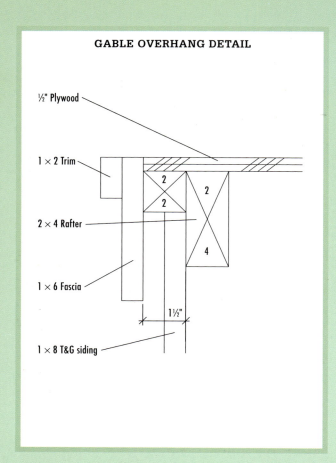

½" Plywood

1 × 2 Trim

2

2

2

4

2 × 4 Rafter

1 × 6 Fascia

1½"

1 × 8 T&G siding

EAVE DETAIL

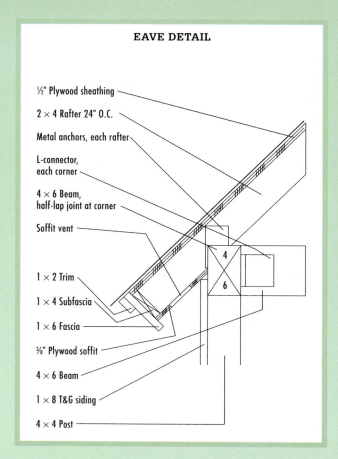

½" Plywood sheathing

2 × 4 Rafter 24" O.C.

Metal anchors, each rafter

L-connector, each corner

4 × 6 Beam, half-lap joint at corner

Soffit vent

4

6

1 × 2 Trim

1 × 4 Subfascia

1 × 6 Fascia

⅜" Plywood soffit

4 × 6 Beam

1 × 8 T&G siding

4 × 4 Post

DOOR JAMB DETAIL

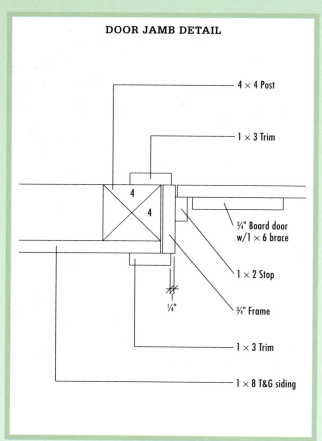

4 × 4 Post

1 × 3 Trim

4

4

¾" Board door w/1 × 6 brace

1 × 2 Stop

¾" Frame

¼"

1 × 3 Trim

1 × 8 T&G siding

DOOR DETAIL

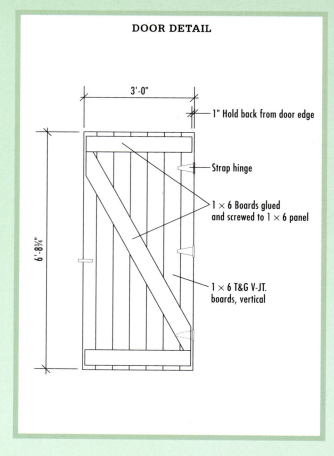

3'-0"

1" Hold back from door edge

Strap hinge

1 × 6 Boards glued and screwed to 1 × 6 panel

6'-8¾"

1 × 6 T&G V-JT. boards, vertical

How to Build the Timber-frame Shed

Prepare the foundation site with a 4"-deep layer of compacted and leveled gravel. Cut three 6 × 6 treated timber skids (120"). Place the skids following the FLOOR FRAMING PLAN (page 184). Lay a straight 2 × 4 across the skids and test with a level.

Cut two 2 × 6 rim joists (120") and nine joists (93"). Assemble the floor frame with galvanized nails, as shown in the FLOOR FRAMING PLAN. Check the frame to make sure it is square by measuring the diagonals.

Position the floor frame on top of the skids and measure the diagonals to make sure it's square. Install joist clip angles at each joist along the two outer skids with galvanized nails. Toenail each joist to the center skid.

Install the tongue-and-groove plywood floor sheathing, starting with a full sheet at one corner of the frame. The flooring should extend all the way to the outside edges of the floor frame.

(continued)

To prepare the wall posts, cut six 4 × 4 posts (90½"), making sure both ends are square. On the four corner posts, mark for 3½"-long × 1½"-deep notches (to accept the girts) on the two adjacent inside faces of each post. Start the notches 46¼" from the bottom ends of the posts.

Mark the door frame posts for notches to receive a girt at 46¼" and for the door header at 82"; see the FRONT FRAMING ELEVATION (page 183). Remove the waste from the notch areas with a circular saw and clean up with a broad wood chisel. Test-fit the notches to make sure the 4 × 4 girts will fit snugly.

Position the post bases so the posts will be flush with the outsides of the shed floor. Install the bases with 16d galvanized common nails. The insides of the door posts should be 29" from the floor sides. Brace each post so it is perfectly plumb, and then fasten it to its base using the base manufacturer's recommended fasteners.

Cut two 4 × 6 beams at 10 ft. and two at 8 ft. Notch the ends of the beams for half-lap joints: Measure the width and depth of the beams and mark notches equal to the width × ½ the depth. Orient the notches as shown in the FRAMING ELEVATIONS (page 183). Cut the notches with a handsaw, then test-fit the joints, and make fine adjustments with a chisel.

Set an 8-ft. beam onto the front wall posts and tack it in place with a 16d nail at each end. Tack the other 8-ft. beam to the back posts. Then, position the 10 ft. beams on top of the short beam ends, forming the half-lap joints. Measure the diagonals of the front wall frame to make sure it's square, and then anchor the beams with two 60d galvanized nails at each corner (drill pilot holes for the nails).

Reinforce the beam connections with a metal post-beam connector on the outside of each corner and on both sides of the door posts, using the recommended fasteners. Install an L-connector on the inside of the beam-to-beam joints; see the EAVE DETAIL (page 186).

Cut eight 4 × 4 corner braces (20"), mitering the ends at 45°. Install the braces flush with the outsides of the beams and corner posts, using two ⅜" × 6" lag screws (with washers) driven through counterbored pilot holes.

Measure between the posts at the notches, and cut the 4 × 4 girts to fit. To allow the girts to meet at the corner posts, make a 1½" × 1½" notch at both ends of the rear wall girts and the outside ends of the front wall girts. Install the girts with construction adhesive and two 20d nails driven through the outsides of the posts (make pilot holes). Cut and install the 4 × 4 door header in the same fashion.

(continued)

Frame the roof: Cut two pattern rafters using the RAFTER TEMPLATE (page 184). Test-fit the patterns, and then cut the remaining ten rafters. Cut the 2 × 6 ridge (120"). Install the rafters and ridge using 24" on-center spacing. Cut four 2 × 2s to extend from the roof peak to the rafter ends, and install them flush with the tops of the rafters; see the GABLE OVERHANG DETAIL (page 186). Add framing connectors at the rafter-beam connections (except the outer rafters). *Note: if desired, you can add framing for a skylight.*

Cut four 2 × 4 collar ties (58"), mitering the tops of the ends at 45°. Install the ties ½" below the tops of the rafters, as shown in the FRAMING ELEVATIONS.

Install the 1 × 8 siding on the front and rear walls so it runs from the 2 × 2s down to ¾" below the bottom of the floor frame. Fasten the siding with 8d corrosion-resistant finish nails or siding nails. Don't nail the siding to the door header in this step.

Cover the rafter ends along the eaves with 1 × 4 subfascia, flush with the tops of the rafters; see the EAVE DETAIL. Install the 1 × 6 fascia and 1 × 2 trim at the gable ends, then along the eaves, mitering the corner joints. Keep the fascia and trim ½" above the rafters so it will be flush with the roof sheathing.

17

Rip the plywood soffit panels to fit between the wall framing and the fascia, and install them with 3d galvanized box nails; see the EAVE DETAIL.

18

Deck the roof with ½" plywood sheathing, starting at the bottom corners. Cover the sheathing with building paper, overhanging the 1 × 2 fascia trim by ¾". Install the cedar shingle roofing or asphalt shingles following the steps on pages 56 to 59. Include roof vents, if desired (they're a good idea). Finish the roof at the peak with a 1× ridge cap.

19

Construct the door frame from ¾" × 4¼" stock. Cut the head jamb at 37¾" and the side jambs at 81". Fasten the head jamb over the ends of the side jambs with 2½" deck screws. Install the frame in the door opening, using shims and 10d galvanized casing nails. Add 1 × 2 stops to the jambs, ¾" from the outside edges.

20

Build the door with seven pieces of 1 × 6 siding cut at 80¾". Fit the boards together, then mark and trim the outer pieces so the door is 36" wide. Install the 1 × 6 Z-bracing with adhesive and 1¼" wood screws, as shown in the DOOR DETAIL (page 186). Install flashing over the outside of the door, then add 1 × 3 trim around both sides of the door opening, as shown in the DOOR JAMB DETAIL (page 186). Hang the door with three strap hinges.

Service Shed

This versatile shelter structure is actually two projects in one. Using the same primary design, you can build an open-sided firewood shelter, or you can add doors and a shelf and create a secured shed that's perfect for trash cans or recyclables. Both projects have four vertical corner posts, a rectangular floor frame decked with 2 × 6s, and gapped side slats that provide cross ventilation. The plywood, shed-style roof is covered with cedar shingles, but you can substitute with any type of roofing.

To adapt the service shed for use as a closed storage shed, you can add a center post (mostly to function as a nailer) and attach slats to create a rear wall. With two more posts in the front, you may define door openings. The adapted shed won't offer secure storage for valuable items like tools, but it will prevent dogs, squirrels, raccoons and other pests from getting into your trashcans.

As for materials, you can save a lot of money by building this project with pressure-treated lumber. Stain or paint the greenish lumber to change its coloring or leave it bare and allow it to weather to a silvery gray. If you prefer the look of cedar lumber, use it for everything but the shelter's floor frame and decking. Also, you might want to set the corner posts on concrete blocks or stones to prevent the cedar from rotting prematurely due to ground contact.

Seasoning Firewood ▸

Proper seasoning, or drying, of firewood takes time. After freshly cut logs are split, the drying process can take six to 12 months, given the right conditions. Stacking split wood under a shelter with one or more open sides is ideal because it protects the wood from rain and snow moisture while letting airflow through the stack to hasten drying.

You can test wood for seasoning by its look and feel and by how it burns. The ends of dry logs show cracks and typically have a grayish color, while unseasoned wood still looks freshly cut and may be moist to the touch. Fresher wood also makes a heavy, dull thud when pieces are knocked together. When it comes to burning, dry wood lights easily and burns consistently, while wet wood tends to burn out if unattended and often smokes excessively as the internal moisture turns to steam.

If you order split firewood from a supplier and can't guarantee how well seasoned it is, have it delivered at least six months before the start of the burning season. This gives the wood plenty of time to dry out. Regarding quantity, a "cord" of neatly stacked split logs measures 128 cubic feet—a stack that's 4 ft. high, 4 ft. deep, and 8 ft. long. A "half cord" measures 64 cubic feet.

Cutting List

Part	Quantity/Size Firewood Shed	Quantity/Size Garbage Shed	Material
Framing			
Side & end floor supports	2 @ 10'	2 @ 10'	2 × 4 pressure-treated
Center floor support	1 @ 8'	1 @ 8'	2 × 4 pressure-treated
Floor boards	3 @ 10'	3 @ 10'	2 × 6 pressure-treated
Corner posts	4 @ 8'	4 @ 8'	2 × 4 cedar
Headers	2 @ 8'	2 @ 8'	2 × 4 cedar
Rafters	1 @ 8' 1 @ 4'	1 @ 8' 1 @ 4'	2 × 4 cedar
Rear center post		1 @ 4'	2 × 4 cedar
Door posts		1 @ 8'	2 × 4 cedar
Door ledger		1 @ 8'	2 × 4 cedar
Slats			
End slats	5 @ 8'	5 @ 8'	1 × 6 cedar
Back slats		5 @ 8'	1 × 6 cedar
Roofing			
Sheathing	1 sheet @ 4 × 8'	1 sheet @ 4 × 8'	¾" CDX plywood
Roof edging	2 @ 10'	2 @ 10'	1 × 2 T
15# building paper	37 sq. ft.	37 sq. ft.	
Shingles	25 sq. ft	25 sq. ft.	18" cedar shingles
Roof cap	1 @ 8' 1 @ 8'	1 @ 8' 1 @ 8'	1 × 4 cedar 1 × 3 cedar

Part	Quantity/Size Firewood Shed	Quantity/Size Garbage Shed	Material
Shelf & Doors			
Shelf		1 @ 24⅝ × 28⅛"	¾" ext.-grade plywood
Shelf cleats		1 @ 6'	1 × 3 cedar
Door panels		1 sheet @ 4 × 8'	¾" ext.-grade plywood
Stiles		3 @ 8' (wide doors) 1 @ 10' (narrow door)	1 × 4 cedar
Hinges		6	Exterior hinges
Door handles		3	Exterior handles
Fasteners			
¼" × 3" lag screws	8, with washers	10, with washers	
Deck screws			
3½"	12	12	
3"	62	62	
2½"	36	48	
2"	50	62	
1⅝"	100	160	
1¼"		116	
6d galvanized finish nails	30	30	
3d galvanized roofing nails	1 lb.	1 lb.	

FLOOR FRAMING PLAN

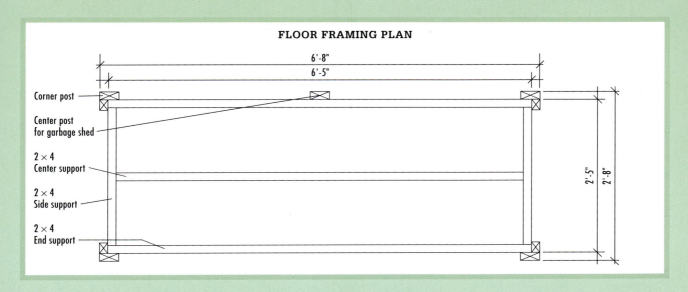

Corner post

Center post
for garbage shed

2 × 4
Center support

2 × 4
Side support

2 × 4
End support

6'-8"

6'-5"

2'-5"

2'-8"

FLOOR PLAN

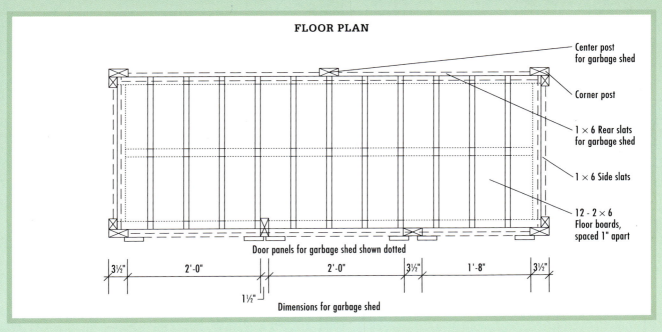

Center post
for garbage shed

Corner post

1 × 6 Rear slats
for garbage shed

1 × 6 Side slats

12 - 2 × 6
Floor boards,
spaced 1" apart

Door panels for garbage shed shown dotted

3½" 2'-0" 3½" 2'-0" 3½" 1'-8" 3½"

1½"

Dimensions for garbage shed

ROOF FRAMING PLAN

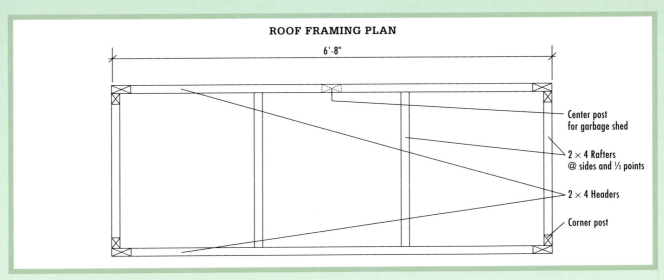

6'-8"

Center post
for garbage shed

2 × 4 Rafters
@ sides and ⅓ points

2 × 4 Headers

Corner post

BUILDING SECTION

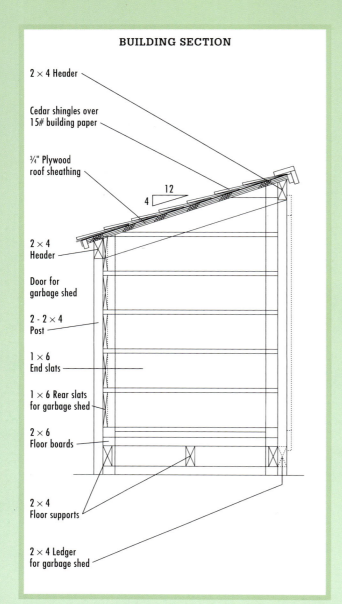

2 × 4 Header

Cedar shingles over 15# building paper

¾" Plywood roof sheathing

12
4

2 × 4 Header

Door for garbage shed

2 - 2 × 4 Post

1 × 6 End slats

1 × 6 Rear slats for garbage shed

2 × 6 Floor boards

2 × 4 Floor supports

2 × 4 Ledger for garbage shed

RAFTER TEMPLATES

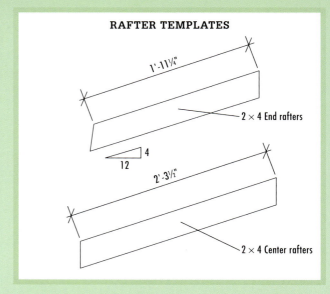

1'-11¼"

2 × 4 End rafters

4
12

2'-3½"

2 × 4 Center rafters

UPPER ROOF EDGE DETAIL

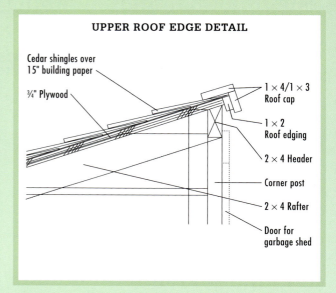

Cedar shingles over 15" building paper

¾" Plywood

1 × 4/1 × 3 Roof cap

1 × 2 Roof edging

2 × 4 Header

Corner post

2 × 4 Rafter

Door for garbage shed

DOOR ELEVATION

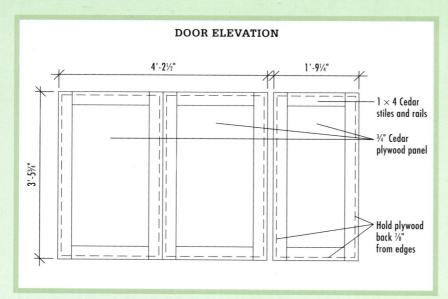

4'-2½"

1'-9¼"

1 × 4 Cedar stiles and rails

¾" Cedar plywood panel

3'-5¾"

Hold plywood back ⅞" from edges

DOOR EDGE & CORNER POST DETAIL

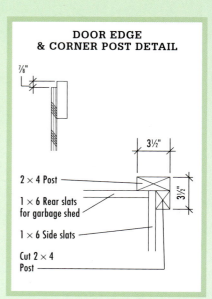

⅞"

3½"

3½"

2 × 4 Post

1 × 6 Rear slats for garbage shed

1 × 6 Side slats

Cut 2 × 4 Post

FRONT ELEVATION

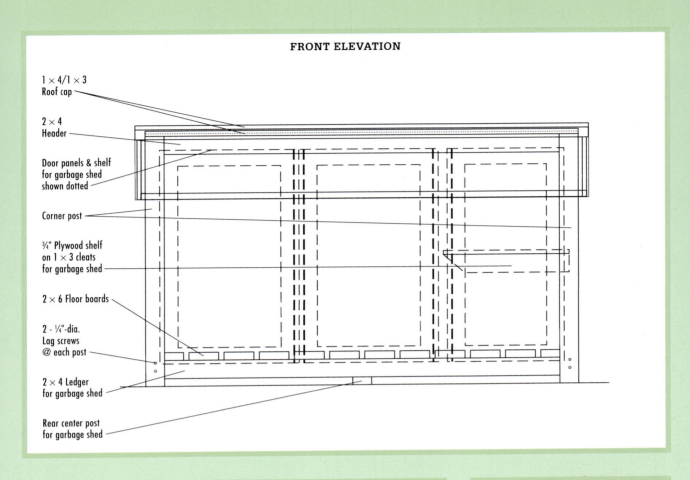

1 × 4/1 × 3
Roof cap

2 × 4
Header

Door panels & shelf
for garbage shed
shown dotted

Corner post

¾" Plywood shelf
on 1 × 3 cleats
for garbage shed

2 × 6 Floor boards

2 - ¼"-dia.
Lag screws
@ each post

2 × 4 Ledger
for garbage shed

Rear center post
for garbage shed

REAR ELEVATION

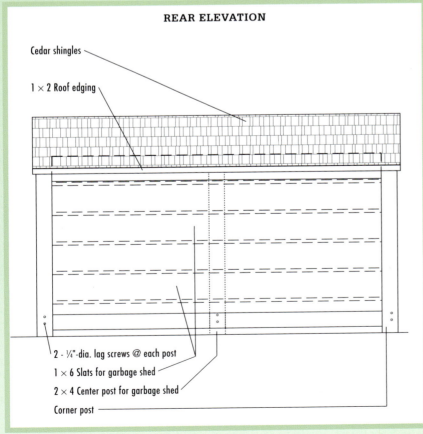

Cedar shingles

1 × 2 Roof edging

2 - ¼"-dia. lag screws @ each post

1 × 6 Slats for garbage shed

2 × 4 Center post for garbage shed

Corner post

SIDE ELEVATION

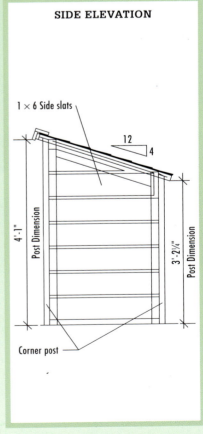

1 × 6 Side slats

12
4

4'-1"
Post Dimension

3'-2¼"
Post Dimension

Corner post

How to Build the Service Shed

Construct the floor frame: Cut the side supports, end supports, and one center support. Fasten the end supports between the sides with 3½" deck screws, as shown in the FLOOR FRAMING PLAN (page 195); locate the screws where they won't interfere with the corner post lag screws (see Step 4). Fasten the center support between the end supports, centered between the side supports.

Cut twelve 2 × 6 floorboards to length. Make sure the floor frame is square, then install the first board at one end, flush with the outsides of the frame, using 3" deck screws. Use 1" spacers to set the gaps as you install the remaining boards. Rip the last board as needed. (For the closed shed, create a 1½" × 2" notch for the left door post, starting 26" from the left end of the floor frame).

Build the corner posts: Rip two 8-ft. 2 × 4s to 2" in width. Make an 18° cut at about 53", leaving a 43" piece from each board. Cut two full-width 2 × 4 pieces at 53" and two at 43", beveling the top ends at 18°. Assemble each front post to form an "L", using the 53" pieces and keeping the angled ends flush; use 2½" deck screws. Assemble the rear posts the same way, using the 43" pieces.

Trim the corner posts to length: First, cut the front posts at 49", measuring from the longest point of the angled ends. Cut the rear posts at 38¼", measuring from the shortest point of the angled ends. Mark the insides of the posts 1½" from the bottom ends. Set each post on the floor frame so the mark is aligned with the bottom of the frame, then anchor the post with two 3" lag screws and washers, driven through counterbored pilot holes.

To begin framing the roof, cut two 2 × 4 roof headers at 73". Bevel the top edges of the headers at 18° using a circular saw and cutting guide or a tablesaw (the broad face of the header should still measure 3½"). Position the headers between the corner posts, flush with the outsides of the posts. Also, the beveled edges should be flush with the post tops. Fasten the headers to the posts with 2½" deck screws.

Cut two upper and two lower rafters, following the RAFTER TEMPLATES (page 196). Install the end rafters between the corner posts, flush with the tops of the posts, using 2½" deck screws. Install the two center rafters between the headers, 25" in from the end rafters. For the closed shed, cut the 2 × 4 rear center post to run from the bottom of the rear header down to 1½" below the bottom of the floor frame (as shown). Install the center post centered between the corner posts.

Plan the layout of the 1 × 6 slats, gapping the slats as desired. On each side, the bottom slat mounts to the outside of the floor, covering the floor from view. The remaining slats mount to the insides of the corner posts. Cut the side slats to fit and install them with 1⅝" deck screws. For the closed shed, cover the rear side with slats, using the same techniques.

(continued)

Sheath the roof with a piece of ¾" exterior plywood cut to 35½" × 81½". Overhang the posts by ¾" on all sides, and fasten the sheathing to the posts, headers, and rafters with 2" deck screws. Add 1 × 2 trim along all edges of the sheathing, mitering the ends at the corners. Fasten the trim with 6d galvanized finish nails so the top edges are flush with the sheathing.

Apply building paper over the sheathing and trim, overhanging the bottom roof edge by 1" and the sides by ½". Install the cedar shingles (see page 58). Construct the roof cap with 1 × 3 and 1 × 4 trim boards. Join the boards to form an "L" using 6d finish nails. Fasten the cap along the top edge of the roof with 6d nails.

For the closed shed only, complete the following four steps

Cut the 2 × 2 door ledger at 73". Install the ledger flush with the top of the floor frame, screwing through the back of the side support with 2½" screws. Cut the 2 × 4 door posts to fit between the ledger and door header, as shown in the FLOOR PLAN (page 195). *Note: The left post is on edge, and the right post is flat. Make sure the posts are plumb, and fasten them with 2½" screws.*

Install 1 × 3 shelf cleats at the desired height, fastening them to the rear and side slats and the right doorpost. Cut the ¾" plywood shelf to fit the space and install it with 1⅝" deck screws.

For the door trim, cut four stiles at 41¾" and four rails at 18¼" from three 8-ft. 1 × 4s. Cut two stiles at 41¾" and two rails at 14¼" from one 10-ft. 1 × 4. Cut two ¾" plywood panels at 23½" × 40" and one panel at 19½" × 40".

Fasten the rails and stiles to the door panels with 1¼" deck screws, following the DOOR ELEVATION (page 196). Screw through the backsides of the panels. Install the doors with two hinges each. Use offset sash hinges mounted to the shed posts, or use standard strap hinges mounted to ¾"-thick blocks.

Metal & Wood Kit Sheds

The following pages walk you through the steps of building two new sheds from kits. The metal shed measures 8 × 9 ft. and comes with every piece in the main building pre-cut and pre-drilled. All you need is a ladder and a few hand tools for assembly. The wood shed is a cedar building with panelized construction—most of the major elements come in preassembled sections. The walls panels have exterior siding installed, and the roof sections are already shingled. For both sheds, the pieces are lightweight and maneuverable, but it helps to have at least two people for fitting everything together.

As with most kits, these sheds do not include foundations as part of the standard package. The metal shed can be built on top of a patio surface or out in the yard, with or without an optional floor. The wood shed comes with a complete wood floor, but the building needs a standard foundation, such as wooden skid, concrete block, or concrete slab foundation. To help keep either type of shed level and to reduce moisture from ground contact, it's a good idea to build it over a bed of compacted gravel. A 4"-deep bed that extends about 6" beyond the building footprint makes for a stable foundation and helps keep the interior dry throughout the seasons.

Before you purchase a shed kit, check with your local building department to learn about restrictions that affect your project. It's recommended—and often required—that lightweight metal sheds be anchored to the ground. Shed manufacturers offer different anchoring systems, including cables for tethering the shed into soil, and concrete anchors for tying into a concrete slab.

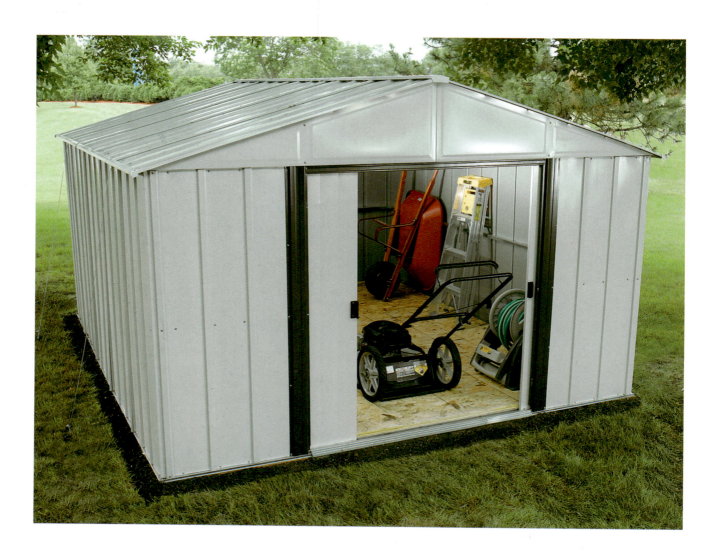

Building a Metal or Wood Kit Shed

If you need an outbuilding but don't have the time or inclination to build one from scratch, a kit shed is the answer. Today's kit sheds are available in a wide range of materials, sizes, and styles—from snap-together plastic lockers to Norwegian pine cabins with divided-light windows and loads of architectural details. Equally diverse is the range of quality and prices for shed kits. One thing to keep in mind when choosing a shed is that much of what you're paying for is the materials and the ease of installation. Better kits are made with quality, long-lasting materials, and many come largely preassembled. Most of the features discussed below will have an impact on a shed's cost.

The best place to start shopping for shed kits is on the Internet. Large manufacturers and small-shop custom designers alike have websites featuring their products and available options. A quick online search should help you narrow down your choices to sheds that fit your needs and budget. From there, you can visit local dealers or builders to view assembled sheds firsthand. When figuring cost, be sure to factor in all aspects of the project, including the foundation, extra hardware, tools you don't already own, and paint and other finishes not included with your kit.

High-tech plastics, like polyethylene and vinyl are often combined with steel and other rigid materials to create tough, weather-resistant—and washable— kit buildings.

If you're looking for something special, higher-end shed kits allow you to break with convention without breaking your budget on a custom-built structure.

Features to Consider ▸

Here are some of the key elements to check out before purchasing a kit shed:

MATERIALS

Shed kits are made of wood, metal, vinyl, various plastic compounds, or any combination thereof. Consider aesthetics, of course, but also durability and appropriateness for your climate. For example, check the snow load rating on the roof if you live in a snowy climate, or inquire about the material's UV resistance if your shed will receive heavy sun exposure. The finish on metal sheds is important for durability. Protective finishes include paint, powder-coating, and vinyl. For wood sheds, consider all of the materials, from the framing to the siding, roofing, and trimwork.

EXTRA FEATURES

Do you want a shed with windows or a skylight? Some kits come with these features, while others offer them as optional add-ons. For a shed workshop, office, or other workspace where you'll be spending a lot of time, consider the livability and practicality of the interior space, and shop accordingly for special features.

WHAT'S INCLUDED?

Many kits do not include foundations or floors, and floors are commonly available as extras. Other elements that may not be included:

- Paint, stain, etc.—Also, some sheds come pre-painted (or pre-primed), but you won't want to pay extra for a nice paint job if you plan to paint the shed to match your house
- Roofing—Often the plywood roof sheathing is included but not the building paper, drip edge, or shingles.

Most shed kits include hardware (nails, screws) for assembling the building, but always check this to make sure.

ASSEMBLY

Many kit manufacturers have downloadable assembly instructions on their websites, so you can really see what's involved in putting their shed together. Assembly of wood sheds varies considerably among manufacturers—the kit may arrive as a bundle of pre-cut lumber or with screw-together prefabricated panels. Easy-assembly models may have wall siding and roof shingles already installed onto panels.

EXTENDERS

Some kits offer the option of extending the main building with extenders, or expansion kits, making it easy to turn an 8 × 10-ft. shed into a 10 × 12-ft. shed, for example.

FOUNDATION

Check with the manufacturer for recommended foundation types to use under their sheds. The foundations shown in the Building Basics section (page 21) should be appropriate for most kit sheds.

Shed hardware kits make it easy to build a shed from scratch. Using the structural gussets and framing connectors, you avoid tricky rafter cuts and roof assembly. Many hardware kits come with lumber cutting lists so you can build the shed to the desired size without using plans.

How to Assemble a Metal Kit Shed

Prepare the building site by leveling and grading as needed, and then excavating and adding a 4"-thick layer of compactible gravel. If desired, apply landscape fabric under the gravel to inhibit weed growth. Compact the gravel with a tamper and use a level and a long, straight 2 × 4 to make sure the area is flat and level.

Note: Always wear work gloves when handling shed parts—the metal edges can be very sharp. Begin by assembling the floor kit according to the manufacturer's directions—these will vary quite a bit among models, even within the same manufacturer. Be sure that the floor system parts are arranged so the door is located where you wish it to be. Do not fasten the pieces at this stage.

Once you've laid out the floor system parts, check to make sure they're square before you begin fastening them. Measuring the diagonals to see if they're the same is a quick and easy way to check for square.

Fasten the floor system parts together with kit connectors once you've established that the floor is square. Anchor the floor to the site if your kit suggests. Some kits are designed to be anchored after full assembly is completed.

Begin installing the wall panels according to the instructions. Most panels are predrilled for fasteners, so the main trick is to make sure the fastener holes align between panels and with the floor.

Tack together mating corner panels on at least two adjacent corners. If your frame stiffeners require assembly, have them ready to go before you form the corners. With a helper, attach the frame stiffener rails to the corner panels.

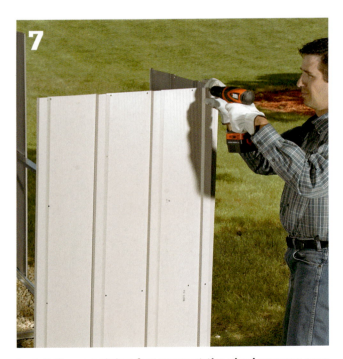

Install the remaining fasteners at the shed corners once you've established that the corners all are square.

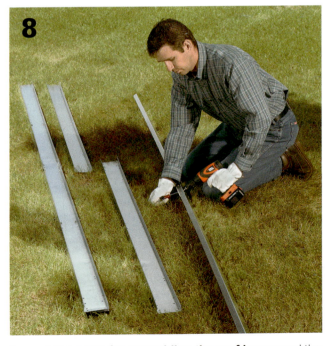

Lay out the parts for assembling the roof beams and the upper side frames and confirm that they fit together properly. Then, join the assemblies with the fasteners provided.

(continued)

Attach the moving and nonmoving parts for the upper door track to the side frames if your shed has sliding doors.

Fasten the shed panels to the top frames, making sure to that any fasteners holes are aligned and that crimped tabs are snapped together correctly.

Fill in the wall panels between the completed corners, attaching them to the frames with the provided fasteners. Take care not to overdrive the fasteners.

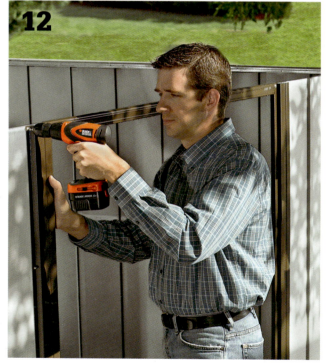

Fasten the doorframe trim pieces to the frames to finish the door opening. If the fasteners are colored to match the trim, make sure you choose the correct ones.

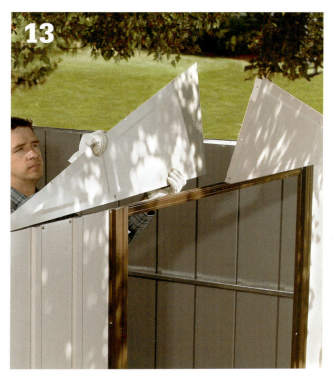

Insert the shed gable panels into the side frames and the door track and slide them together so the fastener holes are aligned. Attach the panels with the provided fasteners.

Fit the main roof beam into the clips or other fittings on the gable panels. Have a helper hold the free end of the beam. Position the beam and secure it to both gable ends before attaching it.

Drive fasteners to affix the roof beam to the gable ends and install any supplementary support hardware for the beam, such as gussets or angle braces.

(continued)

Begin installing the roof panels at one end, fastening them to the roof beam and to the top flanges of the side frames.

Apply weatherstripping tape to the top ends of the roof panels to seal the joints before you attach the overlapping roof panels. If your kit does not include weatherstripping tape, look for adhesive-backed foam tape in the weatherstripping products section of your local building center.

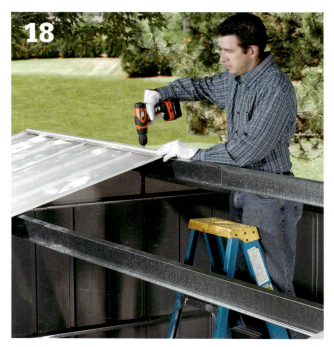

As the overlapping roof panels are installed and sealed, attach the roof cap sections at the roof ridge to cover the panel overlaps. Seal as directed. *Note: Completing one section at a time allows you to access subsequent sections from below so you don't risk damaging the roof.*

Attach the peak caps to cover the openings at the ends of the roof cap and then install the roof trim pieces at the bottoms of the roof panels, tucking the flanges or tabs into the roof as directed. Install plywood floor, according to manufacturer instructions.

20

Assemble the doors, paying close attention to right/left differences on double doors. Attach hinges for swinging doors and rollers for sliding doors.

21

Install door tracks and door roller hardware on the floor as directed and then install the doors according to the manufacturer's instructions. Test the action of the doors and make adjustments so the doors roll or swing smoothly and are aligned properly.

Tips for Maintaining a Metal Shed ▶

Touch up scratches or any exposed metal as soon as possible to prevent rust. Clean the area with a wire brush, and then apply a paint recommended by the shed's manufacturer.

Inspect your shed once or twice a year and tighten loose screws, bolts, and other hardware. Loose connections lead to premature wear.

Sweep off the roof to remove wet leaves and debris, which can be hard on the finish. Also clear the roof after heavy snowfall to reduce the risk of collapse.

Seal open seams and other potential entry points for water with silicone caulk. Keep the shed's doors closed and latched to prevent damage from wind gusts.

Anchor the Shed ▶

Metal sheds tend to be light in weight and require secure anchoring to the ground, generally with an anchor kit that may be sold separately by your kit manufacturer. There are many ways to accomplish this. The method you choose depends mostly on the type of base you've built on, be it concrete or wood or gravel. On concrete and wood bases, look for corner gusset anchors that are attached directly to the floor frame and then fastened with landscape screws (wood) or masonry anchors driven into concrete. Sheds that have been built on a gravel or dirt base can be anchored with auger-type anchors that are driven into the ground just outside the shed. You'll need to anchor the shed on at least two sides. Once the anchors are driven, cables are strung through the shed so they are connected to the roof beam. The ends of the cables should exit the shed at ground level and then be attached to the anchors with cable clamps.

How to Build a Wood Kit Shed

Prepare the base for the shed's wooden skid foundation with a 4" layer of compacted gravel. Make sure the gravel is flat, smooth, and perfectly level. *Note: For a sloping site, a concrete block foundation may be more appropriate (check with your shed's manufacturer).*

Cut three 4 × 4 (or 6 × 6) pressure-treated timbers to match the length of the shed's floor frame. Position two outer skids so they will be flush with the outside edges of the frame, and center one skid in between. Make sure that each skid is perfectly level and the skids are level with one another.

Prepare for the Delivery ▶

Panelized shed kits are shipped on pallets. The delivery truck may have a forklift, and the driver can take off the load by whole pallets. Otherwise, you'll have to unload the pieces one at a time. Make sure to have two helpers on hand to help you unload (often drivers aren't allowed to help due to insurance liability).

Once the load is on the ground, carry the pieces to the building site and stack them on pallets or scrap-wood skids to keep them clean and dry. Look through the manufacturer's instructions and arrange the stacks according to the assembly steps.

Assemble the floor frame pieces with screws. First, join alternating pairs of large and small pieces to create three full-width sections. Fasten the sections together to complete the floor frame.

Attach the floor runners to the bottom of the floor frame, using exterior screws. Locate the side runners flush to the outsides of the frame, and center the middle runner in between. Set the frame on the skids with the runners facing down. Check the frame to make sure it is level. Secure the floor to the skids following the manufacturer's recommendations.

Cover the floor frame with plywood, starting with a large sheet at the left rear corner of the frame. Fasten the plywood with screws. Install the two outer deck boards. Lay out all of the remaining boards in between, then set even gapping for each board. Fasten the remaining deck boards.

Lay out the shed's wall panels in their relative positions around the floor. Make sure you have them right-side-up: the windows are on the top half of the walls; on the windowless panels, the siding tells you which end is up.

(continued)

Position the two rear corner walls upright onto the floor so the wall framing is flush with the floor's edges. Fasten the wall panels together. Raise and join the remaining wall panels one at a time. Do not fasten the wall panels to the shed floor in this step.

Place the door header on top of the narrow front wall panel so it's flush with the wall framing. Fasten the header with screws. Fasten the door jamb to the right-side wall framing to create a ½" overhang at the end of the wall. Fasten the header to the jamb with screws.

Confirm that all wall panels are properly positioned on the floor: The wall framing should be flush with edges of the floor frame; the wall siding overhangs the outsides of the floor. Fasten the wall panels by screwing through the bottom wall plate, through the plywood flooring, and into the floor framing.

Install the wall's top plates starting with the rear wall. Install the side wall plates as directed—these overhang the front of the shed and will become part of the porch framing. Finally, install the front wall top plates.

11

Assemble the porch rail sections using the screws provided for each piece. Attach the top plate extension to the 4 × 4 porch post, and then attach the wall trim/support to the extension. Fasten the corner brackets, centered on the post and extension. Install the handrail section 4" up from the bottom of the post.

12

Install each of the porch rail sections: Fasten through the wall trim/support and into the side wall, locating the screws where they will be least visible. Fasten down through the wall top plate at the post and corner bracket locations to hide the ends of the screws. Anchor the post to the decking and floor frame with screws driven through angled pilot holes.

13

Hang the Dutch door using two hinge pairs. Install the hinges onto the door panels. Use three pairs of shims to position the bottom door panel: ½" shims at the bottom, ⅜" shims on the left side, and ⅛" shims on the right side. Fasten the hinges to the wall trim/support. Hang the top door panel in the same fashion, using ¼" shims between the door panels.

14

Join the two pieces to create the rear wall gable, screwing through the uprights on the back side. On the outer side of the gable, slide in a filler shingle until it's even with the neighboring shingles. Fasten the filler with two finish nails located above the shingle exposure line, two courses up. Attach the top filler shingle with two (exposed) galvanized finish nails.

(continued)

Position the rear gable on top of the rear wall top plates and center it from side to side. Use a square or straightedge to align the angled gable supports with the angled ends of the outer plates. Fasten the gable to the plates and wall framing with screws. Assemble and install the middle gable wall.

Arrange the roof panels on the ground according to their installation. Flip the panels over and attach framing connectors to the rafters at the marked locations, using screws.

With one or two helpers, set the first roof panel at the rear of the shed, then set the opposing roof panel in place. Align the ridge boards of the two panels, and then fasten them together with screws. Do not fasten the panels to the walls at this stage.

18

Position one of the middle roof panels, aligning its outer rafter with that of the adjacent rear roof panel. Fasten the rafters together with screws. Install the opposing middle panel in the same way. Set the porch roof panels into place one at a time—these rest on a ½" ledge at the front of the shed. From inside the shed, fasten the middle and porch panels together along their rafters.

19

Check the fit of all roof panels at the outside corners of the shed. Make any necessary adjustments. Fasten the panels to the shed with screws, starting with the porch roof. Inside the shed, fasten the panels to the gable framing, then anchor the framing connectors to the wall plates.

20

Install the two roof gussets between the middle rafters of the shed roof panels (not the porch panels): First measure between the side walls—this should equal 91" for this kit (see resources). If not, have two helpers push on the walls until the measurement matches your requirement. Hold the gussets level, and fasten them to the rafters with screws.

(continued)

Add filler shingles at the roof panel seams. Slide in the bottom shingle and fasten it above the exposure line two courses up, using two screws. Drive the screws into the rafters. Install the remaining filler shingles the same way. Attach the top shingle with two galvanized finish nails.

Cover the underside of the rafter tails (except on the porch) with soffit panels, fastening to the rafters with finish nails. Cover the floor framing with skirting boards, starting at the porch sides. Hold the skirting flush with the decking boards on the porch and with the siding on the walls, and fasten it with screws.

Add vertical trim boards to cover the wall seams and shed corners. The rear corners get a filler trim piece, followed by a wide trim board on top. Add horizontal trim boards at the front wall and along the top of the door. Fasten all trim with finish nails.

At the rear of the shed, fit the two fascia boards over the ends of the roof battens so they meet at the roof peak. Fasten the fascia with screws. Install the side fascia pieces over the rafter tails with finish nails. The rear fascia overlaps the ends of the side fascia. Cover the fascia joints and the horizontal trim joint at the front wall with decorative plates.

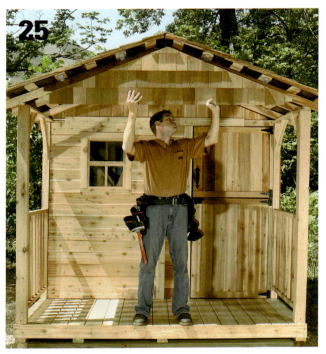

Place the two roof ridge caps along the roof peak, overlapping the caps' roofing felt in the center. Fasten the caps with screws. Install the decorative gusset gable underneath the porch roof panels using mounting clips. Finish the gable ends with two fascia pieces installed with screws.

Complete the porch assembly by fastening each front handrail section to a deck post, using screws. Fasten the handrail to the corner porch post. The handrail should start 4" above the bottoms of the posts, as with the side handrail sections. Anchor each deck post to the decking and floor frame with screws (see *Drilling Counterbored Pilot Holes,* this page).

Drilling Counterbored Pilot Holes ▸

Use a combination piloting/counterbore bit to pre-drill holes for installing posts. Angle the pilot holes at about 60°, and drive the screws into the framing below whenever possible. The counterbore created by the piloting bit helps hide the screw head.

Shed with Firewood Bin

With over 37 square feet of secure storage space and an open-air log bin that holds over a half cord of firewood, this shed is an especially handy outbuilding for backyards, cabin lots, and vacation properties alike. Its economical design makes it easy to fit anywhere and also simple and inexpensive to build.

The shed's footprint measures 6 × 10 ft. At the rear side, the roof stands at just over 7 ft., so the shed fits nicely against a standard privacy fence. In front, the top of the shed rises to nearly 9 ft. above grade, leaving room for two full-height doors and ample headroom inside the storage area. This low-profile shape with no loss of usable space is made possible by the classic shed-style roof. Shed roofs are not only cheaper to build than gables and other roof styles, they're also much easier to frame and shingle (and less likely to leak) because there's only one roof plane and no peak to deal with.

Another distinctive feature of this shed is its timber-frame floor. Instead of using a 2× floor frame set atop timber skids, this floor has 4 × 4 timber joists integrated with the skid foundation. While a standard shed floor requires a step up of almost 12", this integrated design creates a step of only 4¼". An incline of tamped gravel or a short ramp is all you need for rolling equipment right into the shed.

ISOMETRIC

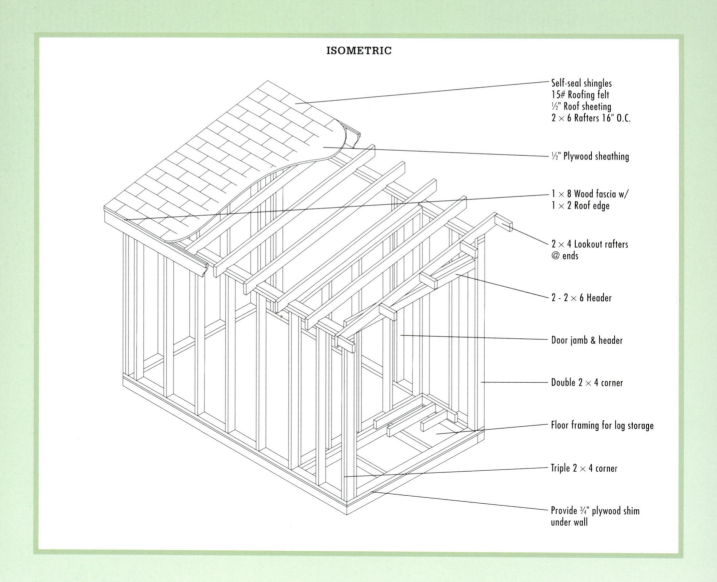

Self-seal shingles
15# Roofing felt
½" Roof sheeting
2 × 6 Rafters 16" O.C.

½" Plywood sheathing

1 × 8 Wood fascia w/
1 × 2 Roof edge

2 × 4 Lookout rafters
@ ends

2 - 2 × 6 Header

Door jamb & header

Double 2 × 4 corner

Floor framing for log storage

Triple 2 × 4 corner

Provide ¾" plywood shim
under wall

Cutting List

Description	Quantity/Size	Material
Foundation/Floor		
Drainage material	1 cu. yd.	Compactible gravel
Skids	2 @ 10'	4 × 4 pressure-treated landscape timbers
Floor joists	3 @ 12'	4 × 4 pressure-treated landscape timbers
Bin joists & floor	5 @ 12'	2 × 4 pressure-treated
Corner brackets	20 @ 3½" × 3½"	Galvanized metal corner bracket
Sheathing	2 sheets @ 4 × 8'	¾" tongue-&-groove ext.-grade plywood
Wall Framing		
Bottom plates	2 @ 10', 3 @ 8'	2 × 4 pressure-treated
Top plates	2 @ 12', 4 @ 10'	2 × 4
Studs	42 @ 8'	2 × 4
Door header	2 @ 8'	2 × 6
Bin header	1 @ 12'	2 × 6
Roof Framing		
Rafters	9 @ 8'	2 × 6
Exterior Finishes		
Siding	2 sheets @ 4 × 9' 7 sheets @ 4 × 8'	⅝" Texture 1-11 plywood siding
Z-flashing	20 linear ft.	Metal Z-flashing
Bin sheathing (optional)	3 sheets @ 4 × 8'	½" ext.-grade plywood
Fascia	2 @ 12', 2 @ 10'	1 × 8 cedar
Corner trim	3 @ 10', 3 @ 8'	1 × 4 cedar
Soffit	1 sheet @ 4 × 8'	¾" ext.-grade plywood
Soffit vents (optional)	6 @ 12"	Metal louvered vents
Door jambs & trim	6 @ 8'	1 × 4 cedar
Door & panel molding (optional)	8 @ 8'	2 × 2 cedar

Description	Quantity/Size	Material
Corner trim at log bin	2 @ 10', 2 @ 8'	1 × 6 cedar
Drip edge, door stops & bottom trim	9 @ 8'	1 × 2 cedar
Roofing		
Sheathing (& door header spacer)	3 sheets @ 4 × 8'	½" exterior-grade plywood roof sheathing
15# building paper	1 roll	
Shingles	1 square	Asphalt shingles—250# per sq. min.
Doors		
Doors	2 @ ⅖ × ⅝ × 1¾"	Exterior wood doors
Fasteners & Hardware		
16d galvanized common nails	10 lbs.	
16d common nails	8 lbs.	
10d common nails	1 lb.	
8d galvanized common nails	2 lbs.	
8d box nails	2 lbs.	
8d galvanized siding nails	5 lbs.	
8d galvanized casing nails (trim)	2 lbs.	
1¼" galvanized roofing nails	2 lbs.	
Door hinges with screws	6 @ 3½"	Galvanized metal hinges
Door handle w/lock	1	
Door head bolt	1	
Door foot bolt	1	
Construction adhesive		

SECTION

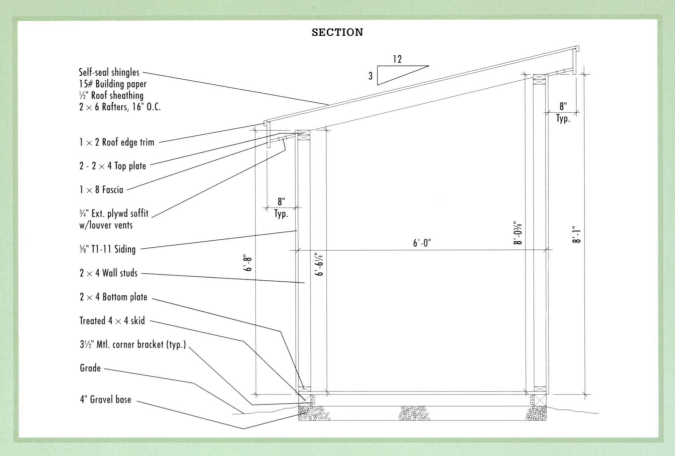

Self-seal shingles
15# Building paper
½" Roof sheathing
2 × 6 Rafters, 16" O.C.

1 × 2 Roof edge trim

2 - 2 × 4 Top plate

1 × 8 Fascia

¾" Ext. plywd soffit
w/louver vents

⅝" T1-11 Siding

2 × 4 Wall studs

2 × 4 Bottom plate

Treated 4 × 4 skid

3½" Mtl. corner bracket (typ.)

Grade

4" Gravel base

12
3

8"
Typ.

8"
Typ.

6'-8"

6'-6¼"

6'-0"

8'-0⅝"

8'-1"

FRONT FRAMING

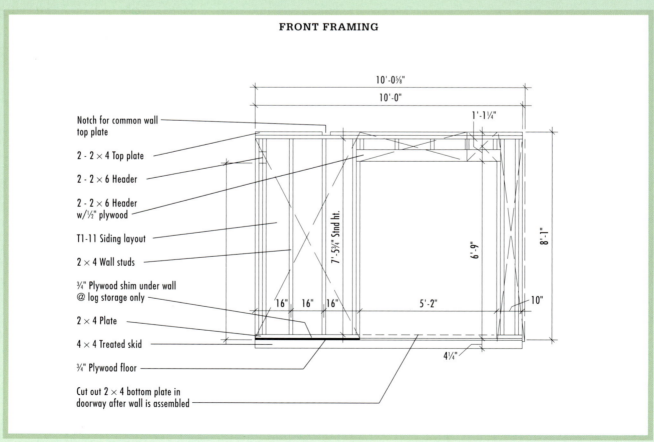

Notch for common wall
top plate

2 - 2 × 4 Top plate

2 - 2 × 6 Header

2 - 2 × 6 Header
w/½" plywood

T1-11 Siding layout

2 × 4 Wall studs

¾" Plywood shim under wall
@ log storage only

2 × 4 Plate

4 × 4 Treated skid

¾" Plywood floor

Cut out 2 × 4 bottom plate in
doorway after wall is assembled

10'-0⅝"
10'-0"
1'-1¼"

7'-5¾" Stnd ht.

6'-9"

8'-1"

16" 16" 16"

5'-2"

10"

4¼"

REAR FRAMING

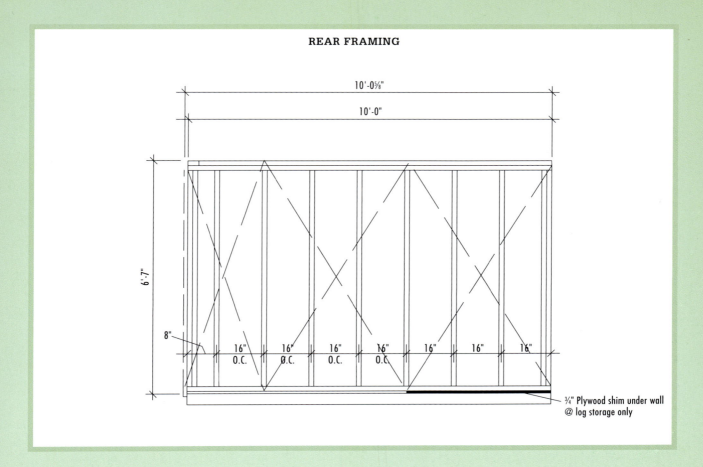

10'-0⅝"

10'-0"

6'-7"

8"

16" O.C. 16" O.C. 16" O.C. 16" O.C. 16" O.C. 16" O.C. 16" O.C.

¾" Plywood shim under wall @ log storage only

FLOOR FRAMING

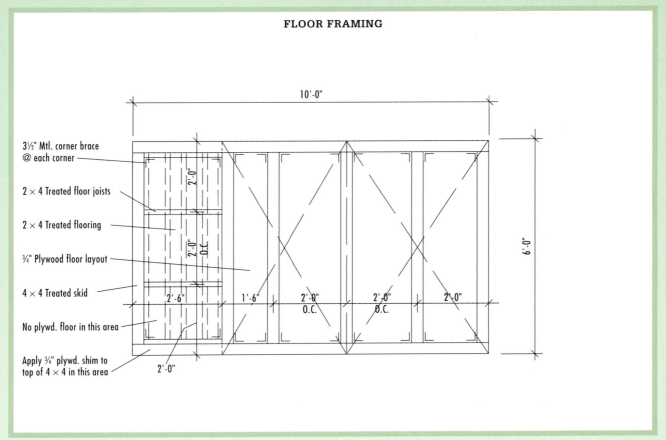

10'-0"

3½" Mtl. corner brace @ each corner

2 × 4 Treated floor joists

2 × 4 Treated flooring

¾" Plywood floor layout

4 × 4 Treated skid

No plywd. floor in this area

Apply ¾" plywd. shim to top of 4 × 4 in this area

2'-0"

2'-0" O.C.

2'-6" 1'-6" 2'-0" O.C. 2'-0" O.C. 2'-0"

6'-0"

2'-0"

COMMON WALL FRAMING

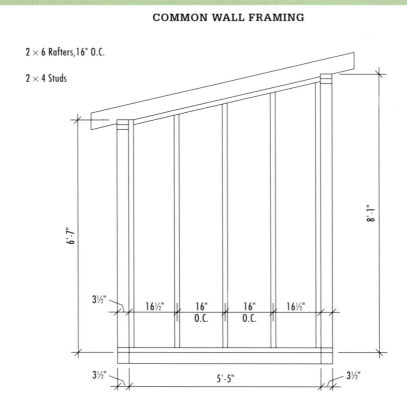

2 × 6 Rafters, 16" O.C.

2 × 4 Studs

6'-7"

8'-1"

3½"

16½"   16"   16"   16½"
       O.C. O.C.

3½"   5'-5"   3½"

RIGHT SIDE FRAMING

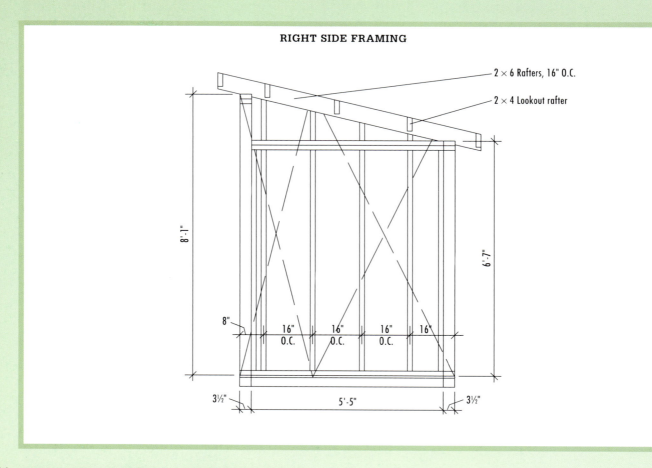

2 × 6 Rafters, 16" O.C.

2 × 4 Lookout rafter

8'-1"

6'-7"

8"

16"   16"   16"   16"
O.C. O.C. O.C.

3½"   5'-5"   3½"

LEFT SIDE FRAMING

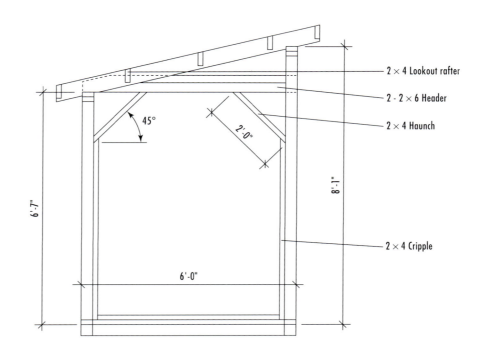

2 × 4 Lookout rafter

2 - 2 × 6 Header

2 × 4 Haunch

45°

2'-0"

8'-1"

6'-7"

2 × 4 Cripple

6'-0"

FLOOR PLAN

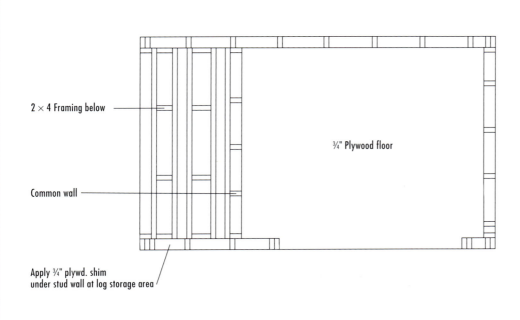

2 × 4 Framing below

Common wall

¾" Plywood floor

Apply ¾" plywd. shim
under stud wall at log storage area

FRONT ELEVATION

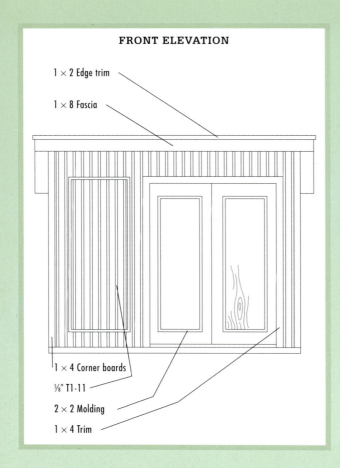

1 × 2 Edge trim

1 × 8 Fascia

1 × 4 Corner boards

⅝" T1-11

2 × 2 Molding

1 × 4 Trim

REAR ELEVATION

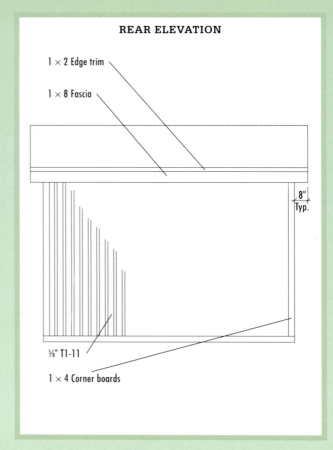

1 × 2 Edge trim

1 × 8 Fascia

8"
Typ.

⅝" T1-11

1 × 4 Corner boards

RIGHT ELEVATION

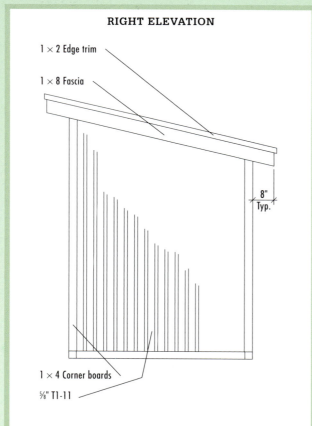

1 × 2 Edge trim

1 × 8 Fascia

8"
Typ.

1 × 4 Corner boards

⅝" T1-11

LEFT ELEVATION

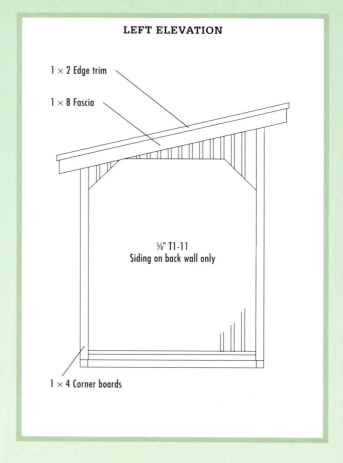

1 × 2 Edge trim

1 × 8 Fascia

⅝" T1-11
Siding on back wall only

1 × 4 Corner boards

RAFTER TEMPLATE

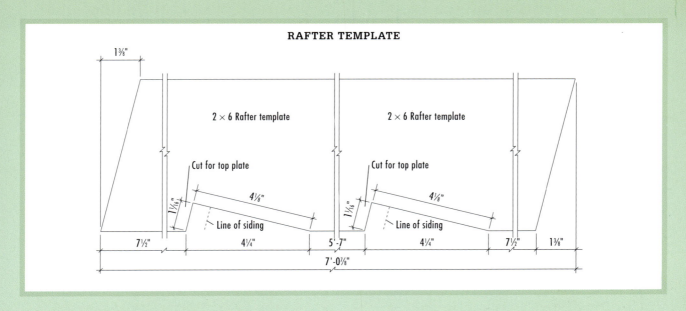

$1\frac{3}{8}$"

2×6 Rafter template

2×6 Rafter template

Cut for top plate

Cut for top plate

$1\frac{1}{16}$"

$4\frac{1}{8}$"

$1\frac{1}{16}$"

$4\frac{1}{8}$"

Line of siding

Line of siding

$7\frac{1}{2}$" $4\frac{1}{4}$"   5'-7" $4\frac{1}{4}$" $7\frac{1}{2}$" $1\frac{3}{8}$"

7'-0$\frac{7}{8}$"

HEAD & SILL DETAIL

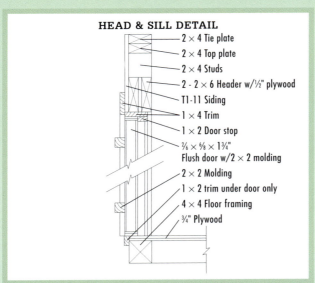

2×4 Tie plate

2×4 Top plate

2×4 Studs

2 - 2×6 Header w/$\frac{1}{2}$" plywood

T1-11 Siding

1×4 Trim

1×2 Door stop

$\frac{2}{8} \times \frac{6}{8} \times 1\frac{3}{4}$"
Flush door w/2×2 molding

2×2 Molding

1×2 trim under door only

4×4 Floor framing

$\frac{3}{4}$" Plywood

DOOR DETAILS

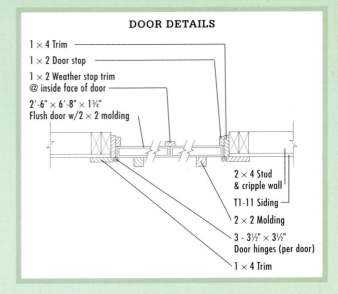

1×4 Trim

1×2 Door stop

1×2 Weather stop trim
@ inside face of door

2'-6" $\times$ 6'-8" $\times$ 1$\frac{3}{4}$"
Flush door w/2×2 molding

2×4 Stud
& cripple wall

T1-11 Siding

2×2 Molding

3 - 3$\frac{1}{2}$" $\times$ 3$\frac{1}{2}$"
Door hinges (per door)

1×4 Trim

HEADER DETAILS

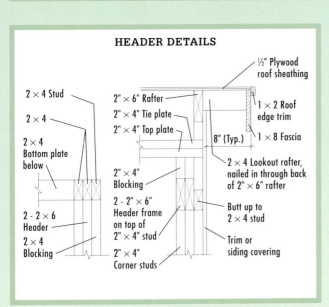

2×4 Stud

2×4

2×4
Bottom plate
below

2 - 2×6
Header

2×4
Blocking

2" $\times$ 6" Rafter

2" $\times$ 4" Tie plate

2" $\times$ 4" Top plate

8" (Typ.)

2" $\times$ 4"
Blocking

2 - 2" $\times$ 6"
Header frame
on top of
2" $\times$ 4" stud

2" $\times$ 4"
Corner studs

$\frac{1}{2}$" Plywood
roof sheathing

1×2 Roof
edge trim

1×8 Fascia

2×4 Lookout rafter,
nailed in through back
of 2" $\times$ 6" rafter

Butt up to
2×4 stud

Trim or
siding covering

CORNER DETAIL

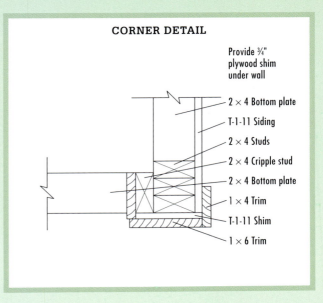

Provide $\frac{3}{4}$"
plywood shim
under wall

2×4 Bottom plate

T-1-11 Siding

2×4 Studs

2×4 Cripple stud

2×4 Bottom plate

1×4 Trim

T-1-11 Shim

1×6 Trim

How to Build the Shed with Firewood Bin

1. Prepare the foundation site with a 4" layer of compacted gravel. Cut the two outer 4 × 4 timber skids (120"). Position the skids on the gravel bed so their outside edges are 72" apart, making sure they are level and parallel with one another.

2. Cut six 4 × 4 floor joists (65") and four 2 × 4 bin joists (26½"). Anchor the joists to the skids with metal angles fastened with 16d galvanized common nails, as shown in the FLOOR FRAMING (page 223). Toenail the inner bin joists to the floor joists. All joists must be flush with the tops of the outer skids.

3. Deck the cabin area of the shed floor frame with two trimmed sheets of ¾" plywood, as shown in the SKID FRAMING. The sheets should be flush with the outsides of the skids and joists over the entire shed portion of the frame. Cover the ends of the skids in the bin area with 3½"-wide strips of plywood floor sheathing.

4. Frame the rear wall as shown in the REAR FRAMING (page 223), using a treated bottom plate and a single top plate. The studs are 73¾" long. Install and brace the wall. Frame and install the square portion of the right side wall as shown in the RIGHT SIDE FRAMING (page 224). Do not install the double top plate or the rake (angled) studs at this time.

5. Construct the front wall following the FRONT FRAMING (page 222). The two studs that will support the bin header are 76¾" long. The jack studs in the door opening are 79½" long, and the built-up 2 × 6 door header is 65" long. Add both top plates on the front wall. Install the front wall, then add the double top plates on the right side and rear walls, overlapping the plates at the right rear corner.

6. Build the common wall in place (see the COMMON WALL FRAMING, page 224). Cut the treated bottom plate (65") and install it flush to the edge of the shed area floor decking. Miter the end of the rear end stud at 14° so the outer edge is flush with the rear wall top plate. Notch the front wall top plates to make room for the common wall top plate, plus 1¹⁄₁₆" of the rafter depth. Cut and install the top plate. Cut and install the four studs as shown.

7. Cut two 2 × 6s (72") for the bin header. Clip the top rear corner of each board: Mark 1⅛" down from the top and 4⅜" from the end; connect the marks, then cut along the line. Join the header pieces with construction adhesive and pairs of 10d common nails driven every 12". Install the header on top of the front wall studs and rear wall top plate. Leave a 1½" space between the header and the end of the rear wall. Add 2 × 4 blocks between the header and front wall top plates.

8. Complete the bin floor following the FLOOR PLAN (page 225). Cut eight treated 2 × 4s (65") and construct the three assemblies as shown in the plan. Install the assemblies using 16d galvanized common nails.

9. Install plywood siding along the front and rear walls as shown in the FRONT/REAR FRAMING. Trim the sheets for the rear wall so they run from the top of the wall down to 1" below the plywood floor sheathing. On the front wall, run full sheets starting 1" below the floor. Add Z-flashing on top of the sheets, and then continue with strips of siding up to the top of the wall.

10. Cut a pattern rafter following the RAFTER TEMPLATE (page 227). Test-fit the rafter and make any necessary adjustments. Use the pattern to cut the eight remaining rafters. Install the rafters using 16" on-center spacing. The outer rafters should be flush with the side walls.

11. Complete the left wall framing as shown in the LEFT SIDE FRAMING: Cut the rear end of the 2 × 4 nailer to follow the end rafter, and install it flush with the bottom edge of the bin header. Cut two 2 × 4 corner braces (24"), mitering the ends at 45°. Install the braces so their ends are equidistant from the corners and their outer edges are flush with the nailer and wall studs. Install a 2 × 4 jack stud to fit between the bin floor and the corner brace on each side of the opening.

12. Cut and install the four rake studs on the right side wall, as shown in the RIGHT SIDE FRAMING. Cover the side walls with siding, starting with a full sheet at the rear of the right side wall. On the left side wall, run the siding to the inside edges of the bin opening. If desired, cover the interior walls of the bin with ½" exterior plywood.

13. Add five 2 × 4 lookouts (7¾") to each end rafter as shown in the LEFT and RIGHT SIDE FRAMING. Install 1 × 8 fascia boards along all four sides of the roof, flush with the tops of the rafters. Cut strips of ¾" soffit material to enclose the rafter bays, beveling the inside edges at 14°. Install the soffits so they are flush with the outsides of the end rafters. Add soffit venting, if desired.

14. Deck the roof with sheathing, starting at one of the lower corners. The sheathing should cover the tops of the fascia boards. Install 1 × 2 drip edge along all sides of the roof, flush with the top of the sheathing. Add building paper and shingles, following the steps on page 56.

15. Trim the sides and top of the bin opening with 1 × 4 and 1 × 6, as shown in the CORNER DETAIL (page 227); use 1 × 6 along the top of the opening. Cover the shed corners with 1 × 4 trim. If desired, create decorative 2 × 2 frames and apply them to the siding and doors (see the FRONT ELEVATION, page 226).

16. Prepare the door opening with 1 × 4 trim as shown in the DOOR DETAILS (page 227). Install the doors using three hinges for each. Add 1 × 2 stops around the opening, plus a trim piece underneath the door. Add a 1 × 2 weather stop to the back side of one door. Install door latch hardware, as desired. Paint or apply clear wood protectant.

Additional Shed Plans

Salt Box Storage Sheds

- Three popular sizes:
  - 8' × 8'
  - 12' × 8'
  - 16' × 8'
- Wood floor on gravel base or concrete floor
- Height, floor to peak: 8'-2"
- Front wall height: 7'
- 6'-0" × 6'-5" double door for easy access
- Complete list of materials
- Step-by-step instructions

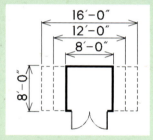

Design #002D-4500

Barn Storage Sheds with Loft

- Three popular sizes:
  - 12' × 12'
  - 12' × 16'
  - 12' × 20'
- Wood floor on concrete pier foundation or concrete floor
- Height, floor to peak: 12'-10"
- Ceiling height: 7'-4"
- 4'-0" × 6'-8" double door for easy access
- Complete list of materials
- Step-by-step instructions

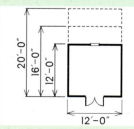

Design #002D-4501

Visit www.projectplans.com to order and view additional projects.

Gable Storage Sheds

- Four popular sizes:
    - 8' × 8'
    - 8' × 10'
    - 8' × 12'
    - 8' × 16'
- Wood floor on 4 × 4 runners
- Height, floor to peak: 8'-4½"
- Ceiling height: 7'
- 4'-0" × 6'-5" double door for easy access
- Economical and easy-to-build shed
- Complete list of materials
- Step-by-step instructions

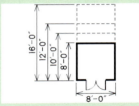

Design #002D-4503

Large Gable Storage Sheds

- Three popular sizes:
    - 10' × 12'
    - 10' × 16'
    - 10' × 20'
- Wood floor on 4 × 4 runners
- Height floor to peak: 8'-8½"
- Ceiling height: 7'
- 4'-0" × 6'-4" double door for easy access
- Complete list of materials
- Step-by-step instructions

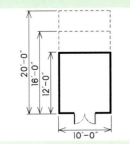

Design #002D-4504

Visit www.projectplans.com to order and view additional projects.

Children's Playhouse

- Size: 8' × 8'
- Wood floor on 4 × 4 runners
- Height, floor to peak: 9'-2"
- Ceiling height: 6'-1"
- 2'-deep porch
- Attractive window boxes
- Includes operable windows
- Complete list of materials
- Step-by-step instructions

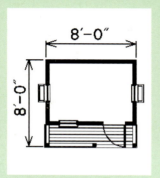

Design #002D-4505

Barn Storage Sheds

- Three popular sizes:
  - 12' × 8'
  - 12' × 12'
  - 12' × 16'
- Wood floor on concrete pier foundation or concrete floor
- Height, floor to peak: 9'-10"
- Ceiling height: 7'-10"
- 5'-6" × 6'-8" double door for easy access
- Gambrel roof design
- Complete list of materials
- Step-by-step instructions

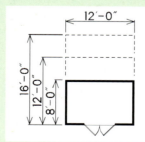

Design #002D-4508

Visit www.projectplans.com to order and view additional projects.

Mini-Barn Storage Sheds

- Four popular sizes:
  - 7'3" × 6'
  - 7'3" × 8'
  - 7'3" × 10'
  - 7'3" × 12'
- Wood floor on 4 × 6 runners or concrete floor
- Height, floor to peak: 9'
- Ceiling height: 7'-4"
- 3'-0" × 6'-8" door
- Attractive styling with gambrel roof
- Complete list of materials
- Step-by-step instructions

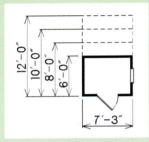

Design #002D-4510

Gable Storage Shed with Cupola

- Size: 12' × 10'
- Wood floor on concrete piers or concrete floor
- Height, floor to peak: 9'-8"
- Ceiling height: 7'-4"
- 3'-0" × 6'-8" door
- Made of cedar plywood with battens
- Complete list of materials
- Step-by-step instructions

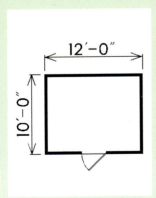

Design #002D-4511

Visit www.projectplans.com to order and view additional projects.

Deluxe Cabana

- Size: 11'0" × 13'6"
- Concrete floor
- Height, floor to peak: 11'-7"
- Ceiling height: 8'
- Unique roof design with skylight
- Convenient dressing room and servicing area
- Perfect storage for poolside furniture and equipment
- Complete list of materials
- Step-by-step instructions

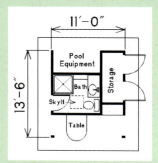

Design #002D-4518

Yard Barn with Loft Storage

- Size: 10' × 12'
- Wood floor on 4 × 4 runners
- Height, floor to peak: 10'-7"
- Ceiling height: 6'-11"
- 6'-0" × 6'-2" double door for easy access
- Loft provides additional storage area
- Attractive styling is suitable for any yard
- Complete list of materials
- Step-by-step instructions

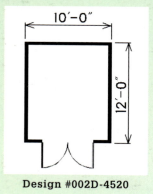

Design #002D-4520

Visit www.projectplans.com to order and view additional projects.

Garden Shed

- Size: 10' × 10'
- Wood floor on 4 × 4 runners
- Height, floor to peak: 11'-3½"
- Left wall height: 8'
- Wonderful complement to any backyard
- Perfect space for lawn equipment or plants and flowers
- Plenty of windows for gardening year-round
- Complete list of materials
- Step-by-step instructions

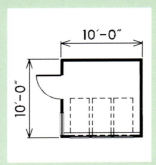

Design #002D-4523

Workroom with Covered Porch

- Size: 24' × 20'
- Building height: 13'-6"
- Roof pitch: ⁶/₁₂
- Ceiling height: 8'
- Slab foundation
- Easy access through double-door entry
- Interior enhanced by large windows
- Large enough for storage
- Complete list of materials
- Step-by-step instructions

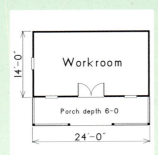

Design #002D-7520

Visit www.projectplans.com to order and view additional projects.

Resources

Asphalt Roofing Manufacturers Association
202-207-0917
www.asphaltroofing.org

The Betty Mills Company
2121 S. El Camino Real, Suite D-100
San Mateo, CA 94403
800-BettyMills
www.bettymills.com

The Big eZee
Metal Kit Sheds
101 N. Fourth St.
Breese, IL 62230
800-851-1085

Cedar Shake & Shingle Bureau
604-820-7700
www.cedarbureau.org

Certified Wood Products Council
503-224-2205
www.certifiedwood.org

HDA, Inc.
*Designs: Clerestory Studio (p. 86 to 99), Sunlight Garden
Shed (p. 100 to 113), Convenience Shed (p. 124 to 137),
Service Shed (p. 192 to 201), Shed with Firewood Bin
(p. 220 to 229)*
St. Louis, MO
800-373-2646/plan sales
314-770-2228/technical assistance
www.houseplansandmore.com

Paint Quality Institute
www.paintquality.com

Simpson Strong-Tie Co.
800-999-5099
www.strongtie.com

Southern Pine Council
*Designs by Bruce Pierce: Simple Storage Shed (p. 154 to
165), Gothic Playhouse (p. 166 to 179)*
Kemer, LA
www.southernpine.com

DuraMAX
Available at the Betty Mills Company
800-BettyMills
www.bettymills.com

Finley Products, Inc.
1018 New Holland Ave.
Lancaster, PA 17601
888-626-5301
www.2x4basics.com

Summerwood Products
735 Progress Avenue
Toronto, Ontario M1H 2W7
Canada
866-519-4634
www.summerwood.com

Photo Credits

Photo courtesy of The Betty Mills Company
p. 204 (top)

Photo courtesy of Finley Products Inc.
p. 205

Dennis Henderson
p. 16, 17 (top & lower)

Douglas Keister
p. 14 (lower)

Photo courtesy of DuraMAX
p. 11 (lower left)

Clive Nichols
p. 11 (lower right), 15, 18 (lower), 19

Dency Kane
p. 8 (lower right), 9 (top)

Eric Roth
p. 6, 13 (lower), 14 (top)

Jerry Pavia
p. 9 (lower), 12 (top & lower), 13 (top)

Photos courtesy of Summerwood Outdoors, Inc.
p. 8 (top & lower left), 10 (top & lower), 11 (top), 18 (top),
62 (left & right), 204 (lower)

Photo courtesy of Spirit Elements
p. 203

Metric Conversion Charts

Converting Measurements

To Convert:	To:	Multiply by:
Inches	Millimeters	25.4
Inches	Centimeters	2.54
Feet	Meters	0.305
Yards	Meters	0.914
Square inches	Square centimeters	6.45
Square feet	Square meters	0.093
Square yards	Square meters	0.836
Cubic inches	Cubic centimeters	16.4
Cubic feet	Cubic meters	0.0283
Cubic yards	Cubic meters	0.765
Pounds	Kilograms	0.454

To Convert:	To:	Multiply by:
Millimeters	Inches	0.039
Centimeters	Inches	0.394
Meters	Feet	3.28
Meters	Yards	1.09
Square centimeters	Square inches	0.155
Square meters	Square feet	10.8
Square meters	Square yards	1.2
Cubic centimeters	Cubic inches	0.061
Cubic meters	Cubic feet	35.3
Cubic meters	Cubic yards	1.31
Kilograms	Pounds	2.2

Lumber Dimensions

Nominal - U.S.	Actual - U.S. (in inches)	Metric
1 × 2	¾ × 1½	19 × 38 mm
1 × 3	¾ × 2½	19 × 64 mm
1 × 4	¾ × 3½	19 × 89 mm
1 × 5	¾ × 4½	19 × 114 mm
1 × 6	¾ × 5½	19 × 140 mm
1 × 7	¾ × 6¼	19 × 159 mm
1 × 8	¾ × 7¼	19 × 184 mm
1 × 10	¾ × 9¼	19 × 235 mm
1 × 12	¾ × 11¼	19 × 286 mm
2 × 2	1½ × 1½	38 × 38 mm

Nominal - U.S.	Actual - U.S. (in inches)	Metric
2 × 3	1½ × 2½	38 × 64 mm
2 × 4	1½ × 3½	38 × 89 mm
2 × 6	1½ × 5½	38 × 140 mm
2 × 8	1½ × 7¼	38 × 184 mm
2 × 10	1½ × 9¼	38 × 235 mm
2 × 12	1½ × 11¼	38 × 286 mm
4 × 4	3½ × 3½	89 × 89 mm
4 × 6	3½ × 5½	89 × 140 mm
6 × 6	5½ × 5½	140 × 140 mm
8 × 8	7¼ × 7¼	184 × 184 mm

Metric Plywood

Standard Sheathing Grade	Sanded Grade
7.5 mm (5/16")	6 mm (4/17")
9.5 mm (3/8")	8 mm (5/16")
12.5 mm (1/2")	11 mm (7/16")
15.5 mm (5/8")	14 mm (9/16")
18.5 mm (3/4")	17 mm (2/3")
20.5 mm (13/16")	19 mm (3/4")
22.5 mm (7/8")	21 mm (13/16")
25.5 mm (1")	24 mm (15/16")

Counterbore, Shank & Pilot Hole Diameters

Screw Size	Counterbore Diameter for Screw Head	Clearance Hole for Screw Shank	Pilot Hole Diameter Hard Wood	Pilot Hole Diameter Soft Wood
#1	.146 (9/64)	5/64	3/64	1/32
#2	¼	3/32	3/64	1/32
#3	¼	7/64	1/16	3/64
#4	¼	1/8	1/16	3/64
#5	¼	1/8	5/64	1/16
#6	5/16	9/64	3/32	5/64
#7	5/16	5/32	3/32	5/64
#8	3/8	11/64	1/8	3/32
#9	3/8	11/64	1/8	3/32
#10	3/8	3/16	1/8	7/64
#11	½	3/16	5/32	9/64
#12	½	7/32	9/64	1/8

Index

A

Accessories
    ideas for, 12
    kits and, 10
Aluminum hardware, 27
Anatomy of sheds, 26
Angles, marking, 47
Approvals needed, 21
Asian style, 15
Asphalt shingles, 52, 56–57
Attached sheds, 11

B

Barn storage shed plans, 230, 232–233, 234
Barn storage sheds with loft, 230
Basic storage shed
    building, 162–165
    considerations, 154–155
    cutting list, 156
    drawings, 157–161
Bird's mouth cuts, 48
Board lumber, 27
Building codes
    building department approval, 21
    foundations and, 28
    siting and, 22
Building paper, installing on roofing, 55
Building section drawings, 24

C

Cabana plan, 234
Cedar
    advantages, 27
    roof shingles, 52, 58–59
    shingle ideas, 14, 18
Children's playhouses. See Playhouses
Clerestory studio
    building, 95–99
    cutting list, 88
    drawings, 89–94
    overview of, 86–87
Closet sheds. See Lean-to tool bin
Collar ties, 47
Components of sheds, 26
Concrete
    building block foundations, 30–31
    building pier foundations, 32–35
    building slabs foundations, 36–39
    estimating amount needed, 39
    foundations and permanent structure
        classification, 22
    lumber for slab foundations, 42
    pouring tips, 39
Construction (CONST) Grade No. 2
    lumber, 27
Construction drawings, working with,
    24–25
Construction stages, 26
Convenience shed
    building, 133–137
    cutting list, 126

drawings, 127–132
    overview of, 124–125
Costs and size, 18
Counterbored pilot holes, drilling, 219
Country style
    exteriors, 9, 180
    interiors, 13, 181
Cupola, plan for gable storage shed
    with, 233

D

Deluxe cabana plan, 234
Dimensions of lumber, 27
Doors
    building platforms to, 82–83
    building ramps to, 74–77
    building stairs to, 79–81
    Gothic, 166, 167
    homemade, 73
    installing flashing above, 73
    installing prehung, 72
    installing trim, 68
    placement of, 8
Dormers, 8
Drainage and siting, 22
Drawings, working with construction,
    24–25
Drilling counterbored pilot holes, 219

E

Elevations (drawings), 25

F

Fasteners, 27
Finishes, 27
Finish lumber, 27
Firewood bin shed
    building, 228–229
    cutting list, 221
    drawings, 220, 222–227
    overview of, 220
Firewood seasoning shed
    building, 198–200
    considerations, 192–193
    cutting list, 194
    drawings, 195–197
Flashing above doors & windows,
    installing, 73
Floors
    framing, 40–41
    installing plywood, 41
Foundations
    building codes and, 28
    building concrete block, 30–31
    building concrete pier, 32–35
    building concrete slab, 36–39
    building wooden skid, 28–29
    taxes and, 22
Framing
    connectors used, 27
    floors, 40–41

lumber for, 27
    roofs, 46–51
    walls, 42–45
Frost lines, 28

G

Gable roofs
    described, 47
    fascia on, 52
    framing, 51
Gable storage shed plans, 231, 233
Galvanized steel hardware, hot-dipped, 27
Gambrel garage shed
    building, 148–153
    cutting list, 140
    drawings, 141–147
    overview of, 138–139
Gambrel roofs
    described, 47, 139
    fascia on, 52
    framing, 51
Garden shed plan, 235
Gothic playhouse
    building, 175–179
    considerations, 166–167
    cutting list, 168
    drawings, 169–174
Gothic style architecture, 166
Greenhouses
    building, 109–113
    cutting list, 102
    drawings, 103–108
    ideas for, 19
    overview of, 100–101
Guest houses, 16–17

H

Hardware
    described, 27
    for metal roofing, 60
    used on siding, 62
Hip roofs, described, 47
Holes, pre-drilling, 219
Homemade doors & windows, 73
Horizontal siding
    installing, 63–64
    trim and, 68
Hot-dipped galvanized steel hardware, 27

K

Kit sheds
    considerations, 202–203, 205
    custom details with, 8, 10
    See also Metal kit sheds; Wood kit sheds
Knotty pine paneling ideas, 13, 180

L

Large gable storage shed plan, 231
Lean-to tool bin
    building, 121–123
    cutting list, 116

drawings, 117–120
overview of, 114–115
Lumber, 27

M

Metal anchors, 27
Metal kit sheds
    anchoring, 211
    assembling, 206–211
    considerations, 202, 204–205
    maintaining, 211
Metal roofing, 52, 60–61
Mini-barn storage shed plan, 233

N

Nailing techniques, 40
Nail types, 40
Neighbors and shed siting, 22
New England style, 16–17
Notched-stringer stairs, building, 80–81

O

Overhead plan views, 25

P

Patios, integrating sheds with, 11, 18
Pier foundations
    advantages, 32
    building concrete, 32–35
    permanent structure classification
        and, 22
Plans
    barn storage sheds, 230,
        232–233, 234
    deluxe cabana, 234
    gable storage shed, 231
    gable storage shed with cupola, 233
    garden shed, 235
    large gable storage shed, 231
    mini-barn storage shed, 233
    playhouse, 232
    working with, 24–25
    workroom with covered porch, 235
    yard barn with loft storage, 234
Plan views (drawings), 25
Platforms, building, 82–83
Playhouses
    building, 175–179
    considerations, 166–167
    cutting list, 168
    drawings, 169–174
    plan, 232
Plywood
    exterior grade, 27
    installing floors, 41
    installing siding, 65
Prehung doors & windows, installing,
    70–72
Pressure-treated lumber, 27, 42
Primers, 27
Privacy, 7

R

Rafters, 47
Rafter ties, 47
Ramps
    building, 75–77
    considerations, 74
Roofs
    finishing overhangs, 69
    framing, 46–51
    installing fascia, 53–54
    installing sheathing & building paper, 55
    installing vents, 58
    knotty pine sheathing, 13
    materials for, 52
    overhangs, 11
    styles, 47
Rubber washered nails & screws, 60

S

Saltbox storage shed
    ideas for, 12
    plan, 230
"Seaside" sheds, 14
Seasonal changes and siting, 23
Select Structural (SEL STR) lumber, 27
Service shed
    building, 198–201
    considerations, 192
    cutting list, 194
    drawings, 195–197
Setback requirements and siting, 22
Shade
    greenhouses and, 101
    overhangs for, 11
Sheathing
    installing on roofing, 55
    knotty pine, 13
    for roof decks, 180
Shed anatomy, 26
Shed roofs, described, 47
Siding
    considerations, 62
    installing horizontal, 63–64
    installing plywood, 65
    installing tongue & groove, 66–67
    trim and, 68
Sites, choosing, 22–23, 101
Skid foundations
    building, 28–29
    permanent structure classification
        and, 22
Slopes of roofs, 47
Soil and siting, 22
Speed squares, 47
Stages of construction, 26
Stainless steel hardware, 27
Stairs
    building, 79–81
    calculating size of step, 79
    considerations, 78
    stepped platforms as, 83

Standard (STAND) lumber, 27
Stick framing
    described, 40
    tongue & groove siding and, 66–67
Storage shed, basic
    building, 162–165
    considerations, 154–155
    cutting list, 156
    drawings, 157–161
STUD lumber, 27
Sunlight and siting, 23
Sunrooms, 18

T

Taxes, 22
Timber-frame shed
    building, 187–191
    considerations, 180–181
    cutting list, 182
    drawings, 183–186
Trim
    considerations, 62
    installing, 68
Trusses, custom, 47

U

Uses, 5, 7
Utility lines and siting, 22
Utility (UTIL) grade lumber, 27

V

Vents, installing roof, 58

W

Walls, framing, 42–45
Windows
    box bay, 124
    clerestory, 86–87
Gothic, 166
    homemade, 73
    installing flashing above, 73
    installing prehung, 70–71
    installing trim, 68
    sheltering with overhangs, 11
Wooden skid foundations
    building, 28–29
    permanent structure classification
        and, 22
Wood kit sheds
    building, 212–219
    considerations, 202–205
    ideas for, 8, 10
Workroom with covered porch plan, 235

Y

Yard barn with loft storage plan, 234

Z

Zoning laws and siting, 22

Also From CREATIVE PUBLISHING international

Complete Guide to Attics & Basements

Complete Guide to Basic Woodworking

Complete Guide to Bathrooms

Complete Guide Build Your Kids a Treehouse

Complete Guide to Carpentry for Homeowners

Complete Guide to Ceramic & Stone Tile

Complete Guide to Contemporary Sheds

Complete Guide to Creative Landscapes

Complete Guide to Custom Shelves & Built-Ins

Complete Guide to Decks

Complete Guide to Decorating with Ceramic Tile

Complete Guide to DIY Projects for Luxurious Living

Complete Guide to Dream Kitchens

Complete Guide to Finishing Walls & Ceilings

Complete Guide to Floor Décor

Complete Guide to Gazebos & Arbors

Complete Guide to Home Plumbing

Complete Guide to Home Wiring

Complete Guide to Landscape Construction

Complete Guide Maintain Your Pool & Spa

Complete Guide to Masonry & Stonework

Complete Guide to Outdoor Wood Projects

Complete Guide to Painting & Decorating

Complete Guide to Patios

Complete Guide to Roofing & Siding

Complete Guide to Trim & Finish Carpentry

Complete Guide to Windows & Doors

Complete Guide to Wood Storage Projects

Complete Outdoor Builder

Complete Photo Guide to Home Repair

Complete Photo Guide to Home Improvement

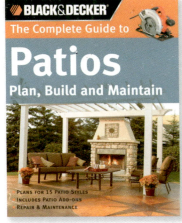

ISBN 1-58923-305-0

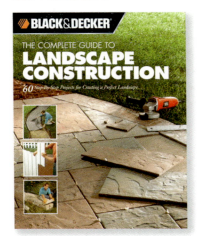

ISBN 1-58923-245-3

ISBN 1-58923-287-9

Creative Publishing international

400 First Avenue North • Suite 300 • Minneapolis, MN 55401 • www.creativepub.com